This Faithful Book

*A Diary
from World War Two
in the Netherlands*

by

MADZY BRENDER À BRANDIS

Translated and edited
by
MARIANNE BRANDIS

This Faithful Book
Copyright © 2019 by Marianne Brandis

For permission, please contact mbrandis@cyg.net
www.mariannebrandis.ca

Tellwell Talent
www.tellwell.ca

ISBN
978-0-2288-1210-4 (Hardcover)
978-0-2288-1209-8 (Paperback)
978-0-2288-1211-1 (eBook)

Table of Contents

List of Illustrations

Acknowledgements

A number of people have helped with this project. I would like to thank Carel Beynen, August de Man, Nando van Ketwich Verschuur, Frank Steensma, Boudewien van Notten, Jim van Notten, Freek Vrugtman, and Charlotte de Josselin de Jong and her father and aunt. Earlier help came from three now-deceased relatives and friends: Hansje van Lanschot–van Vollenhoven, Greet de Beaufort–Blijdenstein, and Addison Worthington.

Special thanks go to my cousin Monica Ellis for her informative and patient answers to my many questions.

I received useful information from Harm Stoel, former commander of the Maarn Fire and Accidents Department and creator of a list of bombings that took place in Maarn during the Second World War.

My particular gratitude goes to Gijs van Roekel and his colleagues of the Cultuurhistorische Commissie Maarn-Maarsbergen and the Regionaal Historisch Centrum Zuidoost Utrecht. For this project I drew on work that I had done in the Netherlands for my earlier book, *Frontiers and Sanctuaries*, but I was unable to go there this time for additional research; therefore Gijs has been my "eyes" in Maarn, my feet on the ground, my colleague in doing tireless and resourceful work in the archives. Without his help this book would lack much of the historical and geographical detail that helped me to bring Madzy's chronicle to life. The map is his creation, based on a map in the archives. Gijs's contribution is far more extensive than is indicated by the items that are explicitly footnoted. Any mistakes in this aspect of the book are my responsibility.

Karl Griffiths-Fulton contributed his artistic eye, computer knowledge, and interested support to the preparation of the illustrations.

The people at Tellwell Talent have been extremely helpful and supportive throughout.

Behind the scenes have been my late father, Wim/Bill Brender à Brandis, and my two brothers, Gerard and Jock. The help that Bill gave me during the writing of *Frontiers and Sanctuaries* was a solid body of information on which I continued to draw for this later project. Gerard and Jock have been interested and supportive, as they always are.

I am especially grateful to Gerard for his drawing of the house in Maarn which appears at the head of each chapter.

There will be factual mistakes in Madzy's diary and in the supporting material that I wrote. Madzy recorded what she knew at the time; my father's memories were written down (and shared orally) when he was an old man; and I have done what I could with what information I had or could find. The significance of Madzy's diary greatly overrides any small errors in detail.

I plan, if it's at all possible, to send you only good and cheerful news. It doesn't help if you make yourself miserable; it's better that you learn about our miseries only later, and that's why I'm writing this faithful, truthful book.

—Madzy Brender à Brandis
writing to her imprisoned husband, Wim,
16 June 1942

Preface: The Diary

On the morning of Friday, 15 May 1942, a young woman named Madzy—who had given birth two days earlier to a baby boy—kissed her husband good-bye as he set off to keep an appointment. She expected him home that evening, but as it turned out he would not return for more than three years.

Separations of this kind have always happened, but few have been chronicled in as much detail as this one was because Madzy wrote a diary. She recorded details about not only her outer life but also the inner one—the *whole* experience: the anxiety, longing, loneliness, fear, and despair, and also the hope and humour and beauty. Her experience resonates beyond itself, in other lives and different circumstances. It is the universal story of a person suddenly confronted by a huge and dangerous obstacle. It is a survival narrative; it tells us something about human courage and endurance.

*

When she began writing the diary, Madzy Brender à Brandis was thirty-one years old, the mother of a three-year-old daughter as well as the just-born son, Gerard Willem. Her husband was Wim Brender à Brandis. They lived in Maarn, a village in the centre of the Netherlands, between Utrecht and Arnhem. This was the middle of the Second World War, and the Netherlands had been under German occupation for two years. Wim was a demobilized cavalry officer; on that May day, he and his fellow officers were, without warning, taken captive by the Germans and sent to a prisoner-of-war camp.

The diary describes Madzy's life during his absence—how she dealt with the hardships, shortages, and hunger, and also with the dangers involved in warfare and enemy occupation. This is the kind of life story that vividly illuminates large-picture public history.

The diary is essentially one long letter to Wim, for him to read when he returned from the camp (*if* he returned). She began writing it three days after he left and ended it with his safe arrival back home. After the first six weeks of his imprisonment, they were able to carry on a skimpy (and censored) correspondence; what could not go into those letters went into the diary.[1]

For Madzy, writing the diary was at first a way of maintaining a make-believe contact with Wim. However, equally important, she used the act of writing to figure out how to live, how to manage in the real world, and how to survive in both practical and emotional terms. It was not only half of a dialogue with Wim but also a dialogue with herself.

*

The narrative, though it sounds like an uncensored outpouring, is more circumspect than it appears. Madzy, knowing that the diary could fall into enemy hands, avoided writing anything that might endanger herself or her friends. The German police regularly raided private houses looking for hoarded food, Jewish people in hiding, men evading conscription to labour camps, and evidence of Resistance activity. These "razzias" were arbitrary, sudden, often brutal, and always frightening.[2]

Long after the war, however, Madzy wrote about some things not mentioned in the diary. In a 1976 taped narrative she recorded that in the area around Maarn, which was well-wooded

---

1   We have only three of the letters he wrote to her, and none of hers to him, so we don't know what they were writing to each other.
2   She must have had a very secure hiding place for it in the house, but I don't know where that was. "Keeping a diary, however carefully it was hidden, was extremely dangerous." (Caspers, *Vechten voor vrijheid*— "Fighting for Freedom," p.47)

and comparatively thinly populated, there were many people in hiding (called "divers" because they went underground), and there was much Resistance activity. An underground newspaper was being published very nearby. An English officer, being sheltered by a friend of hers, had a clandestine radio transmitter.[3] Madzy lent English-language books to a Canadian airman shot down nearby and hidden by another friend. The omissions we know about suggest she could have written a great deal more had it been safe to do so.

Madzy's narrative shows what daily life becomes in perilous conditions and under enemy occupation. Fearful of endangering herself and the children, she mostly obeyed regulations, but the need for safety struggled against her strong principles and self-respect. Many Dutch people who opposed the occupying forces were defiant, even militant. Madzy's resistance was quieter. But the portrait of the Dutch queen, Wilhelmina, that hung in the house was a form of resistance: Madzy could have been punished for it. She helped divers, although we have no idea to what extent because she records it very rarely. No doubt she read the underground newspapers. But her priority was the survival of her family and close friends. She knew German, so in her contacts with the occupying administration, she could understand what they were saying and reply appropriately— which meant carefully and, most of the time, submissively.

Her account also reveals something of how a community as a whole functioned. Madzy wrote about help received and given, and about amusing incidents. It is a fragmentary image of a village—*that* village, during *those* years, viewed through *her* eyes. Conditions, especially as they pertained to food, differed from town to town, even from family to family. Farm families ate better than urban ones, even though much of what they

---

3   Henri van der Zee, *The Hunger Winter*, p. 139. A friend and neighbour of Madzy's, Dientje Blijdenstein, also recorded this in her diary (private papers).

produced was requisitioned and sent to Germany. Some people managed to hoard food. There was a black market for those who could afford it.

Her picture of daily life reminds us that, even in the middle of a war, some semblance of ordinary existence has to be maintained. The details, though humdrum, resonate because of the unusual and stressful circumstances; shopping for groceries is not humdrum when there are warplanes flying low overhead. Shortages and restrictions required constant invention and adaptation. Life focused on the basics: food, shelter, family, health and illness, and, above all, safety. There was little entertainment or relaxation, and often little variety except for the different kinds of hardship. The only "shopping" was the endless, urgent, often difficult provision of food. But there were cups of tea (usually imitation) with friends and the all-important arrival of the mail.

*

Like most diaries, this one is fragmentary. Threads of the story are begun and then dropped. There are gaps and obscurities, not only because of Madzy's self-censorship but also because, being written for Wim, it does not explain things that he knew already. Often it sounds like one side of a casual conversation over a cup of coffee.

In the first weeks, before she had Wim's address, Madzy wrote voluminously in the diary. Once she had his address, she wrote long letters to him. However, as the families of the other 2,060 imprisoned officers were no doubt doing the same thing, the censors could not handle the amount of correspondence, so the authorities in the prisoner-of-war camp set up a system whereby each officer, every month, received a specific number of forms, each of which allowed only a few lines of writing and had an attached blank form for the reply. For Madzy, that was completely inadequate, so again the overflow went into the diary. However, in the diary she probably did not record what had she already put in a letter, so that left gaps.

Moreover, she had limited time to spend on writing and, with wartime shortages, only so much paper.

*

This was not my first encounter with the diary. Some years ago I wrote *Frontiers and Sanctuaries: A Woman's Life in Holland and Canada*, which is the story of Madzy's whole life. The diary was the principal source for the chapter dealing with the Second World War, but there I used only a very small part of the whole. The importance of the diary as a document justifies this present edition of the complete work.

In preparing this edition, I wanted to be as faithful as possible to the original, not only to the factual content but also to the feel and tone; but I needed to create a readable text. The original is repetitious, in part because Madzy was using the writing as therapy. Her longing for Wim appears over and over again; so does the increasingly severe problem of providing food for her family. I removed some of the repetition but kept enough to convey the realities of her life, both inner and outer, which, as she wrote, was what she had set out to record.[4]

Other editing involved issues of translation. The original is in Dutch, but Madzy sometimes used foreign words: she knew English, French, German, Latin, and some Greek. I translated most of these terms into English but kept a few in the original because they are part of the flavor of her writing. And I wanted to reflect the idiomatic expressions, the fragments and hesitancies and awkwardness typical of diaries. Once I had a complete translation, I edited it to produce the version given here.

The diary contains inconsistencies—not surprising in a narrative covering more than three years. Conditions changed. The inconsistencies are part of the evolving story. Inconsistencies about public events are no doubt the result of the fragmentary and often inaccurate information available to her. The Dutch

---

4   I did not indicate where these deletions took place. Madzy used ellipsis as punctuation, and all the ones in the text are hers.

media, German-controlled, were not reliable. More reliable, perhaps, were the underground newspapers. There was the grapevine: some of what she records was rumour, what was "known" at that time. There was also the BBC, but what Madzy was hearing was the day's news as the BBC knew it, and because of the disrupted communications it was not always accurate or up-to-date. And of course she was often writing in haste and simplifying.

To sketch the context for Madzy's narrative, I have provided some information about the larger picture of the war and living conditions, but these notes are brief and based on only a few sources. Interested readers can easily find further details. I have generally not tried to discover whether what Madzy records about the larger public situation was correct. What she wrote is what she—and the BBC, and the grapevine—knew on that day.

There are probably other inaccuracies. She was sometimes uncertain about the spelling of local names; she had no telephone and therefore no phone directory so, even had she wanted to, she had few handy sources for checking.[5]

*

As I worked on this project, I realized that in fact there are two stories. In addition to the diary itself, there is a second, retrospective layer. It consists partly of Madzy's post-war writings, the principal one (for this project) being the narrative, already mentioned, that she taped in 1976 while rereading this diary. She also wrote short stories and memoirs about the war period, and she referred to it occasionally in her journalism.[6]

Furthermore, there are Wim's writings. In this book, Wim appears in two guises. He is Wim, the young man in the POW camp, the nearly-invisible participant in the dialogue. But he is also Bill, the name used in Canada after 1947, who, in old age,

---

5   I have checked spellings where I could, but sometimes no documents are available. Moreover, my research assistant in Maarn, Gijs van Roekel, tells me there were indeed variations in the spelling of names.

6   See Conclusion and Appendix C.

wrote memoirs and helped me with the first phase of work on the diary. To maintain this important distinction, I use "Wim" to refer to the young man and "Bill" for the older one.

In that earlier phase of the work, Bill helped me by identifying the people and places named in the diary, familiar to Madzy and him but often not to me. He did an extremely rough translation of the whole diary. That translation contained many inaccuracies and omissions but was useful to me in a general way.

Bill also wrote an account of his time in the POW camp—two versions, in fact. They are not long, but they give some of the unheard half of the dialogue.[7]

And there is a further strand in this second story. I was the elder of those two children, three-and-a-half years old in May 1942, and I include some of my memories.

This second story, given in the headnotes and footnotes, enhances the diary's significance by placing it a larger, retrospective context.

*

The first entry of the diary makes it clear that this is, at one level, an extremely private document. That raises the question of whether it should have been made public.[8]

There are several answers to this. In the first place, although Madzy did not give the diary to Wim when he returned from the camp (most likely she felt that all the anguish and hardship should be allowed to slip into the past), she did keep it. In 1976 she reread it and prepared the taped narrative based on it. After that she still kept it, along with most of her other writings. Before her death in 1984, she requested that some later diaries be destroyed, but she decided to preserve this one.

Moreover, as the writing of the diary proceeded, she clearly recognized that it was becoming an important document.

---

7   This, and some other material about the POW camp, can be found in Appendix A.

8   Vera Brittain, faced with a similar decision, wrote: "Time, in the end, reduces all private things to history" (*Testament of Experience*, p. 178).

Beginning in September 1944, as we shall see, she became consciously a chronicler of public events.

A further indication of Madzy's recognition of the diary's larger importance is that, four weeks after Wim's return from the camp, she wrote the account of his homecoming, to complete the story. By then she was not addressing him (because he was right there), but for other readers she needed to give the story an ending.

The most decisive answer comes from Madzy herself. Among her papers there is the beginning of yet another diary, written about two years before her death. In it she wrote (in English):

> My aim is to be as free and uninhibited [as possible] in putting down my very inner thoughts, knowing that no one will read them as long as I live. After my death I do not care what [any]one thinks or knows of me; the more of me and my thoughts the better, for then they won't put me on an unearned pedestal. Rather let my real self appear, something I so often try to hide. For they often think or pretend to think that I am a better or more honest person than I am. This really worries or bothers me.

This passage explains her careful preservation of her writings, published and unpublished, and it also gave me—or someone—permission to write her story. The war diary shows both the outer life and the inner, the public face and the one that she tried to hide. Two years before her death, she was giving permission for her "real self" to be revealed so that she would be seen more wholly than she had ever been during her lifetime.

*****

Nuts and bolts:

- Madzy used weights and measures in her references to food, etc. I have usually not translated these into imperial measures; what she wrote conveys clearly enough the general fact of shortages. In dealing with distances, I convert the ones referring to the neighbourhood of Maarn, many of which relate to Madzy's expeditions in search of food and were therefore important to her, but usually give the ones that are part of the war news only in the form she uses—often miles, because she is quoting the BBC.
- In one or two cases the spelling of a place name has changed: I have kept the form she used.
- The diary is full of people. In the Introduction I deal with the more important ones, and others are identified in the footnotes and listed in the index. Minor characters are sufficiently identified by the context.
- Madzy always addressed Wim as "Dicks."[9] I appear under many different names. There are variations of "Marianne," but the most common is "Pankie" and variations on that. Gerard Willem, the baby, also appears under various forms of the name, sometimes "Geert."
- To maintain some of the flavor of Madzy's Dutch life, I have kept the Dutch terms of address that she uses: Mevr[ouw] (Mrs.), Juffr[ouw] (Miss), Mijnheer, Meneer, M[r], and de heer (all meaning Mr.). Family members are Grootvader (Grandfather), Oma (colloquial for Grandmother), Vader (Father), Moeder (Mother), Oom (Uncle), Tante (Aunt).
- For quotations from family papers, I have given the location in *Frontiers and Sanctuaries* where the passage is used; interested readers will find that book easier to locate than the (mostly unpublished) documents.

---

9   In the diary there are, confusingly, several people—mostly men, but one woman—named Dick, but only one "Dicks."

Inevitably this book sometimes overlaps with *Frontiers and Sanctuaries*. Where there are inconsistencies between the two, this book, which is more detailed and incorporates more recent information, is the more accurate. In cases where the same diary passage appears in both books, there might be slight differences in my translation; revisiting a passage, I sometimes reconsidered a precise bit of wording or shade of meaning.

Introduction: The Author

Mattha Cornelia van Vollenhoven (always called Madzy) was born on 25 August 1910, in Scheveningen, just outside The Hague. Her parents, Joost and Iete, had been living in the Dutch East Indies for some years and had just returned permanently to the Netherlands, where they set up a large household. Madzy, recording memories late in life, said (with a touch of wry humour, because she had simpler tastes), "We couldn't do with less than a cook, and an assistant cook who also served at table, a butler, and one or two servants (who lived in) for cleaning the house; then we had the chauffeur, and a charwoman or two who came in to help with the cleaning. We also had a man who came once a week to wind the clocks and set them, and a man who came once a week to polish the shoes and the silver."[1]

Not mentioned in this list of servants is the nanny. This was Juus (or Juusje) Egner, who was to live in the van Vollenhoven family from her early twenties until she moved to a seniors' residence. Like all nannies, she was a very important person to her young charges, and she was a major figure in Gerard's and my wartime lives.[2]

---

1   More details can be found in *Frontiers and Sanctuaries.*
2   We know little about Juus's background, except that she was of Huguenot descent. Her older sister was employed in the van Vollenhoven family in the Dutch East Indies, and when Joost and Iete returned to the Netherlands in 1910, that older sister stayed behind. Juus entered the household upon the family's return in 1910, and when the children were grown up, she remained in Iete's service.

Upon returning to the Netherlands, Joost van Vollenhoven ran for Parliament (as a Liberal) and won. Then, in 1916, he became managing director of the Bank of the Netherlands, and his services in trade negotiations during the First World War resulted in his being knighted by King George V of England and being made a member of the Order of the Lion of the Netherlands, the country's highest order.

Joost was a somewhat unconventional and fun-loving man, and Madzy adored him, but she was not equally fond of her mother, a socialite who left the children's care mostly to the servants. There were eventually four children. Iete had a son, Paul Adama van Scheltema, from a previous marriage. She and Joost had a son, also named Joost, who had Down syndrome. Madzy was born three years later, and Johanna (Hansje) nine years after that.

Madzy's father died in 1923, and for Madzy it was a major loss.

In her teenage years, Madzy's young and forward-looking ideas often clashed with Iete's more conventional ones. Madzy wanted to wear her hair short and to take a university-entrance school curriculum rather than a lower-level one; she wanted to study law and sing in the university choir. She won all these contests, but the relationship was uncomfortable until, decades later, living geographically far apart, they were able to work out a better one.

Madzy's health was never good. When she was about four, she had frequent colds and fever; it was feared that she had tuberculosis, and she had to lie quietly for months. Later she developed a goitre, which kept her out of school for two years until it was operated on when she was eighteen.

After recovering, she spent nearly a year at an apparently modest finishing school in England. Back in the Netherlands, with the help of a tutor, she put herself through an intensive course of home study so she could write her university entrance exams, in which she obtained very high marks. From 1931 to

1936 she studied law at the University of Leiden but left just before doing her final examinations because she had become engaged to Wim Brender à Brandis.

*

Wim was born in The Hague in 1911, the younger of two children. His father, Gerard Brender à Brandis, was a chemical engineer, a recognized expert in his field; besides being director of the municipal gas works in The Hague, he was also a part-time professor in gas technology at the University of Delft. Wim's mother, Hans Hoogewerff, was a prominent member of the Anthroposophical Society. It was not a happy marriage, and when Wim was fourteen, his parents divorced. His subsequent education suffered. He was shuttled from school to school, the choice made sometimes by his mother, sometimes by his father, and in the end he lost two years.

Wim was interested in country life. He loved gardening and horses, and as a child he had rabbits and pigeons. Some of his best childhood memories were of holidays spent in Maarn, where his uncle and aunt, Ferd and Betsy de Beaufort, had an estate called de Hoogt.

Because of his disrupted education, Wim lacked the qualifications to go to university. After completing school, he did a year's compulsory military service in the field artillery, which at that time was equipped entirely with horses. By the time he finished, it was 1932, the middle of the Depression. He found work in a Rotterdam grain-importing firm headed by a cousin, and two years later he was transferred to the firm's very small New York office.

He was miserably lonely in the United States, but Madzy began a lively correspondence with him. They were distantly related and knew each other slightly because they had played on the same field-hockey team at school. Iete was a close friend of Wim's aunt Betsy de Beaufort. At Christmas 1935 Wim spent his leave in the Netherlands, and he and Madzy became engaged. Madzy, who had been preparing to do her final exams and then join her half-brother Paul in the Dutch East Indies to practice law, found her life suddenly and completely changed.

After the Christmas holidays, Wim returned to New York, and in September 1936 Madzy went there to marry him.[3]

Wim had hoped that Madzy's companionship would make him less lonely in the United States, but in fact they were both homesick. He disliked his work, and he hated the densely urban area around New York. Madzy looked for a part-time job or some kind of volunteer occupation, but it was the Depression, and as a foreigner she was not accepted for anything.

So she began to write. She had done some writing at university and even before that, although only two pieces from that time survive. Now, in the United States, she began writing occasional columns for a Dutch newspaper, *Het Vaderland*. We have eight of those columns, published under the title "Impressions of a Dutch Housewife in America," and also some other pieces from that time, published and unpublished. The best of this work is lively, informative, and very readable.

*

In 1938, with war threatening, the Netherlands began to enlarge its army. Wim, a reserve artillery officer, learned that he could become a career officer and switch to the cavalry. In September 1938, they moved back to the Netherlands, and I was born there in October. We first lived in Amersfoort, where Wim took a training course for cavalry officers. During the five days of fighting between the Netherlands and Germany in May 1940, he came under fire several times.

After the Dutch surrendered, the Netherlands was occupied by the Germans, and the Dutch armed forces were demobilized. Bill, writing memoirs in his old age, recorded: "Normally we should have been made prisoners of war, but the Germans, expecting Dutch cooperation in their war effort if they treated

---

3   Appendix B contains part of a narrative Madzy wrote shortly after the wedding and honeymoon.

us well, allowed the entire Dutch army to go home. However, career officers had to sign a document saying that they would not engage in activities against the German army or their occupation of the country. Except for a few officers who considered that against their honour, we all signed."[4]

Wim, glad to be out of active service, enrolled in an agricultural school in Leeuwarden, in the northeastern part of the country. Being older than the other students, he was allowed to complete the two-year program in one year. On Saturdays he worked as a volunteer on a big farm to learn about practical farming. He also began taking a correspondence course in estate management. He loved it all, but Madzy later recorded: "We made it through that winter, but it wasn't a very enthusiastic winter, as you can imagine." She knew no one, and they had unpacked only the bare necessities, so no doubt the house did not feel very homey. Besides, having a toddler to look after would have tied her down. We lived there from August 1940 to spring 1941 and then moved to Maarn, where Wim had spent those enjoyable summer vacations and where, since there were a number of country estates in the area, he hoped to find work in estate management.

*

One of these estates, already mentioned, was de Hoogt, but there were others. In a memoir written in his old age, Bill set the scene.

> In that general area, adjoining properties were owned by other prominent families. One of them was the Blijdenstein family, who had large properties, mostly wooded. There were two daughters in that family, Dientje and Christie, and two sons, Jan and Willem. Jan had married Greet de Beaufort,[5] Christie married Piet van Notten, and Dientje remained unmarried. Dientje

---

4   *Frontiers and Sanctuaries*, p. 91.
5   Greet was Wim's cousin, daughter of Betsy and Ferd de Beaufort and a close friend of Wim's because of those summer holidays at de Hoogt.

and Christie managed the estate. I knew the family—not very well, but there were many connections. During the war, therefore, when I was demobilized and had spent one year at the agricultural school in Leeuwarden and wanted to find a job, Madzy and I decided to move to Maarn. I asked Christie van Notten and Dientje Blijdenstein if we could temporarily stay in a small apartment attached to the game warden's cottage. They agreed. They didn't know Madzy before that, but it became a very close friendship. Dientje then asked whether Madzy and I were interested in living in the small gardener's cottage ("het Tuinmanshuisje") on the estate. It was very modest but had just been renovated and now had running water and indoor plumbing. Madzy and I gladly accepted the offer. And that's how Madzy and the children came to spend all those war years in Maarn.

Wim, still an army officer and receiving a portion of his salary, found part-time and volunteer work. His principal employer was Jhr. M[r] J. G. Stratenus,[6] owner of Broekhuisen, an estate in Leersum, about seven kilometres (four and a half miles) away, for whom Wim worked as part-time estate manager, and he was also employed by a forestry service marking trees for cutting and thinning, and doing some surveying.

Madzy, in the 1976 memoir, said, "I was a little bit afraid because it was again lonesome; it was again *away* from people and friends—and with the Germans around, and a depot of explosive materials not very far away, it was dangerous. But it was the right thing for Wim. He just loved it and I thought, 'I

However, she never appears in Madzy's war diary because she and her husband spent the war in the United States.

6 "Jonkheer" is a Dutch honorific of nobility. (Wikipedia, "Jonkheer," accessed July 31, 2016, and Wikipedia, "Kasteel Broekhuisen," accessed May 27, 2012).

will love it too.' Finally, actually, in Maarn I had a fairly nice time because I made a lot of contacts."

*

This is the house where the Brender à Brandis family lived from 1941 to 1947, as it was then, showing the street side. The figures in front are probably Marianne and the goat, Trixie.

The house we lived in had been built perhaps a century earlier[7] as a labourer's cottage consisting of one main ground-floor room with a scullery off it and an enclosed bed, like a deep cupboard. Upstairs, under the sloping roof, was a small bedroom. About the beginning of the twentieth century, an addition was built, containing two rooms downstairs and two up, none of them large. Shortly before we moved in, an indoor bathroom was added and, as is typical in the Netherlands, washbasins installed in the two main bedrooms. The original ground-floor room was now a fairly roomy squarish kitchen, with the new bathroom and the older scullery opening from it. Cooking was done on a wood stove; there was also a propane-burning unit, but during most of the war there was no propane. The living room and dining room

---

7　This is information from Bill, either conjecture or something he had learned in the course of his work as estate manager in the neighbourhood. The description of the house is based partly on my memories and partly on his notes.

in the new addition were warmed by a wood-burning heater, and there was a small coal-burning fireplace. The upper floor was unheated.

Behind the house was a small barn and a good-sized vegetable garden. There was an orchard on one side (not part of the property we rented from the Blijdenstein estate) and woods on the other side and behind. The area across the road was also wooded, and there was a long driveway leading to Huis te Maarn, the "big house" on the Blijdenstein estate. What Madzy meant by "lonesome" was that from our house no others were visible. As noted, we had no telephone.

Socially speaking, however, it was not lonesome. There were old friends of Wim's nearby, and the two of them immediately began making new ones. Wim's aunt Betsy, one of his favourite relatives, was at de Hoogt, about four kilometres (two and a half miles) away. Dientje Blijdenstein and Christie van Notten quickly became friends; so did the local doctor, Ad van Kekem, and his wife, Dick, and our close neighbours VaVa and Edward Hoogeweegen. Nine kilometres (six miles) away in Leusden, near Amersfoort, were Dick and Charlotte Kolff, friends from the Amersfoort days who would be an important resource for Madzy during the war. It was a circle of intelligent and congenial people, with similar backgrounds and interests.

Several of Madzy's family were also quite nearby: her sister Hansje lived in Utrecht, eighteen kilometres (twelve miles) away, and her brother Joost six kilometres (four miles) away in Driebergen. A beloved uncle, Willy Schüffner, lived in Hilversum, twenty-one kilometres (sixteen miles) away.

Also part of the circle, but less congenial, was Madzy's mother, Iete, who for periods of time during the war was evacuated from The Hague and, being a close friend of Betsy's, usually stayed at de Hoogt.

*

Madzy seems to have done no writing at this time except for numerous letters, but she sporadically kept a baby book to record details about my growth. On 15 February 1942, after a gap of nearly two years, she wrote:

> Wars and misery passed over Marianne's head, and left no mark except that she is terrified of airplanes. The food-rationing problems don't affect her. The war continues. This is the day of the fall of Singapore.[8] But here we look out on peaceful woods decorated by snow and hoarfrost, and all we notice of the war is sometimes bombing either nearby or farther away and the rationing of food. What preoccupies us most is the coming of Marianne's little brother or sister in the beginning of May, and the exam that Papa has to write.

This gives a glimpse of how things stood three months before Wim was taken prisoner.

*****

In the Preface I quoted Madzy's words about wanting her inner life to be known to others. I learned about that inner life from her writings, which came to me after her death; among them was work that none of us had seen before. Almost everything was fragmentary, and almost all of it was strongly autobiographical. As I put those writings together, mosaic fashion, I realized I was doing what she had never managed to do: creating a portrait and a coherent narrative. A few aspects of what I learned will serve to introduce the young woman who wrote the war diary.

For Madzy, the painful gap left by her father's death would be filled by Wim. When he was taken prisoner, the gap abruptly opened again and remained open until he returned.

One thing that helped her to survive was religion. The diary as she wrote it contains many appeals to a God whom she sees

---

8   Madzy followed events in the Far East because her half-brother, Paul Adama van Scheltema, and his wife, Mita, and four daughters were in the Dutch East Indies. After the colony fell to Japan, they spent the rest of the war in Japanese prison camps.

in an uncomplicated way as a father figure who takes a personal interest in her.[9] I was struck by this because she never revealed such feelings in her other writings, nor in her outer life during the time when we children knew her. Perhaps, in her busy pre- and post-war existence, surrounded by family, she was less in need of such support. Her parents were not particularly religious. Madzy and Wim were Remonstrant,[10] but in Maarn there was no Remonstrant church, so she attended a Reformed one.[11] In the diary she once mentions having attended a Remonstrant service ("I felt more at home"[12]). During the war, attending church was not only a matter of seeking spiritual comfort but also an opportunity for exchanging information with neighbours and for offering and receiving moral support.

I wrote that Madzy was forward-looking in demanding a good education and studying law in Leiden, but the diary also reveals attitudes from her more old-fashioned upbringing. For instance, before the war she had been used to having the guidance and support of authority figures; her pre-war world had, generally speaking, been protective of well-born young women. During the German occupation, that framework was abruptly replaced with an authority that was far from benign.

She saw her role as being that of a submissive wife: her husband was the head of the family. When Wim was taken prisoner, Madzy suddenly became the head; now *she* was the authority. The diary shows what an upheaval this was and how she adapted.

---

9 I edited a number of those passages out to remove unnecessary repetition.

10 Bill explained to me that both his and Madzy's families belonged to the Remonstrant church, a small Protestant denomination whose ideals were described by K. H. D. Haley as "flexible and tolerant" (*The Dutch in the Seventeenth Century*, p. 108).

11 De Hervormde Kerk.

12 Entry of 7 March 1943.

Madzy's pre-war image was that older people looked after younger ones—a not unnatural view, perhaps, for someone who was still young. She was disconcerted to find, during the war, that her mother and Wim's parents were often less supportive than she expected them to be. At one point she wrote that it seemed strange that she, a young woman, should be so much looked to by older people for help and support.[13]

The war slashed across these inherited and unexamined attitudes, forcing her to become independent and indeed to become a leader and a supporter of others. We see these qualities emerging in response to the pressures of the time.

We also see how the sometimes almost unbearable stress distorted her thinking and emotions, and her relationships with other people. Under stress, that is what happens. Judgment falters. "Small" things bulk large. A fortress mentality sometimes takes over, but it is yoked to a desperate need to stay connected to others. This is part of Madzy's story and of humanity's.

The diary, therefore, provides insight into a mental space that is in some ways different from ours. Madzy records not only her own wrestling with these issues but also her observation of the wrestling process itself. We see attitudes from the pre-war world being replaced with ones that became prevalent after 1945 and that are familiar to us. This is social change happening.

*

The diary shows a writer finding her voice. She sketches characters, chooses the telling detail, shapes the day's events into narratives, and includes direct or indirect dialogue. She had an energetic and probing intellect, and loved reading. She had a lively sense of humour and enjoyed absurdities; flashes of this show up in the diary at the most unexpected moments.

---

13 Entry of 8 October 1943. Vera Brittain writes about "that curious mixture of maturity and childishness which was so long characteristic of our dislocated generation" (p. 537). Brittain was born in 1893, but it seems to me that her observation applies very well to Madzy.

Her fluent pencil records it all.[14]

*****

In the outer world, meanwhile, there was a war on. The occupation was, at first, not unduly severe.[15] The Germans, thinking of the Dutch as "cousins," expected cooperation. But relations rapidly became strained. Bill wrote that he and Madzy were in no danger provided that they did not do anything to oppose the Germans. So long as they kept their heads down, therefore, life was comparatively simple and peaceful.

Nonetheless, as Madzy wrote in the baby book, it *was* a time of "wars and misery." The bombing was worrying, especially because, at this early stage of air warfare, bombing was very inaccurate.[16] Airplanes were still a comparative novelty—and low-flying, bomb-dropping warplanes were an extremely frightening novelty. Maarn was on a major east-west transportation corridor that the Germans used for moving troops and *matériel* and that the Allies regularly bombed.[17] During major raids, planes flew over in massive concentrations. In the camouflaging woods close to de Hoogt, an area known as Noordhout, the German army

---

14 She mostly used a pencil because she often wrote while lying in bed, and as she remarks in the 1976 narrative, she did not want ink blotches from her fountain pen to stain the sheets. She used two large hard-cover notebooks; both have the first few pages removed, indicating they had been previously used for something else. The solid structure of the books made it possible for her to write while lying in bed. When the second book was full, she used a school scribbler.

15 Walter B. Maass, *The Netherlands at War*, passim. Also Werner Warmbrunn, *The Dutch under German Occupation*, p. 11.

16 Ronald Bailey, *The Air War in Europe*, passim. Also Richard Overy, *Why the Allies Won*, passim.

17 The construction of an east-west highway from Utrecht to Arnhem had begun just before the war. The Germans continued to work on it for their own purposes, but it was not finished until after the war (Lägers & Veenland-Heineman, *Maarn: Geschiedenis en architectuur*—"Maarn: History and Architecture," p. 42).

built a big antiaircraft battery, which was the target of Allied bombing; when its guns were fired, our cottage trembled. The woods provided hiding places for German armament depots and concentrations of troops and also for Dutch divers.[18]

Moreover, the country was governed by an enemy dictatorship, and the Dutch were suffering from restrictions and shortages. Life was dominated by identity papers, ration coupons, uncertainty, and danger. After the milder regime at the beginning of the occupation, the situation deteriorated rapidly. The refusal of many Dutch people to cooperate with the Germans led quickly to friction. Friction led to repression and then to a reign of terror, with the enemy administration and several different police forces controlling almost every aspect of the Dutch people's lives and imposing arbitrary and brutal punishment, such as sudden raids ("razzias") on private property.[19] They imprisoned innocent people as hostages for the good behaviour of the rest of the population. When there were acts of sabotage or other disobedience, a number of the hostages would be shot.[20] This happened numerous times, so there was always a reservoir of hostages. Prominent public figures were particularly at risk of being taken.[21]

*

When the diary begins, in May 1942, we had been living in Maarn for a year and were settling in. Wim had planted an extensive vegetable garden, partly because he loved gardening and partly

---

18 For Resistance and divers, see Chapter Six headnote.
19 Maass, passim.
20 "The killing of even a minor German functionary ... invariably resulted in the executing of a dozen or more hostages" (Lynne Olson, *Last Hope Island*, p. 237).
21 Warmbrunn (p. 12) and elsewhere. Maass (p. 127). Overy (p. 304) writes: "In the occupied territories German apparatchiks became a byword for criminality and violence—their rule was harsh in the extreme, their economic policies a mixture of looting and exploitation. This was not true of all German officials ... but the dominant image abroad was dictated by those who did thrive on crime and vice."

because of the rationing and shortages. I helped him; a child of three-and-a-half can be useful in matters of seeding, weeding, and fetching things, and I loved it. I remember helping to hold the twine (each end wound around a stake) that was used so that the seeds and seedlings would be set in a straight line. My father and I would hold the twine straight and taut above the ground, each of us at one end, and then push the stakes into the soil.

We had a goat—a young one not yet bred and therefore not giving milk—and four hens. Wim ordered additional pullets; having your own eggs was also useful, though we had to hand over a certain number of eggs per hen if we wanted to receive poultry feed.

Wim did his paperwork at home, so in the living room there was a desk with ledgers and correspondence. He was still taking courses in estate management and was studying for an exam. Once a month he and the other demobilized career officers reported to the German authorities; the office where he had to report was in Amersfoort, ten kilometres (six miles, bicycling distance) away.

Madzy, pregnant, made preparations for the birth of the baby, which would take place at home, as was customary in the Netherlands at that time, and she would remain in bed for about two weeks afterward. A private nurse, Wendela van Tuyll van Serooskerken, a friend of a friend, came to stay in the house. To make it easier for attendants to look after her, Madzy had her bed raised on blocks (she and Wim slept in separate beds). She had part-time household help from Marietje de Bruin, a young woman who lived in one of a cluster of houses called the Knorrebuurt, just along the road.

On Wednesday, 13 May, Madzy gave birth to a boy, Gerard Willem.

Friday, 15 May, was Wim's regular day for reporting to the German authorities, but this time he had received notice to go to the German army unit in Ede, which was about twenty kilometres (fifteen miles) away and meant going by train.

It was lovely spring weather. After telling Madzy that he would be back at six o'clock, he rode his bicycle to the station to catch a morning train to Ede. He took along a scribbler of notes so that during the train trip he could study for his exam. He wore an ordinary suit and, because of the fine weather, did not take a coat.

However, Madzy was uneasy. In the prevailing atmosphere of uncertainty, it was worrying that he had been told to report to a different location.

She was right to worry: all the officers (just over 2000 of them, in several different reporting locations) were taken captive and sent to a prisoner-of-war camp.[22] It was to be more than three years before Wim returned.

To Madzy the shock of his sudden disappearance, and under such frightening circumstances, was very severe indeed, especially because she was already vulnerable after having just given birth. Her way of grappling with the crisis was to write it down and shape it in the form of a letter to Wim. This gave her some illusion of having contact with him.[23] So on Monday, 18 May, still lying in bed, she began writing. Abruptly a shutter opens on her life, a life at once individual and representative.

----

22 In his old age, Bill wrote an account of this event: see Appendix A.

23 In 1963, Madzy, then in Canada, wrote to Bill, then visiting the Netherlands: "Darling, as usual when you are away I am completely lost unless I am writing to you; I did that when we were engaged, tried to do it when you were in camp (then I wrote everything in a large book we still have) ...." (*Frontiers and Sanctuaries*, p. 283).

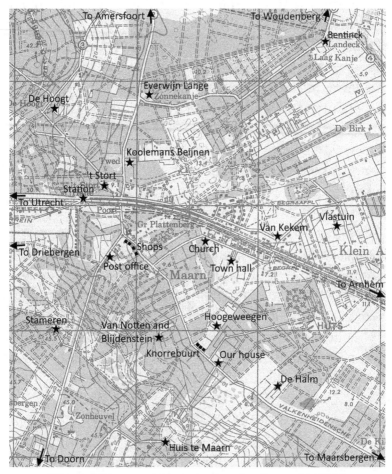

This is Maarn as it was during the Second World War; the basic map was prepared for the Allied troops. The stars indicate local shops and the houses of friends to which Madzy refers.

[Collection of the Cultuurhistorische Commissie Maarn-Maarsbergen. The later additions were made by Gijs van Roekel.]

Chapter One

18 May to 23 May 1942

Monday, 18 May 1942
Maarn

My dearest,

This book is intended only for you.[1] It will be a description of the life that I and the children lived without you while waiting for the happiest day of our lives—the day when you return to our midst and the champagne cork pops.[2]

I could write a thousand things about what happened during the first days, but let's skip over them quickly. It's still too difficult for me to write very much about it. I worried during the whole of Friday the 15th, but when you didn't return at 6:30 and also no telephone message came I almost panicked.[3] At 8:30 Wendela went to phone Amersfoort and came back with alarming news.[4] At 9:30 Moeder Iete [Madzy's mother] came from de Hoogt with

---

1   This indicates Madzy's intention at that very moment. Over the years she came to recognize the diary's larger importance.
2   There actually was a bottle of champagne in the cellar. A couple of years later Madzy gave it to her sister, Hansje.
3   Though Madzy had no telephone, people could phone one of her neighbours, and the message would be brought to her.
4   Wendela was the nurse staying in the house. Bill translated this as "telephoned with the Kolffs in Amersfoort." Dick Kolff, a good friend of Wim's and a reserve cavalry officer, was often a source of information. Madzy doesn't say what the alarming news was.

the news that all of you had been imprisoned. The doctor came at 10:30.[5] Pankie slept that night with me.

The next day was spent anxiously waiting for news. No letter. Moeder Hans came and stayed for the night.[6] On Sunday Marietje fetched the mail and we got your so-called letter.[7] Oh, my dear boy, then I cried more than I had done during all my birth-givings together. Let's not think about it ....

I thought only of you and of the moment when you had to choose between your conscience and your wife. I can never hope to understand what that must have cost you.[8]

And then I worried about your well-being.

But I had to think of your son. I consider Gerard Willem more as your son than as mine—no, more as a gift from me to you, for whom I now have to care with my very best efforts in order to give him to you healthy and sound when you come home.

I will not talk about the countless signs of interest, the visits, and the tears shed around the baby's cradle. But I must tell you

---

5   Dr. Ad van Kekem was the village doctor; two days earlier he had assisted at the birth of the baby. He and his wife, Dick, were part of Madzy and Wim's social circle.

6   Moeder Hans was Wim's mother, Anna Nancy Hoogewerff, who lived in The Hague. She was divorced from Wim's father and used her maiden name.

7   This was a printed card instructing the family to send the imprisoned officer's uniforms and other personal effects to a specified address in the Netherlands. On the card, the prisoner was permitted to write only his home address, no personal message. The first real news from Wim would not arrive until 9 June.

8   In the absence of reliable information, there were many rumours. Madzy had apparently heard that the officers had been given a choice between upholding their honour as officers (and therefore submitting to imprisonment) or signing some "dishonourable" statement so they could be released. Bill's note: "There was absolutely no choice; we were just put on the train to Germany."

that Kraaloogje—out of grief—disappeared for two days but showed up again this morning.[9]

There were innumerable arrangements to make. I asked Vlastuin to fetch the goat; none of us knew how to look after it.[10] They asked me where the chicken feed was, etc. I didn't know anything. How unprepared we were, tumbling into this!

I asked Oom Willy to come so that I could ask him if he could make personal contact with you in Ede to tell you that I was well, and Gerard Willem also—not knowing that you had crossed the border long ago.[11] I also asked him whether, if there was a

---

9   This was one of the hens, "Beady-eye." In the midst of all the grief and anxiety, this is a little outcropping of Madzy's delight in the absurd. We remember that she visualized herself as writing to Wim and knew he would enjoy this tiny bit of droll humour.

10 Bill's note: Vlastuin was a small-scale dairy-farmer living nearby.

11 During the next few months, this motif runs through the diary: whether Madzy's uncle, Willy Schüffner, could get a message to Wim or even pull some strings to obtain his release.

    Wilhelm Schüffner (1867–1949) was Madzy's uncle by marriage, the widower of an aunt of Madzy's. He was a German-Dutch professor of microbiology and immunology who, while living in the Dutch East Indies around the turn of the century, had researched malaria. He was, in 1942, a member of the Royal Dutch Academy of Sciences (Wikipedia, "Wilhelm Schüffner," accessed July 20, 2017; Nederland's Patriciaat— "Patrician families of the Netherlands", p. 300). He was still a German citizen, and lived in Hilversum where, in 1942, the German Wehrmacht for the Netherlands, headed by Friedrich Christiansen, established its headquarters (Dutch-language Wikipedia, "Hilversum," accessed May 23, 2018). Madzy's wording here is cautious in case the diary fell into enemy hands. In a footnote to the entry for 11 June 1942, Bill identified "Kristiansen" [sic] as "a German connection" of Willy's and also as "a top German official," which makes it very likely that Friedrich Christiansen is the man referred to.

    However, as Bill wrote in a note to the entry of 11 July 1942: "[Had this contact succeeded, it] would be terrible in the future to be judged as accepting a favour from the German authorities. Fortunately it never had any success. After the war [people who had received favours from the Germans] were in very bad trouble during the purification of the Dutch people."

chance, he would speak in connection with the possibility that some officers would be released because of work they did.[12] He said that if there was one person for whom he could speak, that would be you. "But not against our conscience," I warned him, and so he left again after five minutes.

Your suitcase had to be packed.[13] I spent all day fretting about what to include. Everybody helped, but I was unable to walk and check on everything. Moeder Iete dug in the trunk of winter clothes and found your uniform. I selected the shoes and put new laces in them. Finally, in the evening, Wendela and I packed it with incredible care. On my behalf she walked all through the house, and she brought rolls of toilet paper, and your windbreaker. Moeder Hans packed your toilet articles. And in the evening at 9:30 came VaVa begging to be allowed to add something: the chocolate and peanut butter and something else are from her.[14]

---

12 Agriculture, with which Wim had a connection because of his work as estate manager, was a "privileged" occupation.

13 I remember, as a small child, kneeling beside the suitcase and "helping" to pack it. It was a leather one; Bill later wrote that, in the camp, realizing that a suitcase would be an awkward piece of luggage to carry if they had to flee suddenly, he cut it up and made a backpack of it. See Appendix A.

14 VaVa Hoogeweegen and her husband, Edward, were very near neighbours, living at a house called de Boerderij. VaVa was active in the Resistance (Caspers, *Vechten voor vrijheid*—"Fighting for Freedom," p. 144). Sometime after this, Edward (Major Hoogeweegen) escaped to England and (presumably on his return to the Netherlands) became the first commander of the Rotterdam brigade of the RVV, a Resistance organization involved in sabotage and espionage (Caspers, p. 306). (By the end of the war, Edward was on the staff of Prince Bernhard; see entry for 8 May 1945.) VaVa provided shelter for a couple of neighbourhood children who had insufficient food at home and for some Resistance workers. Their house was, in the beginning of 1944, the location of a clandestine radio sender and, later, of the radio service of the RVV (Caspers, p. 144). VaVa also sheltered two of the Allied soldiers who had fought at Arnhem but had been unable to escape to the Allied-held territory south of the rivers (van der Zee, p. 139).

And now I realize that when I wrote the label I omitted a part of the address! Will you get the suitcase soon? I will be glad to hear that you received everything.

Oh! I forgot your slippers! That's terrible! But we included nine hard-boiled eggs, half a pound of butter, a tin of pâté, and pipe tobacco, and cookies. Tante Betsy provided labels. Finally Tante Betsy's Piet brought it personally to Ede.[15]

Today Vader Gerard and Jet came; more tears around the cradle.[16] The little one is really being sprinkled. We will never forget his first days, full of sorrow and sadness about your departure. But nor will we forget the cordiality and help that we received from everybody, including Vlastuin, where the goat is staying.

---

15 Bill's note: "The suitcase arrived in good shape some three to four weeks later. Most of the food I shared with friends, as they had done also. But the Germans had taken all the food from the suitcases at another assembly point. Madzy had included a small English Bible which I read during the first month as there were no other books. It was of course marvellous to get all these things and also to get underwear and be able to brush teeth and shave; besides, I had no coat with me." (NOTE: The Bible was actually a Dutch one—clearly, sixty years later, Bill was misremembering. We still have it; Madzy inscribed it, in Dutch: "To my own dearest Dicks from his Mappie, 15 May 1942.")

16 Gerard Brender à Brandis, Wim's father, and his second wife, Jet, were living in Wassenaar, adjacent to The Hague, at the beginning of the war, but Bill told me that at some point they were forced to leave so that the buildings in the area could be demolished to make way for a launching site for V-1s and V-2s, which were pilot-less bombs and rockets. As noted in the Introduction, Gerard was the director of the municipal gas works in The Hague. An article that appeared on his ninetieth birthday in the newspaper *De Telegraaf* (9 September 1971) noted that during the war "the labyrinthine complex [of the gas works] functioned as a hiding place for divers during razzias; the hiding place itself was camouflaged as an infirmary." In 1947 he was made ridder in de Orde van de Nederlandse Leeuw (Knight in the Order of the Dutch Lion).

This morning de heer and Mevr. Stratenus came by in their car.[17] Moeder Iete received them. They remain loyal to you and told her, "We don't know how we will manage without your son-in-law."

It's now Monday evening. Juus came and the household is again running quite well.[18] Gerard Willem is still drinking too much. He slept all day, but Wendela says that that's because yesterday I took tranquillizers and sleeping pills.

Now I'm going to sleep with full confidence that I will be able to carry out the task which God has entrusted to me, and that I can be proud to have such a courageous husband. May God bring us together again. We both will then have learned a lesson, namely that happiness like ours is not just dropped in one's lap. You have a heavy task—to keep up your spirits far from everything you love most. I hope that your friends will help you.[19]

My task is, all of a sudden, to take responsibility for our two children, the house, the garden, and the animals.[20] I will try to do everything in the way you would have done it; the garden with help from a labourer, the animals with advice from Dick Kolff.[21] In all this I will miss your help and advice, but I will have the feeling that I'm doing everything for you to the best of my ability.

---

17 These were the people for whom Wim had worked as part-time estate manager before his imprisonment (see Introduction). Madzy's mentioning that they came by car shows that automobiles were still comparatively rare. In conversation, Bill told me that in the Netherlands at that time "it looked very rich to have a car."

18 Juus Egner (see Introduction) lived in Iete's household in The Hague but had clearly been summoned to Maarn help Madzy.

19 Wim had many friends among the imprisoned officers.

20 Bill's note: "The 'animals' consisted of four chickens; the goat was with the farmer." But Madzy was a city person, and to her the establishment in Maarn seemed like a small farm.

21 Dick and Charlotte Kolff lived on their family's estate in Leusden, just southeast of Amersfoort, nine kilometres (six miles) away. There were greenhouses on the estate, and before the war there had been an extensive staff. Dick grew orchids and vegetables (information from Bill and from Carel Beynen, Charlotte's nephew).

I need to fill the days with this work, and it *will* fill them. May it not last too long: that is my deepest wish.

I need this lesson badly because I have been until now too self-centred and selfish. From now on my thoughts and deeds will be only for you and Marianke and Gerard Willem. I will count myself out entirely and live only for the three of you. *That* will be my life.

I will leave everything in the house as it is: your coat and hat hanging in the hall, the books on your desk, your pipes in the rack. I still base my hopes on the one chance you have: that you will be released because of your work in agriculture. That hope supports me and makes me strong.

You may be safer where you are than here with us. There's less danger of bombing there, and in case of an English invasion you wouldn't have to fight.[22] Prisoners of war don't have it too bad in general.[23] We'll try to make sure that you get as much food as possible. If you make sure that you survive it in your spirit, and if you are strong, I will do the same.

My dearest darling, the rain from a thunderstorm is falling on the roof above my head. And fortunately it's becoming a little cooler, because I'm swimming in perspiration in bed. I am going to dream of your homecoming, and I will pray to God to keep you safe for us.

Tuesday, 19 May. Today little Gerard is six days old. This evening I played with him. I lifted him out of the cradle myself (today the stitches were taken out so I can move more easily). I said to him, "My dear little chap, tears stream around your cradle, but you'll have to grow vigorously, and together we will make sure that

---

22 Throughout the diary, Madzy uses the term "the English" for the Allies, probably as a form of shorthand.

23 The living conditions of prisoners of war were regulated by the Geneva Convention, and POWs' lives were indeed not as dreadful as (for instance) those of the men from the occupied countries who were drafted to work in factories and on farms in Germany.

you become a big boy, and then when Pappa comes home we'll walk to meet him and he'll be amazed at you." Then I saw in my thoughts all the growing stages of the little boy: as a baby lying down, then when he is sitting up. Then as a little boy walking. At which of these stages will you see him again?

Today Pankie had a *crise de nerfs*. She suddenly had a bout of very unhappy crying. The poor child has been very deprived, with all the other emotions. I held her close in my arms and let her cry herself out and then read her beloved chicken story to her.

Tante Betsy came today, with tears in her eyes. She brought buttermilk. There's an avalanche of visits and presents.

I hear dreadful stories: that on Friday 150 women in Ede were chased with bayonets, rumours about the Green Police, about the food that you're being given, etc.[24] It makes me miserable. Then when I think about you I again feel the pain that lies in my heart like a stone. Are you very unhappy? Are you already over it a bit? I'll be so glad when you at least have your suitcase. Have you been able to shave and wash? What do you have to do? Hard work? Do you hang around? Do you get fed? Can you sleep? Do you understand a bit what we wives are going through in the way of fear, anxiety, uncertainty, loneliness, wretchedness?

Enough. I can't agonize any more. It has to be endured.

VaVa brought strawberries with sugar!

Annetje Nahuys and Anneke de Jonghe were here.[25]

This evening Wendela went on my behalf to Mevr. Stratenus. The bookkeeping is to be delivered on Thursday. If it doesn't last too long they will try to keep the job open for you.

---

24 The Green Police were the executive branch of the police force (the Sicherheitsdienst) that the Germans had brought with them to enforce their laws and administer punishment. They were "the incarnation of German terror" (van der Zee, p. 48; Warmbrunn, p. 41).

25 Annetje Nahuys was a good friend of Madzy's. She was manager of Stameren, a small hotel in Maarn that was later requisitioned for use by German officers. Anneke de Jonghe was probably the wife of Emiel de Jonghe, another estate manager with whom Wim had worked.

Wednesday, 20 May. The whole village wept over you. Juffr. Steenbeek[26] is still crying. All of them are grieving about your absence. I hope that they've cried themselves out by the time I go to the village again because if not I will join them in a lusty bout of blubbering. I'll provide myself with a large handkerchief.

Wendela and I have made a thousand plans for this last week of her stay here. We're going to preserve koolmoes,[27] put eggs in brine (we have about 30 eggs on hand, all gifts), sow flower seeds, etc.

We ate spinach from the garden; Dientje[28] said that it had to be thinned, and Teus de Bruin did it with Pankie.

Evening. This afternoon I sat in the garden.[29] The joy of Pankie—"Mammie is better!"—was moving. All of a sudden she is entirely manageable and sweet again. She missed Mammie so much, she told me, and over and over again she came to kiss me.

---

26 Steenbeek was the local grocer.

27 Koolmoes is a leafy green vegetable, *Corchorus olitorius*. There is no good English term for it.

28 See Introduction. Dien (Dientje) Blijdenstein and her sister Chris (Christie) van Notten were by then close friends of Madzy's. Christie's husband, Piet, is mentioned at the beginning and end of the diary as being in Maarn, but in the interval he spent a couple of years in the same POW camp as Wim. Christie and Piet had two sons, Jim and Bem, who were about my age. The big house on their estate, Huis te Maarn, was just up the hill from ours, but at that time the family were living in a smaller house nearby.

29 In the 1976 narrative Madzy says, "The first days I spent in bed. In Holland that was the usual way; we had to stay in bed for at least twelve or thirteen days after the birth of a baby. However, I had been in America and I had told my Dutch doctor, Ad van Kekem, that in America they had a different system, that after five days women were sent home from the hospital. Of course I also had many stitches and they were very painful so it was very hard to get up. But as soon as Dr. van Kekem could he took out the stitches. He was a very wise man and he let me get up and go outdoors."

Madzy and Pankie. The stress and worry have left a mark.
In the background are the vegetable garden and barn.

The garden has grown unbelievably in this week and we have to start preserving koolmoes and spinach immediately. We don't know what to do with it all.

I'm washing myself again, and I again have a slender figure to be proud of. Today Wendela photographed the children and me—I'll send the pictures to you.[30]

One of the hens has pitched her tent in the orchard and is laying her eggs there. From time to time she comes home to eat oyster shells and drink water and then disappears again into her retreat. Strange behaviour, but we're just letting her do what she wants. We can't tie her up with a piece of string.

If I can arrange for you to be released on account of your work, not you as a single case but if more officers are released for a similar reason, would you be in favour of my trying it? Oom Willy could perhaps, later, intercede for you.

Everyone here rejoices at this plan, except Moeder Iete, Hansje,[31] and Tante To,[32] who attack me with idealized talk about the nobility of this sacrifice that you are making for your fatherland. They don't consider that if you're away for too long you'll lose your job at Broekhuisen, after all the effort that you've

---

30 Madzy seems to have disliked being photographed when she was pregnant. We have only two photos of her in that condition. One was taken from behind as she was leaning over the rail of the ship *Statendam* when she and Wim were leaving the United States, and in the other one I am sitting on her lap. In neither one is her pregnancy very visible.

31 Hansje was Madzy's sister, nine years younger; in the summer of 1942 she was twenty-two years of age and living in Utrecht, where she worked in a government office that had been moved from The Hague.

32 This was Catharina Maria van Vollenhoven, a sister of Madzy's father. At that time she was living in Wolfheze, a town near Arnhem, sharing a house with another of Madzy's aunts, Cornelia de Gijselaar, "Tante Cor." Tante To was one of Madzy's favourite relatives, though at this point they do not seem to have been seeing eye to eye.

put into building it up. I also discussed it with Wendela and she agreed with me.[33]

Pankie is very interested in my nursing of the baby. "Do you have only milk in your tummy? In both your tummies? Is it the milk from the dairy?" And: "Mammie, how thin you are now!" Yes, my darling boy, you will also be amazed at my slender figure! All my clothes fit me again and I have no "pot" anymore.

Thursday, 21 May, in bed in the evening. It's a strange feeling to have to divide my attention between two children. I helped Pankie on the potty, and then I hopped into bed at quarter past nine. Then I had to check whether my little boy was still lying comfortably. Because although Wendela and Juus divide the children between them and talk about "your child" and "my child," they are after all still mine—no, yours and mine.

Now I have to admit something very intimate, and that is that I have such a great physical longing for you, and this longing is growing so strong that I will have to fight it. Do you remember that on Wednesday or Thursday I said to you: "I long to crawl into bed with you"? Well, that was not just an offhand remark but a deep longing. I also feel so deeply guilty that in the last while I gave absolutely nothing of myself to you. I was often on the point of offering it and then thought: "No, between us something like that has to be spontaneous and not forced. And besides, we still have to wait for 6 weeks after my giving birth, so don't stir anything up." Now I don't know whether I did the right thing. Do you long very much for me or has this last period of abstinence been a good preparation for a period of separation?

I have so much the feeling that if I am very brave God will grant that I will be able to welcome you back alive and well. I

---

33 This passage gives a glimpse of the discussions going on and also of the divisions within the family, which would have increased the stress for Madzy. Bill's note, given above, about the danger of asking favours of the Germans indicates that Madzy's plan was in fact ill-advised and that her family's opposition was wiser, even if insensitively expressed.

feel that I'm standing above reproach as a person responsible for my actions and for my children. That's why I'm also staying here in the country and hope very much to have you back again before the winter, when the evenings are long.[34] On the first of July Lies is coming to stay here for an indefinite time.[35] Juus will stay until then.

But you'll understand that I'm again having to cope with the contrary advice and the meddling from Moeder Iete and Hansje. Also in the matter of Oom Willy. I wrote to you in the letter that I put in the suitcase (did you get it?): "My uncle, Professor Schüffner, was here: very helpful." I also told Vader Gerard and Jet, who were here today, and they agreed with me. Moeder Iete and Hansje, on the other hand, carry on in such a sentimental way about your "making a sacrifice for the Queen and the Fatherland" and "I think it's fine that Wim is gone," that there's nothing to be done with them. They asked me, "Aren't you proud of Wim?" to which I replied, "Why should I be extra proud? I actually hadn't expected anything else from him; I find it very normal. As a member of the NSB he would have no life here. Then he's better off in a camp."[36] They always express things in such an exaggerated way. But on the other hand they very generously want to send two-kg Red Cross parcels to you three times per month. I'm allowed to use your rationing coupons for such parcels.

---

34 Later she explains that Wim's parents and Iete were urging her to come and live with one or the other of them until Wim returned.

35 Lies was Wim's only sibling, three years older and a nurse. Her daughter, Monica, was aged two.

36 Bill deduced from this that there was a rumour circulating that in order to be released he would have had to join the (small) Dutch Nazi party, the Nationaal-Socialistische Beweging (NSB). This group was collaborating with the German Nazis, and its members were feared and despised by the rest of the Dutch population. Bill wrote that no such offer was ever made and that if it had been he would not have accepted.

The "fat" ration has been decreased again, and potatoes are harder to get.[37]

Today I had to gather all the Broekhuisen papers and deliver them. I enclosed a letter explaining the 650 guilders that I found with them. I'm still weak but I can manage such little tasks.[38]

Jet is coming to do the income tax.[39] Vader is helping us financially. People are saying that you will again receive your full pay, you one-third and I two-thirds.[40]

Will you have received your suitcase already, and exactly as we packed it?

Goodnight, my dearest—someday probably the sun will shine again. Every day I pray for an invasion by the English and an end to the war.

There is one thing which I simply can't stand yet. That is lying in bed and hearing the trains.[41] Then I get the same feeling that I had on the unhappiest evening of my life, Friday the 15th of May,

---

37 Many Dutch families at that time ate potatoes as part of every hot meal, so the shortage of potatoes was a big issue.

38 Presumably one of Madzy's or her friends' helpers did the actual delivering.

39 Jet had worked in a financial institution before her marriage and was good at such things.

40 Bill did not translate or annotate this. As a demobilized cavalry officer, he had presumably been on reduced, "non-active" pay and had taken part-time work to supplement this as well as keep himself occupied. As a POW, he was regarded as being again in active service, and his salary was apparently 125 guilders per month. However, earnings from his part-time work would now have stopped. In addition to Vader Gerard's financial help, Iete also helped Madzy later in the war by buying some food on the black market, but Madzy still had to be careful with the money.

41 The sound of passing trains had very painful associations for Madzy. When she and Wim were living near New York, he commuted by train, and every evening she would go to the railway station to meet him. In writings dealing with that time (see Appendix B), she recorded how train after train would disgorge other commuting husbands but not Wim. The sound of trains was therefore always associated with Wim's absence and her longing and loneliness.

when I lay listening and waiting for you, not knowing that you were already no longer in Holland.

Friday, 22 May. With each day it becomes harder to bear; I can almost not carry on but I have to move forward, there's nothing else to do.

But my dear boy, what were your thoughts when you left here last Friday? Everything was so wrong and contrary. You shook hands with Wendela and gave her the key to your desk. You laid down some papers, but no farewell note to me. And you didn't even take a coat with you! How could you do that, my boy? I discovered that just today; I thought you had taken your good raincoat, but today it arrived back from the dry cleaners! Oh, how wretched! Why was I lying in bed? Why didn't I go to the door with you? Why wasn't I even able to watch you leave, or hug you, or prepare something for you to take along?[42]

Fate is cruel.

I brought out your portrait, and again the tears are pouring. I'm weak and tired and my heart is a painful lump in my chest. But I must not complain. I have to trust in God and pray every day that He will let you return home soon.

Little Gerard is becoming angelically sweet. He blinks his eyes so delightfully and makes such lovable little grunting sounds, and today he gave me a little laugh—he really did. But I have such mixed feelings when I hold him in my arms, and often the tears spring to my eyes when I think how much of him you are missing, so I really can't enjoy it totally. I can't enjoy anything

---

42 Some of these actions, which clearly Madzy had pieced together after the fact, suggest that she thought that Wim suspected that he might *not* return that evening, but in a memoir titled "Our Lives Together" (see Appendix A) Bill wrote that he had no suspicion of this until he arrived at the railway station and met a fellow officer carrying a small suitcase. In the annotation to this diary passage he wrote: "I was convinced myself that I would return on that Friday." Madzy, in her anguish, is grouping all kinds of things together without analyzing them very critically.

without you; that's something that you know about me. I only feel grateful that I have little Gerard; I get more comfort from him than from Pankie.

Saturday, 23 May. I've discovered that Pankie has your character trait of not wanting to think about dreadful things. She doesn't want to be reminded of you and therefore she acts as if she doesn't miss you. This morning I showed her your portrait and she didn't want to look at it; she put her hands over her eyes.[43]

Gerard Willem doesn't allow us much sleep. By day he is sweet as an angel, but this past night (after a feeding session that didn't end until quarter to twelve) he began to scream again at half past two, and by five o'clock the noise was so loud that I fed him. So we don't get much rest at night.

I have absolutely no appetite; I just stuff food into myself. Everyone tries to find something to tempt me. From Edward [Hoogeweegen] I received some red wine; he felt that I needed a boost. He is angelic and helps me in every possible way.

Evening. "Is that the Pappie who is now in Germany?" Pankie asked today, pointing at your photo. "Those Germans are awful grabbers, aren't they, Mammie?" Pankie notices more of the situation than appears on the surface.

I will be glad when I can again look after my children all by myself. When Wendela leaves on Friday I will take Gerard entirely into my own care, though Pankie will still be in Juus's

---

43 In the 1976 narrative, Madzy gave a different interpretation: "Marianne took Dad's disappearance very silently. She didn't react at all at first, and I felt that that wasn't the right thing. When I was thirteen years old and my father died I never talked about him any more, and that has had a very bad effect on me. So I knew that [in 1942] I should talk about Dad and about Dad's coming back and so on. So after a week I found a very nice photograph of Dad and I showed that to Pankie and immediately she put her little hands in front of her eyes and turned away and ran away, so I knew at that time how much the little sweetheart suffered too and couldn't express her suffering."

hands. I can't deprive Juus of the pleasure of looking after a child. But I'm going to take everything over and do it myself: the children and the housekeeping (at least the organization of it) and the garden and the animals.[44] I will keep everything as it is for when you return.

I get plenty of visitors. Charlotte [Kolff] came this morning. Dick has packed a suitcase already: she is very worried.[45] It's expected that at any moment the reserve officers and the noncommissioned officers will be taken prisoner. The construction industry has come to a standstill because building materials have been requisitioned by the Germans, and the labourers have to go [to German labour camps].[46] Vader has to supply 46 labourers. He was told to select them but he refused.[47]

---

44 In the coming years, Madzy would do a lot of gardening. Though she seems to have done some at the school in England, the sudden need, now, to do heavy, necessary work in the vegetable garden was new to her.
45 At this point, it was only the Dutch career officers who had been taken prisoner, but the reserve officers were afraid that at any moment the same would happen to them. Several of Madzy's friends, including Piet van Notten and Dick Kolff, were reserve officers. Piet was eventually imprisoned, but, according to information I received from Charlotte's nephew, Carel Beynen, Dick more or less went underground and never did go to a camp.
46 Dutch men were conscripted to work in labour camps in Germany to replace German workers who were by then in the army. Olson (p. 218) writes that the Germans needed labourers because they had lost so many men in the savage fighting along their eastern front. It was a gradual process, but van der Zee (p. 29) states that by the end of the war more than half a million Dutch men had gone to German labour camps.
47 These would be employees at the gas works.

Today Mevr. Everwijn Lange[48] came to visit, and also—unexpectedly—Dr. Plomp, very nice of him.[49] The fact that I'm still feeding the baby one extra time per day, and that from Day 7 I've been up and sitting in the garden, is a sign that I'm managing well.

This evening visits from Annetje Nahuys and Hans van K. V., who stayed chatting until 10:00.[50]

They say that the 65 Dutch prisoners of war who were taken two years ago have been put with you in Austria. They say that you are in Linz, Heiligenblut, Graz, Innsbruck. They say that we can send you three parcels (two kg each) per month and that you will get two parcels from the Red Cross, for which we have to use your coupons, and that we can send you parcels of five kg with books and clothes. They say that you'll be able to write four postcards and two letters per month, and we as many as we want (everything in Dutch). They say that it's good to be able to think of you wearing your uniforms and that you'll be well looked after. However, they say so many other things (that you aren't allowed to wear your shirt-collar and tie,[51] and that you've had your heads shaved) that I had better stop because thinking about them makes me wretched.

I'm longing to receive some sign of life from you and pray to God every moment that he will keep you safe and healthy for the three of us.

Now Gerard has to be fed.

---

48 She was the wife of the mayor, F. E. Everwijn Lange. In the Netherlands, mayors are appointed, and he was the mayor from 1924–1951 (Lägers & Veenland-Heineman, p. 98). During the war most/all of such officials were replaced by men who supported the Germans; in Maarn the wartime mayor was J. P. A. de Monyé, a member of the NSB (Caspers, p. 181).

49 Dr. Plomp had been our family doctor when we lived in Amersfoort and also a next-door neighbour.

50 Hans van Ketwich Verschuur was at that time married to Wim's cousin Els, daughter of Betsy and Ferd de Beaufort.

51 Shirt collars were detachable from the neckline of the shirt.

Wim Brender à Brandis. On the back Bill later wrote: "Drawing made in Prisoner of War Camp in Stanislau (Ukraine) 1943."

Chapter Two

24 May to 28 May 1942

Madzy, along with the inevitable worrying, continued to pick up the strands of Wim's Maarn life and to reconstruct her own after the disruptions of childbirth and Wim's departure.

She always had helpers. For a few weeks in the summer of 1942, and then again from November 1942 to the end of the war, Juus Egner lived with us. Juus benefited by being able to find a home in Maarn because, as Iete's live-in servant, she would also have had to evacuate from The Hague. She was company for Madzy, who was living in an isolated house under dangerous conditions. Her presence was invaluable during the later war years when Madzy had to go out scrounging for food. But Juus was not young (she was in her late fifties at this time and had worked as a nanny and personal attendant rather than a cleaner), so for the cleaning and other heavy work there was a part-time servant. In the house, as in the garden, Madzy did a considerable amount of the work herself, but her health wouldn't allow her to do the heavy work.

The housework was labour-intensive. We had no washing machine; the smaller laundry was done by hand, and the large items were sent to a commercial laundry. The "smaller" laundry by now included the washing for two small children. Later in the war, when the electricity was shut off, water came from a hand pump in the garden, and the required hot water was heated on the stove with inadequate fuel, wood which had to be found, split or broken up, and then carried indoors (and the ashes taken out). Most fabrics had to be ironed. Floors were swept with a broom. There were virtually no prepared foods. The grain Madzy obtained later in the war had to be ground up or processed in some other way.[1]

Even with help in the house and garden, Madzy's days were extremely busy. She shopped in the village. Later, as the food situation worsened, she went farther afield to farms and elsewhere to obtain food, some of which she shared with others. Writing letters, and visiting friends and family, were essential for keeping in touch in a time of increasing crisis. There were the children to look after. There were clothes to be mended or altered—a never-ending job because, as the war continued, it became impossible to buy new clothing.

One of my sources for information about wartime conditions is the correspondence that Madzy had with Virginia Donaldson and her daughter Rosalie Worthington, distant relatives of Wim's. Their ancestor had moved to the United States in 1812; the contact had been maintained, and Madzy and Wim had visited Virginia on their honeymoon. During the war, civilian correspondence between North America and the Netherlands ceased, but after the war Virginia reconnected with Madzy through the Red Cross and immediately asked her what she needed so that she and Rosalie could send parcels. Madzy's side of this correspondence,[2] even though it mainly describes how things were in 1945, sometimes alludes to earlier conditions. For instance, Madzy wrote in 1945 that she was wearing five-year-old stockings, much mended, and that she had only one sweater, much patched. Her other sweaters had been bartered away or unravelled so that the yarn could be re-knitted into garments for us children. She had cut up underwear of her own and Wim's to make underwear for us. Madzy's letters of thanks itemize the contents of each parcel: staples like scarves, winter hats, tea, toilet soap.

*****

---

1 In the 1976 narrative, when describing how she made rye bread at home, Madzy said that she ground the rye in the coffee grinder. See entry for 24 October 1944.

2 Madzy's letters were returned to me by Addison Worthington, Rosalie's son.

Sunday, 24 May. The stream of visitors is becoming overwhelming.[3] Constantly talking about you, about the whole matter of the prisoners of war, about your chances of coming home, your work here, your life there, your ability to bear up—it's driving me crazy. This morning Tante Gusta and Tante Ida and Els, then Oom Wim and Tante Caro Roest van Limburg.[4] Oom Wim envies you: he says, "I wish that I were with Wim and not constantly in danger of being taken hostage for Amsterdam." The situation is becoming daily more frightening; the tension in the air is almost tangible.

Meanwhile I'm waiting with anxiety, hope and ... fear for the first word from you. From now on I will always go to the post office on Sunday to get the mail.[5] Juus did it today. I'm afraid of what you will write and how I will be able to bear the first sign of life from you. Because outwardly I'm being brave, but inside

---

3   In the 1976 narrative she said, "I think that I got on the average about six to eight guests a day." Clearly her friends and family were concerned about her.

4   Gusta was Wim's aunt. Ida was Wim's great-aunt by marriage and also a distant relative of Madzy's.

    Willem Roest van Limburg, a cousin of Wim's father, had a prominent position at the Nederlandsche Bank (the Bank of the Netherlands). In May 1940, at the time of the German invasion of the Netherlands, Queen Wilhelmina had to be urgently evacuated to England, and she was driven to Hoek van Holland in an armoured car (Olson, p. 29). The vehicle belonged to the Nederlandsche Bank, and Wim Roest van Limburg drove it (information from August de Man). His prominent position at the bank increased the risk of his being taken hostage.

    The fact that Madzy speaks of this couple so casually and refers to them as "Oom" and "Tante" indicates that she knew them well; it's possible that that friendship was based on the fact of Madzy's father having formerly been managing director of the bank. In the Netherlands at that time, children addressed close friends of their parents as "Oom" and "Tante."

5   On weekdays the mail was delivered, but the post office was just a room in the house of the postmaster, Mr. Niewenhuizen (information from Jacob Heerikhuisen, March 10, 2019) and Madzy obviously knew that on Sundays he would give the mail to her or one of her helpers.

is one large wound. I'm aching to hear some news so that at last I will know where you are, how you are, whether you caught a cold during the trip because you didn't have a coat, etc. Everything hurts me inside.

But I've resolved that my own "me" is no longer an important subject, however much the attention I'm receiving from the outside world would lead me to believe that. What I have to do in this time is to learn to forget myself, remove my own feelings from the calculation, and base myself on you and your wishes, and those of the children. Only then will I be really satisfied with myself.

After this week my days will be full. The barn is a mess,[6] the chickens have to be looked after better, the goat has to be brought back here eventually. In the garden the weeds are shooting up, and the lawn has to be mowed. I have to find someone who will cut grass to make hay to feed the goat during the winter. The grass cuttings will make hay, won't they? Once we can correspond calmly you will have to give me advice. I have many questions to ask you.

Evening. For a woman who gave birth 11 days ago I've done a lot of work. This morning I tidied the house and packed the silver because it will be stored at Tante Betsy's. I don't like the idea that we, as women living alone in such an isolated house, should have so many nice things here. This afternoon we did some hoeing and raking in the flower garden. Then came Dientje, and afterwards we walked to de Boerderij.[7] This evening we sowed flower seeds. The garden is growing like mad. In several beds where I thought that nothing had been sown yet there are now young plants: according to Dientje there are beets, winter carrots, beans, and cabbage. The day after tomorrow Gijs will hoe the potatoes. Tomorrow I will hoe the gravel paths, which

---

6   It was not a very big barn, but it had a loft.
7   De Boerderij was the Hoogeweegens' house, a couple of minutes' walk from ours.

look like a lawn. I also gave the hens potato peelings again, which they devoured. I really feel that I'm the master in my own house again. There is an unbelievable amount to do. I also want to go to the barn-loft to fetch that mattress down, otherwise the mice will eat it.[8] I can't find those swords of yours.[9] The air gun I'll keep: a good weapon to have in this isolated place.

I read in the paper that we have to supply 15 eggs per chicken per year [in order to receive poultry feed]. Fortunately, just yesterday, I put 32 eggs in preservative.

I sent all your papers to the Forestry service.

All the work gives me a push to dare to tackle life again and to hope for a happier time. Don't think, just work hard and drop into bed in the evening fagged-out. That's best.

I gave Pankie her own little flower garden where she may do the sowing herself. She is so excited about it that just now, when I put her on the potty, she asked if there's already anything coming up.

We don't read aloud in the evening now, but instead we work in the garden. The corn is coming up, some plants with four leaves already. When will I have to transplant them? I don't think I'll get your reply in time.[10]

I'm also going to learn to milk the goat. And I'll clean its pen, wearing your coverall. Also the chicken pen, which is very dirty.

Gerard was in the bath today for the first time and found it quite amusing.

---

8   Bill explained, in the annotation to a later entry, that the mattress had been put there to provide a hiding place for him if he had suddenly had to go underground.

9   Bill noted that swords were part of his equipment as a cavalry officer. He had buried them in the woods.

10 This is one of the places where she writes as though this is a letter to be sent directly to Wim. In fact, of course, she had not yet been able to ask him this or any other question.

Monday, 25 May. In the mornings everything is difficult; then there's still a whole day ahead of me and then I think how you would have loved it, the garden and the beautiful weather and the animals, and then I hurt so much inside. Will that pain ever wear off a bit? Will I ever miss you less? How do you feel? Will you ever tell me about it?

In the mornings Pankie always comes to lie in your bed for a few minutes to eat a rusk. We get rusks with the children's coupons. But potatoes are not to be had anymore, not for money or fine words.

"Are you thinking about Pappa?" Pankie just asked.

"Yes, sweetie."

"Are you missing Pappa?"

"Oh, darling, so much."

"*How* much?"

"A hundred times a hundred thousand."

"I only a thousand," she says, and then: "Shall I go and have a look to see if Pappa has already come home?"

"Oh, sweetheart, if only it were true!"

"Yes, but *really*, Mamma?"

"Where would you look, darling?"

"Downstairs in the garden, naturally."

So now she's quickly dressing herself so that she can go and look at her own little garden. She's still full of excitement about that.

I'm going to read a bit, because then for a little while I don't think about you. For three more days I *have* to eat breakfast in bed and then I can get up again as normal. Wendela gladly pampers me with breakfast in bed, but I find it awful. I'd much rather throw myself into my work at 7:30 but I'm still too weak for that. If only I perk up quickly now. And if only my milk doesn't decline when I work harder.

Afternoon. There are moments when I think I'm becoming a bit used to having to do without you for an indefinite time. There are other moments when everything seems insurmountable and then I wish that I were also a career officer. This is one of those moments. I wish I were with you. Today someone said that you were in Silesia.[11] I had just made myself somewhat happy about the thought that you were in Austria—people said that that was not too bad. Now all of a sudden I'm down in the dumps. Ach, not only about that "Silesia" but about the uncertainty and the indefinite duration and about every moment of missing you. I long so much for your first sign of life, but on the other hand I'm afraid. Oh, if I could only snuggle against you and find comfort and support from you! Or if only I knew how long it will still be! Then I could start counting the days. How does that uncertainty affect you?

Sometimes you disappear from me in a mist. Then I have to remind myself of how you stood shaving, how you lay in bed with your hair in a messy topknot, how you tied your tie in front of the mirror, how you worked in the garden, and how you came home from Broekhuisen on the bicycle. Then I feel very, very close to you again. Because we love each other so very much that every fading of your image into nothingness can be reversed by evoking such memories.

Would I dare to hope that in six weeks I might see you back? Ridiculous. Six months? Unthinkable that it might be that long. By then it will be winter, the evenings long and dark. No, no, dear God, not that long! Instead please let us have the conclusion of the war, with fighting here in our fatherland—even if we have to flee from the house with children and baggage—give us that whole ordeal, but in God's name let there be an end to the wretchedness. Because Holland is at the moment very wretched, with all those lonely, sorrowing wives and mothers, the shortage of food, the fear ... the fear of what tomorrow will bring us ....

---

11 Silesia was near the Polish border. For Madzy, the farther away Wim was, the worse. Moreover, with the fighting between Germany and Russia, Eastern Europe was not a safe place to be.

For the first time Gerard Willem lay in the baby carriage outdoors, on his twelfth day! Why do you have to miss out on all those joys, and why are they for me also, therefore, no longer joys? I can't take pleasure in a life without you. But I have to be brave; I must and will bear up at all costs.

During dinner Pankie said suddenly: "Pappa telephoned this morning to say that he is coming home tomorrow! And then he will come on the bicycle from Broekhuisen, and then he will jump off the bicycle, and then I will give him a really big kiss." She misses you too, darling. Do you see now how the three of us can't manage without you?

Evening. This afternoon I again cried for half an hour. Then I tackled my life again. This afternoon Gerard W. was photographed. It's for you; I'll send the pictures as soon as I have contact with you.

This evening Tini came, just while I was sweeping the barn.[12] She brought a koek and rye bread.[13] The welcome gifts keep streaming in. But I have absolutely no appetite. When Tini left, Dick van Kekem came, and then also the doctor [Ad]. They stayed until past 10 o'clock. If you had been here you wouldn't have been able to study for your exam: if there aren't 6 to 8 visitors per day, mostly unexpected, then I'm surprised.

Tuesday, 26 May. This morning Eddy[14] and Annemarie came pedaling through the pouring rain. Soaking wet. Eddy full of hope that he as reserve officer would be interned one of these

---

12 Tini Sandberg was a doctor and one of Madzy's closest friends. She was one of a little group that, in their university years, made a walking tour in Cornwall.

13 The typical Dutch koek is a delicacy somewhere between bread and cake.

14 Eddy van Vollenhoven, though he had the same surname as Madzy's maiden name, was (according to Bill) not a close relative. Annemarie was his wife.

days.[15] His suitcase is packed and everything in order. Pictured himself walking into your barrack-room and bringing you the latest news about us. Promised me that when the call-up was announced, and if he had the time, he would come here and pick up some things to take to you. To me, all this looked far too rosy to be true. If Eddy were to join you, though, I would be easier. He is so reasonable and always gives you such support. But I'm sure it won't turn out like that. Besides, there are 15,000 reserve officers! But these days anything is possible.

It's becoming oppressive here. There is tension and expectation in the air.

Today I had Gijs working here for the whole day in the garden and he hoed all the gravel paths. They look beautiful! But how can I keep that up? I feel obliged to keep it all neat.

Vlastuin says that the goat isn't pregnant. We're going there [to Vlastuin's farm] tomorrow. I'll discuss with him whether she can be bred again. I also have to talk to M[r.] de Jonghe about firewood; we have almost none left, also not enough to do the preserving.[16] I arranged with van Ee that your bicycle will be hidden here.[17] The tires will be taken off; one of them I'll have mended and then all those things hung in the cellar. I'll have the bicycle put in the loft of the barn. I'll put the saddlebags behind the hot water tank, waxed.[18]

I hope that I do everything right. I worry all the time in case I forget something. You really spoiled me by doing everything, and

---

15 So long as Eddy was in the Netherlands he was in danger of being taken hostage or of being sent to a labour camp in Germany.

16 This is probably Emiel de Jonghe, whom Bill identified as another estate manager living nearby. Because of his work he would likely have access to firewood.

17 Bicycles, especially men's, were regularly being confiscated by the Germans; there was less demand for women's, which is no doubt why Madzy was able to keep using hers until nearly the end of the war, although at a certain point it broke down and she was forced to use Wim's.

18 Presumably they were of leather, and the wax would preserve them.

now you've suddenly left me unprepared in the busiest season. All of a sudden I have such a "masculine" feeling; everything comes on my shoulders, everybody asks me about everything. I have to work with carpentry tools. The iron bars in Pankie's room are loose; a notice saying "Pull" has to be mounted on the front gate; the back gate is broken; the leg of the laundry-drying rack is still broken; the seat of my bicycle has to be raised; I have to climb the ladder to the loft of the barn to get the mattress and take it back to the house, etc. etc. I knew that you did a lot of chores, but not that it was *this* much, and I knew that I left a lot to your care, but that I was *this* lazy—no, I wasn't aware of that!

Last night I dreamed that many refugees came past here and that we ourselves had to flee to a strange country (it seemed to be Belgium) and that my bicycle had been stolen.

I'm a bad mother because when I wake up in the morning my first thought is not, "What's the wonderful thing that has happened? Oh, yes, little Gerard," but "What horrible thing has happened? Oh, yes, Dicks." My milk is already seriously diminishing and Wendela stuffs me full of milk and porridge.

I concluded yesterday that the longest that you could and might be away is six months and therefore I'm going to make a calendar in the back of this book and cross off the days.[19]

Wednesday, 27 May. Gerard Willem is 14 days old today, but his birth feels like months ago.

How does it feel to be a prisoner of war? Very claustrophobic and limited in freedom?

---

19 There is no indication of how she reached this conclusion; maybe it was just an attempt to create what then seemed the worst possible scenario. However, she did set up a calendar on the inside back cover of the diary, beginning on May 16. It ran to 31 December 1942. She began another on 25 September 1944, and kept it until 25 December, then added the note: "Churchill says that it could still go on for 3 months."

I've had an active day today. First Marietje and I tidied and swept the barn. I locked your carpentry cupboard.[20] We got the mattress from the loft, with me above and her below, and aired it. Then I bicycled to Vlastuin—somewhat painful but manageable. Trixie [the goat] came to meet me and licked my finger. She looked better, less thin along her spine but also less round of belly. No, there's no kid coming. I arranged with Vlastuin that as soon as she is ready she'll go to the buck again and then be brought back to us. Then I'll pay him for everything.[21]

There's word from The Hague that you're all together in Tyrol and are doing well.

Did you throw a note out of the train? Some women have still been receiving such things. Are you very hungry? We're choking with food now that we have your coupons and Gerard's, and now that we all eat so much less.[22]

Evening. Wendela mowed the lawn and I raked the cuttings together and loaded them in the wheelbarrow and spread them in the barn to dry. That will be hay for the goat. The corn is being crowded out by the koolmoes and almost impossible to find. And when I dig over that area[23] what do I do with those tiny unfindable plants in between the thick, jungly koolmoes? Problems. And what should I plant instead of the koolmoes?

---

20 Wim loved working with wood and always had a carefully maintained set of carpentry tools.

21 The goat would begin providing milk when it had a kid, and as food supplies dwindled it would be helpful to have fresh milk, especially with two small children.

22 This would have been a temporary and probably local glut; in the country as a whole, food was scarce enough to be rationed. See entry for 28 May 1942.

23 She was referring to the fact that after the koolmoes was finished, that bed would be dug over to prepare for a crop (of other vegetables).

Endives?[24] Carrots? I'll ask Dick [Kolff]. Charlotte is coming tomorrow.[25]

I asked de Jonghe about firewood. In two weeks I'll have firewood, he said. All you have to do is be the wife of a prisoner of war and all doors open for you! But, ach, I'd rather be the wife of a working estate manager, who returned cheerfully home from work every evening to his wife and children.

Thursday, 28 May. Daily life is absorbing my attention more and more, and so I can bear your absence a bit better. All the same my milk is not as abundant as it was with Pankie, and if I want to feed our little boy well I have to try very hard not to worry. Such problems are difficult but can be overcome.

A prominent Gestapo officer in Prague has been attacked. The poor Czechs! He is not dead yet. Apparently it is the "worst" man, "Killer" Heydrich.[26]

---

24 She was probably referring to the dark endives with loose, curly leaves rather than to Belgian endives.

25 On the flyleaf at the back of this volume of the diary, she wrote gardening notes. They are undated, but since they precede the calendar (see entry for 26 May), they were probably made at this time. She wrote:
   - Have the cabbages been manured? I did it again.
   - Spinach and koolmoes sowed too close together. Corn in between them is *not* a success. I moved the corn and now it's OK.
   - Strawberries are under a net. How do I do the hoeing between them?
   - Sow the chard in spring: more salad greens.
   - Too much fertilizer to the beans and potatoes? Both are too big. The beans fall over with the least bit of wind.
   - [Plant] herbs in flower garden; [they] take up too much room from the vegetables.
   - Potatoes (red) *above* the ground.

26 R. T. E. Heydrich was one of the main architects of the Holocaust as well as the chief of (among other things) the Gestapo. He died a week after this attack (Olson, 234; Wikipedia, "Heydrich," accessed March 30, 2017). Madzy's phrase "the poor Czechs" refers to the fact that there would inevitably be savage reprisals. There were. "Altogether, more than five thousand Czech citizens died in the aftermath of the assault on Heydrich" (Olson, p. 241).

This morning we gathered six wheelbarrows of firewood.[27] It's wet because these days it rains almost every night (the sun shines during the day) but it will dry in the shed.[28] I'll chop it up. Wendela is afraid that I'm doing too much, because of the milk supply, but I'm overflowing with energy.

I tried to persuade Wendela to come here for August and September, and perhaps for the winter (although I can't picture a winter without you) because I've decided not to spend the winter in The Hague (at most a week or two) because I won't give up my personal freedom.[29] If necessary rather a children's nurse and lonely evenings but not a dependent position with parents or parents-in-law. You know how well they mean it but also how it will actually be. If only I can manage financially, and if the winter isn't too severe and the isolation too unbearable! But I won't think about the winter. By October or November you'll be home again, won't you, my darling? (I love you!)

Evening: The following story I got from Tante Betsy's Mevrouw LeHeux.[30] One of the imprisoned officers found a chance to write a postcard to his wife from Nuremberg, writing as though he was one of the children in that group that were sent from

---

27 This would be mostly kindling, gathered in the woods next to the house. I remember doing this with Madzy all during the war.

28 There was a woodshed attached to the barn. I remember Wim explaining to my small self that the shed had slatted (not solid) walls so that the air circulation would dry the wood.

29 In the 1976 narrative Madzy says: "I didn't want to leave Maarn. I was happy there and I wanted to stay on my own, but they [Wim's parents and Iete] said, 'Why don't you come and stay with us? It will be so much cheaper for you, and you won't be so lonesome. You have no telephone. You have no man to defend you, and the Germans are all around.' And they were right, but I just wanted to stay where Dad had left us so that when he came home he would find us back, if that was possible." For part of the war The Hague was evacuated, but at this time Wim's parents and Iete were evidently still living there.

30 Bill's note: Mevrouw LeHeux was the wife of a doctor in Doorn, presumably Betsy's doctor.

Holland to Austria "to recuperate." He wrote something like this: "We arrived after 24 hours of traveling (stiff but healthy and cheerful) in the city of toys.[31] The people who have to look after us do their best. We are considered to be so grown-up that we will make the rest of the trip without supervision. We get alternately pea- or bean-soup, sourdough bread with *lots* of butter, and sausage and lots of cold water to drink. We beg our mothers not to worry about us because we're doing fine." Later you have to tell me whether this could have been true![32]

Later, oh later, my boy! After the war? Peace? Can it ever happen? And what is still awaiting you? And us here? Food is very scarce, butter hard to get, potatoes and vegetables entirely finished, milk in very short supply. My milk is declining. You see, a person can keep a cheerful face but be exhausted inside, and normally there will be no consequences—unless you're nursing a baby. But the milk has to come from inside, and if things aren't quiet there it doesn't work. It takes me an unbelievable amount

---

31 Nuremberg was known for its production of handmade toys (Wikipedia, "Nuremberg," accessed July 19, 2016).

32 This sounds to me as though it could have been deliberate disinformation. What I was able to discover about children being taken to Germany/ Austria (Austria had been annexed to Germany in 1938) was this: Dutch children who looked "Aryan" were being kidnapped and sent to Germany for Germanization, and this was a permanent displacement. Therefore, the notion that they were being sent there to "recuperate" is improbable. That makes it equally improbable that a POW would use that story as a cover for getting a message to his wife. The rosy picture of care and food, whether purporting to relate to the children or to the POWs, is equally hard to credit. Bill, in his translation of the diary, wrote an emphatic "No!" beside this passage. Madzy records the rumour, perhaps innocently (grasping at anything that sounded like information) but perhaps tongue-in-cheek. Interestingly, she alludes to the sending of children to Austria "to recuperate" as though it were a well-known fact, but that could be self-censorship, pretending to accept the official explanation of the kidnapping of children (Wikipedia, "Kidnapping of children by Nazi Germany," accessed April 4, 2017; http://members. iinet.net.au/~gduncan/1942.html#lesser_known_1942).

of self-control and all my inner strength to keep a brave face towards the outer world, and God helps me enormously because by myself I wouldn't be able to manage.

Today Charlotte was here with groceries. I saved out 2 kg of rice and some oatmeal and 4 kg of sugar and put them away.[33] Charlotte is seriously worried about the possible internment of the reserve officers; Dick's suitcase is ready.

Sometimes I think: "For Dicks I actually don't have to stock up on food; he won't be coming back until there is peace and food." But then I also think: "The war could be finished here and the POWs liberated while the rest of the world is still at war and there would still be no supply of food." That again makes me want to save food for the winter. After all, you can never know. But every evening I make up a story about how the war could end and how you would all of a sudden be standing here at the door (that's why I'm not leaving the house). And still it's so hard to visualize that.

Wendela is, unfortunately, leaving tomorrow.

---

33 Hoarding food was heavily punished, but everyone did it when they had a chance.

Chapter Three

29 May to 15 June 1942

The food situation continued to be a major preoccupation. Food was rationed, but having a rationing coupon did not always mean there was food in the stores to match the coupon.

There was also the black market. In the Netherlands at that time it took various forms. Some people bypassed the rationing system by obtaining food directly from the farmers, usually by barter. Commodities not grown in the country, like tea or coffee, were presumably smuggled in. Black market commodities were expensive, and Madzy could rarely afford them, though later in the war she did barter our belongings for locally grown food.

Her reports on the large-scale food situation were based on what she read in the underground press or heard via the grapevine. Writing in haste, as she often did, she did not always indicate whether she was talking about the general situation or our particular one. With our garden, we had fresh vegetables in season, though we seem always to have been short of protein.

*

In this chapter, the Dutch royal family is mentioned. Queen Wilhelmina had escaped to England on 13 May 1940, at the time of the German invasion.[1] Once there, she became "the soul of her country's resistance,"[2] largely by means of her regular talks on the BBC's "Radio Oranje" programs, which were immensely heartening to her subjects

---

1   Olson, pp. 28–29.
2   Olson, pp. 123–124.

in the occupied Netherlands.[3] Her daughter, Crown Princess Juliana, was living in Ottawa with her young daughters.

Juliana's consort, Prince Bernhard, spent most of the war in England; early in the war he had trained with the Royal Air Force and flown bombers over occupied Europe. Toward the end of the war he was based in the by-then-liberated southern provinces of the Netherlands. He was one of Queen Wilhelmina's chief advisors. "In 1943, she appointed him liaison officer between the Dutch military and the rejuvenated resistance forces" in the Netherlands. "A year later, he was named commander in chief of the resistance."[4]

*

On 9 June Madzy recorded receiving the first communication from Wim, a printed card. Though containing nothing personal, it gave her his address. Bill told me (see Preface) that she immediately began writing long letters to him—until the system of forms was set up by the officials at the POW camp. "From then on," Bill wrote, "we could write 2 letters and 1 card per month but on lined forms and not beside these lines. A blank half was attached for a reply by [the recipient]." At first they had to be written in German because there were not enough Dutch-reading censors. "That was also the reason for the delay of the first letters—no censors. Later it could all be in Dutch."[5] The space was extremely limited, and the awareness of censorship further restricted what people felt free to write.

I have been unable to confirm Bill's information about how many of these forms each prisoner was allotted; another source states that the officers were allowed to write four letters and three postcards per

---

3　The BBC was a great support for the morale of the residents of all the countries in occupied western Europe. It broadcast programs in the languages of the occupied countries; the daily Dutch-language broadcasts were titled "Radio Oranje" ("Radio Orange") because orange was one of the country's national colours (the royal family is the House of Orange).

4　Olson, p. 379.

5　This information about the system of forms comes from Bill's note to the entry of 10 July 1942. However, Madzy first refers to the forms on 10 February 1943, mentioning them as though they were then a recent imposition, so Bill's memory, sixty years later, was likely less accurate.

month, and it does not refer to them as forms.[6] Yet another website also says it was four letters and three postcards per month.[7] For our purposes this is almost irrelevant because we have only two of the letters Wim wrote on these forms. His letters arrived irregularly, and some never reached Madzy at all.

*

Beginning with the entry for 13 June, Madzy recorded that some army doctors had been sent home from the POW camp. As non-combatants, they should apparently not have been sent to the camp in the first place. Moreover, sick or elderly officers were also returning. The fact that early release was possible added greatly to Madzy's anxiety. She had *hoped* that Wim might be eligible for this because of his work in agriculture, but to find that it was actually happening with other people adds a sharp and painful edge.

*****

Friday, 29 May. This will be brief because it is already 11:30 p.m. Wendela left today; we were both almost in tears. Now I have the entire care of Gerard myself. All the baby things are here in my bedroom and his cradle is standing right here. Wonderful that I'm not sleeping entirely by myself, though even Gerard's cradle doesn't fill the gap of the empty, cold bed beside me.

Irma Pahud[8] still had a note from her husband that was found between the train rails. Did you also throw something from the train?[9]

---

6   www.eindhovenfotos.nl/levensloop_frans_de_waal.htm

7   This is the correspondence of Henk de Pater and his wife, Coby, published (with supporting and explanatory material, all in Dutch) online: http://oorlogspost.yolasite.com. Henk was imprisoned about a year later than Wim but was sent to the same camp.

8   Bill's note: "She was the wife of a cavalry officer whom I knew at Amersfoort." Mrs. Pahud seems to have been living in Doorn at this time—see entry for 29 June 1942, in which Madzy records visiting her during the same trip that involved a session with her dentist in Doorn.

9   Bill's note: "No."

It's a beautiful night. So still. And yet the atmosphere in the country is oppressive. There is not a single potato to be had, nor any vegetables, and everything is finished: cheese and butter and milk. I'd better go to Vlastuin.[10]

We have to deliver 15 eggs per chicken per year, and that has to be done by the middle of June. That's also hard luck!

I have to weed the garden urgently. The nursing doesn't go well. My nipples are raw—G. W. has sucked them to pieces. It's extremely painful.

Now I'm going to sleep. Have to feed him again at 5 or 5:30, and get up at 7:30 at the latest. Good night, my dearest.

Saturday, 30 May, in bed in the afternoon. In a few minutes Juus will bring Gerard upstairs for the feeding so I'm just taking a moment's break in the busy day. Sometimes I think that I can't manage to do everything.

During the night a plane flew so scrapingly low over our roof that the house trembled. It's so strange, but I—who formerly had all kinds of objections to living here without a man in the house and without a telephone—I now think nothing of it, close the shutters in the evening (except the one in the scullery, which no longer fits) and the door, and I sleep like a rose, saying to myself, "When the English arrive, they'll wake me." For the rest it was cozy to sleep with Gerard next to me. I dreamed of you, that you were back home and how happy I was ...!

So often I ask myself what you're doing at that moment. If only I could visualize it!

De heer van H. Goedhart is gone, has just disappeared. His wife [Erna] was here yesterday. She doesn't know where he is, only that he is still free.[11]

---

10 This is Madzy's first reference to obtaining food from other sources besides her garden and the food shops.

11 Madzy gave the name in this abbreviated form; Bill spelled it out as "van Heuven Goedhart" but didn't identify him. I was able to piece a few things together. Van Heuven Goedhart was a journalist and later

Suddenly there is a lot of flying; there is once more a fuel depot in Soesterberg.[12] They say that all the Germans here have civilian clothes with them so that they can leave immediately when the English arrive.

I'm going to pack a knapsack and put the pram in the kitchen at night.

This morning I bathed G. W. myself for the first time. He screamed just as loudly as he did with Wendela. But then what did he do? All of a sudden he peed in a neat arc in the direction of Mamma!—who didn't know how to stop it so quickly and therefore let it spray to the floor. Pankie's shrieks of delight were deafening.

I will have Juus here until 1 July, and from 15 July to 1 September Lies is coming with Monica.

Here comes G. W.! He is a real boy, with a boy's little round head and a boy's body (broad shoulders and narrow hips). He already has such a conceited little expression.

This afternoon I'm going to do some weeding in the vegetable beds.

Evening: It's already almost 11:30. Nursed and changed G. W., had a shower myself, and now just a good-night kiss for you, my dearest dear. Because no matter how dear my children are and how deeply happy I am with them, nothing on earth is more dear to me than you. I miss you more than I'll ever be able to tell you in words or actions, but I *want* to be brave and I *will* be brave.

---

a politician and diplomat. According to Madzy's diary, he and his wife, Erna, lived in Maarsbergen, three kilometres (two miles) from Maarn. Up to this time he had been editor-in-chief of the Resistance newspaper *Het Parool*. Madzy here records his disappearance from his home; presumably he went underground and escaped to England. In 1944 he was in London and became Minister of Justice in the Dutch government-in-exile (Wikipedia, "Gerrit Jan van Heuven Goedhart," accessed July 18, 2017; *Biografisch Woordenboek van Nederland*; van der Zee, p. 165ff).

12 Bill's note: This was a now-German air-force base about eight kilometres (five miles) from Maarn.

This afternoon de heer Koolemans Beijnen came on behalf of the Red Cross about the food parcels, and I'll look after that.[13] If you actually receive what's on those lists of what will be sent, you'll have more than we, but I'm afraid that the food supplies in the Netherlands won't permit it.

Still waiting for your first letter. Oh, if only I receive it soon!

Sunday, 31 May. The third lost Sunday for our cozy little family—our precious Sundays, each of which used to be a festive day and is now only a day of missing you even more painfully. Every Sunday I think back to the last Sunday we had together, when we were with the three of us (actually four), all alone, and when I could for the last time cosset you with nice things to eat. Remember the canned pears? Did I have a premonition that it had to be now or never?

But I *have* to keep going, not look back (like Lot's wife who was turned into a pillar of salt) but forward, forward to our reunion and our new life....

During the night there was an unbelievable uproar from Noordhout[14] with screaming artillery over our heads, bomb explosions that made our house tremble, and everywhere in the distance sirens.[15] In the past, on a night like that, with all that uproar, I would have been frightened even with your comforting presence. And now? I slept until Pankie called me and came to sleep in your bed.

---

13 According to Bill's note, Mr. Koolemans Beijnen had known Madzy's parents in the Dutch East Indies and felt protective toward Madzy. He and his wife were among Madzy and Wim's friends in Maarn.

14 Noordhout was an area of woods near de Hoogt, three or four kilometres (two and a half miles) from our house. The Germans had built a large anti-aircraft installation there (information from Bill), and it was frequently a target for Allied bombardment, which is what Madzy means in the next paragraph with the phrase "the English arrived."

15 In the diary, Madzy never mentions searchlights, but when we arrived in northern British Columbia in 1947, she likened the northern lights there to the searchlights that were familiar to her from the war.

However, the night *was* very broken up. I got to bed at 11:30 but was not yet asleep when the English arrived at midnight and the "party" started; Pankie called at 1:00. At 4:00 Gerard woke me and I gave him a clean diaper and took Pankie back to her bed. At 5:00 I nursed the still-crying Gerard and at 8:00 I quickly got up, opened the blackout curtains, looked after the chickens, bathed and fed Gerard, had a bite to eat myself in between, etc., etc. In this way the night as well as the day is very busy and I'm so tired that I have no time to worry. When I smell the pillow I go to sleep immediately.

I have trouble with heart palpitations but don't dare to admit it yet.[16] There's so much to do, and already I don't know how to manage it all.

I'm just going to Nieuwenhuizen to see if there's a letter from you. He'll let me in.

Afternoon: No, nothing yet. Sixteen days ago I said to my husband, "Well, till 6:00 or 8:00,[17] then." Since then I've heard nothing from him. I don't know whether he's alive nor, if so, where he is or how he is. Whether he is well or sick, and whether he gets enough to eat. But that doesn't matter to the Germans. As far as they are concerned we can wait for months still.

Evening: I tried to visit Mevr. de Boer in Maarsbergen, whose husband, as captain in the infantry, shares your fate.[18] She seems to be still very depressed and I wanted—as someone sharing her situation—to cheer her up a bit. But she wasn't at home so I went

---

16 Bill's note: "She had that also in the U.S. when she was very unhappy there, and she said that the palpitations first started after her goitre operation in her late teens."

17 It would have depended on which train he was able to catch.

18 Mrs. de Boer was to become one of Madzy's regular contacts during the war, not a really close friend but a person toward whom Madzy felt protective. Her husband, Captain de Boer, was apparently in the same camp as Wim.

on to Mevr. Goedhart, another person in a similar situation, but not quite the same.[19]

The Maarn police had phoned her: "Is Mijnheer Goedhart there?"

"No," she answered.

"Do you know when he will be home?"

"No, I don't even know where he is."

"Damnation!" was the brief reply!

Yesterday Cologne was very heavily bombed, hence the uproar here.

Gerard is screaming for his meal! I'll go and feed him. Good night, my only dearest.

Monday, June 1, afternoon. As soon as Gerard had had his bath and was nursed and outside in the pram, I went to the garden. First I weeded the bed with the carrots and beets. Then I dug up the bed where the koolmoes had been, and raked it, and sowed more carrots. Then I put in a row of lettuce where the radishes and cress had been. Then it was 12:30. After my rest, I'll weed the potatoes, and this evening I might just weed the beans still. Soon the spinach bed will also be dug over but we are still cutting from it, and because in all of Holland there are absolutely no vegetables to be had we have to eat the spinach up to the last bit.

It's beautiful weather and Gerard, in his pram, stands all day outside in the sun. Pankie played with Bemmie [van Notten] and rode on the wagon with Legemaat, who was delivering firewood.

Evening: Mevrouw de Boer came this afternoon and we became friends. She still saw you when you sat in the train, in the station in Maarsbergen![20] Her husband had gone to sit beside you; you

---

19 i.e., Erna van Heuven Goedhart's husband had also disappeared, though not into a POW camp.

20 This would have been on Wim's trip to Ede, on the day when he was taken prisoner.

were sitting with other officers, two military police officers, and a bald gentleman.

Tuesday, 2 June, afternoon: Today I'm again a bit more depressed. I received a message from Hansje that you are in Nuremberg and therefore not safely in Linz or somewhere in Austria. She sent me the complete address. I doubt whether it's correct, but I sent a letter there as well as a postcard. It's high time that you heard news from us. It's also time that I heard from you.

Last night again a hellish uproar for hours on end; hundreds of airplanes flew over our heads, and Noordhout fired back so fiercely that the house frequently trembled and the bottles and glasses on the washstand rattled. So I didn't get to sleep until 2:30, and at 3:00 G. W. began to cry, until 4:30. Can you understand that it was hard to wake up at 7:15?

Marietje dug up the spinach bed and I sowed the rest of the beans, and celery in a small corner. When the second koolmoes bed is empty I'll sow carrots there, and on 21 June winter endives and on 13 August autumn turnips. Then plant cabbage and then I'm more or less ready, I think.

Evening, 11:30: Just now someone stood outside whistling. It was VaVa, in her pyjamas, to say that Davy, her dog, had escaped and she was afraid for our precious chickens.

This afternoon Els and Dientje to tea, and de heer Bentinck,[21] and this evening Annetje Nahuys. No shortage of visitors.

We're already saving eggs for the levy: we have to deliver 21 eggs before 24 June, 45 before 13 August. Therefore we can't eat any ourselves. That's too bad, just at this time. Moreover they're searching houses to look for stockpiling. There's nothing for them to find here. De heer Everwijn Lange phoned Piet [van Notten] to warn us.

---

21 Baron Bentinck and his wife lived in Maarn in a house named Landeck (Lägers & Veenland-Heineman, p. 107).

Now I'd better go to sleep. Will they be flying again? When will the English come themselves?

I've been very sad again today and have trouble keeping going. That I should miss you *so* much! That I would be *so* worried about you! Never again will I worry if you're an hour or more late coming home, because that's nothing compared with what I'm experiencing now.

Wednesday, 3 June, afternoon. Jet is here doing the income tax. It's a brilliant day, now blazingly hot, and G. W. is lying in the crib outdoors under the apple tree. Vader Gerard is terribly depressed, Jet says. He is very miserable about you.[22] G. W. received a bank account with 75 guilders in it and I received 100 for the nurse.[23] Now I'm going to have a nap. The heat is, alas, not good for my heart. Just like before.[24] Ach, everyone's thoughts are constantly with you. Only G. W. can distract us sometimes. But G. W. comes second by a long way.

Evening. Well, the tax is done and immediately put in the mail.

Our Pankie is being a great nuisance; she won't go to sleep at night, is lying now (at 10:15) awake still. She scratches Juusje or pulls her hair, and the least little thing sets her off crying. "I'm so sad that now I can't go with Pappa to Broekhuisen," she said today. "Pappa *promised* me—in bed, you remember, Mamma?" The child is really having too many difficult experiences for a three-year-old.

To Jet's great delight, Gerard made an enormous dirty diaper, so that I had to change all his clothes and Jet could watch it all.[25]

---

22 Wim was his only son, and the baby (at that point) his only grandson.
23 The context indicates that they were gifts from Wim's father.
24 See note above. Madzy is probably referring to how ill she felt in the United States in the summer of 1938 when she was expecting me. In a tape of memories that she made in her old age she said that it was a very hot, sticky summer, day after day (weather conditions that the Dutch were not used to).
25 Jet had no children of her own.

Deep in my heart I'm still hoping to see you very soon. That helps me to keep my courage up. Maybe you'll be back before your exam? Maybe another three weeks? Maybe before November? My God, it's so difficult.

Thursday, 4 June, evening. This morning Tante Lotje Suermont to visit, well-meant but boring.[26]

I've sown leaf lettuce and weeded, and the corn had to be transplanted. This afternoon I gathered firewood and chopped it up. This evening suddenly a wagonload of firewood from Broekhuisen; for a moment I didn't know what to do with it but it will all get sorted out. Saturday there will be another. Schut's son-in-law is coming in a week or two to pile the wood.[27]

Dick [Kolff] will ask someone at the garage to drain off the gasoline and I'll go and pick it up.[28] So everything comes to rights—in half an hour this problem was also solved.

I again had the thought that you might after all still have a chance of being released from the camp because of your work. Why else have you been prevented, so far, from writing to us?[29] Perhaps they're making a selection among the officers. Why else would you have had to report everything about your work on

---

26 This was an aunt of Wim's.

27 Bill's note to the entry of 11 June 1942: Schut was an elderly neighbour who sometimes did odd jobs for Madzy.

28 The reference here is to Wim and Madzy's car, a Ford coupé, which they had bought second-hand in the United States and brought back to the Netherlands with them in 1938. After the beginning of the occupation, to prevent it from being confiscated, Wim hid it at the Kolffs' estate under a pile of firewood. Perhaps all the talk about firewood brought it to Madzy's mind now, or perhaps burying the remark in the middle of other information was a way of concealing it from any hostile reader of the diary. The Germans did eventually find the car and confiscate it, but (surprisingly) they paid Madzy for it. See entry for 22 November 1944.

29 Because Madzy had received no letters, she assumed that the officers had been prevented from writing, but in fact the problem seems to have been that the mail was not getting through. See headnote for this chapter. The lack of letters led Madzy to conjecture all kinds of things.

those two lists?[30] Maybe you'll be released before your exam on 9 June or a bit later? May I make myself happy with such a hope or is that wrong? But if I don't talk to myself in a hopeful way I can't keep going. The heart palpitations continue. If only I can deal physically with the stress. Every day I pray to God for that, because if I get sick what will happen to the three of us? *Enfin*,[31] I had better not fret before the dreadful things actually happen. But if it's going to last a long time, I fear for my ability to endure.

Friday, 5 June. Three weeks have passed, feeling like three long months. How much longer?

Charlotte was here, and Annetje [Nahuys], and Miss de Lanoy.[32] The stream of visitors continues. Charlotte heard that, because you sang the "Wilhelmus"[33] during your departure, you are being punished by being forbidden to write home for six weeks.[34]

To record all the unrest that we're suffering here, there is no book long enough.

Little Gerard is so sweet. I have adorable photos of him to send to you, as soon as I know where you are.[35]

---

30 Madzy seems to be referring to documents that Wim, before his imprisonment, had had to fill out for the occupying authorities. However, see note to entry of 30 June 1942.

31 She uses the French word, as she frequently did when she reached a point of conclusion, resignation, or resolve.

32 Miss de Lanoy Meyer was the Dutch woman who had operated the small finishing school in London that Madzy attended (see Introduction). Madzy's use of the word "Miss" here, rather than "Juffrouw," indicates that she was accustomed to addressing the lady in English.

33 The Dutch national anthem.

34 Bill's note: "Not true." However, the fact that the Dutch were prepared to believe such things indicates how accustomed they had become to arbitrary and apparently senseless decrees, and to reprisals and punishment.

35 She clearly did not trust the information that he was in Nuremburg, though it was in fact true.

Saturday, 6 June. Last night again I dreamed repeatedly about you and woke up crying, so that all morning I was on the verge of tears. I think this is the most miserable time of my life. No, I can't say that, but of what has already happened to me in my life this is by far the greatest grief and the severest trial. Even my father's death didn't affect me as much as this. It's impossible for me to take real, deep pleasure in Gerard, even though the little chap is dearer than I can ever express in words. But I have pleasure in nothing, neither in the fine weather, nor in the beauty of nature, nor in my children, nor in my life. There is only resignation and the hope for better times. Wia wrote in a letter: "What a strange idea, that we will see our husbands back only when there is peace again in our country. What will still happen to us here before that day comes?"[36] Well, fortunately we *don't* know: evacuation, fighting, upheaval, bombardment? In any event more screaming artillery shells, because last night they were again flying over us to the Ruhr and the artillery fire was deafening.

Today Pankie received a beautiful little summer coat from Moeder Iete which we really need in case something happens some night. I'm going to pack the rucksack, if I can find it. There's still so much that I can't find: the screen for the basement window, batteries for the flashlights.[37]

I'm seriously considering inviting no one to come and stay from 1–15 July[38] but just to stay cozily alone with the children. All the visitors sometimes make me tired. There's so little time to be quietly by myself. And Marietje will come and sleep here.

There are rumours that a captain from Woudenberg might be coming back because he works in agriculture and that those people will be allowed to return. Such a hope regarding you lives deep in my heart. But sometimes I don't know whether I may

---

36 Wia Kloppenburg was the wife of one of Wim's best friends, Wim Kloppenburg, who was also in the POW camp.

37 These are things that Wim would have put away, never thinking to tell Madzy where.

38 This would be the interval between Juus's departure and Lies's arrival.

hope for such a thing, because in the final analysis it's probably more dangerous here than there. And therefore I say to myself: "God's will be done."

This morning I went to de Hoogt.[39] I asked Martijn [the gardener] about cabbage plants, because the ones you planted aren't successful. The cauliflower plants also all died. Tante Betsy has a great shortage of vegetables and potatoes. And we also have nothing any more. 50% goes to Germany, 30% to the German army here, 10% to the Germans living in the Netherlands, and 10% for the Dutch.[40] Most of that goes to the big cities, to prevent unrest and because people in the countryside are more likely to have something. But no one has anything. We have to wait until the end of July for potatoes. We still have 5 kg potatoes here. We got nothing on last week's coupons and now they've expired.

This afternoon I put the goat pen in order. At the beginning of this week I cleared out the manure and scrubbed the pen clean, and I spread dry leaves and straw. After dinner Pankie and I went to Vlastuin; the goat is coming home on Monday. The [Vlastuin] boys will bring her on Monday to a buck in Woudenberg, and after a week again. He said that I should ask him if I needed anything.

---

39 De Hoogt, home of Betsy and Ferd de Beaufort, was about three and a half kilometres (two and a half miles) from our house. As the war progressed, it accommodated numerous refugees and evacuees— as many as one hundred at any one time (information from Nando van Ketwich Verschuur, son of Els and Hans). During the last winter of the war (and perhaps earlier), the ground floor was occupied by Germans (Briedé, *Maarn-Maarsbergen in de loop der eeuwen*—"Maarn-Maarsbergen through the centuries," p. 177).

40 Van der Zee, referring to the earlier years of the occupation, writes (p. 72) that "some sources" say that 60 percent of Holland's agricultural produce went to Germany. Madzy's figures may be incorrect in detail, but nevertheless they reflect a situation that was dire for the Dutch.

I cleaned my bicycle and watered the garden.[41] And now I'm going to sleep—that is to say, first have a shower and then nurse Gerard and then at about 11:30 turn off the lights. Doing the blackout is also my job. I'm becoming half a man.

Sunday, 7 June, afternoon. This morning I went to the church in Maarsbergen, something which for a long time we had intended to do together. But many things we planned remain *in petto*,[42] which we really should have done and for which neither of us took the initiative. That will change later. I have to admit honestly that when Ds. Stekhoven[43] prayed first for the Queen and all her family and then for all prisoners and the lonely and worried families left behind, the tears came. I hope no one noticed. Except for the minister, the mayor, and de heer Bentinck there was no one I knew. But I've resolved to put your life and those of the children into God's hands.

Evening: And yet resignation is so difficult. When, as on this evening, I've been busy watering and hoeing in the garden, and the goat's stall is so clean and the barn so tidy—all of it done for you—I think: "If Dicks came walking in right now, he would say, 'Matje, how neatly you've done all that',", and all at once I'm convinced that you will *certainly* come home today, and also that I can't keep going without you for a single day or night longer. Then it is as though I break inside and I don't know where I will find the strength to put on a cheerful face when I say goodnight to Pankie and to whisper to her, as I do every evening, "Pappa will come home soon." Then I feel how much I love you, how badly I showed that in the last while, and how wretched I feel about that.

---

41 Watering was done with a watering can filled at the hand pump in the garden, a laborious process for a whole sizable vegetable garden.

42 The Latin phrase, commonly used by the Dutch, refers to something that is still "in store," to be done in the future.

43 The clergy are titled "Dominus," abbreviated to Ds.

I love you so intensely and so much that I would give everything to have you quickly back in my arms. Let the English come and bomb our house to pieces and chase us out of the land so that they can fight here; let hardship and difficulties come over us, if only you can return very, very soon to your Matje, who can't live without you, not one day, not one night, not one hour. At this moment I'm not an ordinary human being any more; my soul has gone with you and only my body walks around doing its tasks, looks after the children, looks after the house and garden, laughs and "bears herself bravely," as everyone says.

Monday, 8 June, evening. Dearest, it is already past 11:30 and if they start flying in a few minutes there won't be much sleep for me, especially with crying Gerard. And Pankie also frequently calls me during the night because she has had a bad dream. Therefore, briefly: this afternoon I visited the Stratenus family, exceptionally friendly and welcoming. We talked about everything and they hope very much for your speedy return, and they also want to write to you. They gave me some chard and also chard seed, because I couldn't buy that any more. They are enormously cordial and well-disposed.

This morning I received your salary for May: 125 guilders.[44]

The trip to Broekhuisen was melancholy; in my mind's eye I saw how we two had looked forward to doing it together and I saw you bicycling here, all those many times in the winter and the snow.... But I mustn't think, only *do*, and for the rest sleep-walk.

Sometimes I ask myself: is he asleep now, or is he eating, or what is he doing? Do you think often of me, Dicks, and do you say, just as I do, "Keep up your courage, keep up your courage"?

They say that the war will end by 16 July. May God grant it! But it would take a miracle.

---

44 In the entry for 25 June 1942, Madzy writes that she will receive two-thirds and he one-third; it's not clear whether this payment of 125 guilders is the whole amount or only the two thirds.

Tuesday, 9 June, afternoon. This morning came your first sign of life from Nuremberg! But what a sign! A postcard, in German, printed, with only your signature and the address in your handwriting, and the date. Besides, the fact that you have a *number* upset me terribly.

And it arrived, after all the waiting, at a strange time. I was standing on the station platform with Pankie and Gerard, to meet Moeder Hans [Wim's mother] who was coming towards us, and then Marietje came waving the card. What a deep disappointment, this horrible little card! Yes, my boy, now I have to be thankful because you're alive and healthy and I know that on 29 May you were in Nuremberg. But ... I'm dreadfully unhappy, because I had already imagined your first card: "Dearest Matje," etc. etc. In my imagination I had already received so many cards, but not this, not this ....[45]

Since then my heart is beating at a roaring pace. It's not possible to stop it. I hope that Moeder doesn't notice it. She is staying until 8:00. I'll see if we can send a Red Cross parcel, and I will try again to write to this address.[46]

Last night again there was a hellish uproar and Pankie crying and sleeping in your bed. The nights become steadily shorter.

Evening: When I had brought Moeder back to the railway station (she was nearly in tears as we stood on the platform) I went to de heer Koolemans Beijnen about your first Red Cross parcel, and I showed your postcard to the van Nottens and the Hoogeweegens. All of them were equally indignant about this impersonal communication. And how long do we have to wait now for something personal?

---

45 It is probably at this point that Madzy began to write long letters to him, though possibly she had been writing to the address that Hansje had given her.

46 Wim, in the first real letter Madzy received (see entry for 17 June 1942, and Appendix A) indicated that he was receiving at least some of Madzy's letters.

Vader sent me cabbage plants, which I'll put into the ground tomorrow. This evening it's suddenly bitterly cold, and the soil will have to be worked a bit tomorrow.

Wednesday, 10 June, afternoon. Gerard fed, Pankie in bed, peace in the house. Van Setten came to change the stove pipe. That was something that I couldn't do. But I can saw a little board and screw it over the hole in our bedroom ceiling. This morning I dug over the cabbage patch. I have to sow a few more flat beans—I just saw that they didn't all come up. We ate the first strawberries. The first things that I sowed are coming up: lettuce, small cucumbers, and green beans. I'm very proud because I was sure that nothing I sowed would grow. The beans seem to me to be coming up very soon; I didn't even soak them in advance, as Droffelaar had advised. It is very dry and the watering takes my whole evening, together with looking after the animals and closing the shutters.

Every time I hear a train, I think of you. Those trains... those trains....

During the night I suddenly started to worry that I hadn't packed enough warm clothes in your suitcase and that I should have sent your heavy winter coat. Did they give you a blanket? If only I had been able to walk around when we were packing your suitcase! But those wretched stitches meant that I couldn't move a step. The reserve officers will be better prepared when their hour strikes.

Evening: I'm writing with fingers that are crooked from the work in the garden. My hands haven't developed the calluses for that kind of work. My back and arms also sometimes protest violently, but I'm certainly becoming limber. Later on will you take me on as a gardener's boy and let me do a lot of the work with you? It's healthy for me and gives me enormous pleasure. Will you let me take a really *active* part?

I think I will let Pankie sleep permanently in your bed. With all that uproar at night, she is becoming steadily more restless; almost every night I have to get up for her once or twice. And with nursing Gerard and all the noise from the artillery fire the nights are not particularly restful, and having a nap in the afternoon is difficult when you're worrying as much as I am. Speaking of worrying: my goitre is swelling again. If, in Heaven's name, I can only stay healthy! And if only it doesn't last too long, this misery. Some people are asking: "And are you going to spend the whole winter here alone in this isolated place?" And then I say, "But, dear people, Wim will be home long before the winter." Do I believe that myself? Don't I actually visualize myself sitting here with two children for another year—if not two—in anxiety and wretchedness about you? Oh, I don't know how I would survive that. The day after tomorrow it's four weeks since you left. It feels like four months, endless, unmentionable, frightful months ....

I've just paid all outstanding bills and the rest of the tax. If something happens to me, there's no one who can do it and that would be such a nuisance.

Thursday, 11 June. Today I was busy again; I'm having my afternoon rest now and am sitting up in bed writing. This morning at 8:00 I watered the cabbage plants, then bathed and fed the baby (that took until about 10:00). Then I sowed flat beans. Then I did some weeding. Then I put those long stakes in the woodshed and sawed off the tips that protruded. Fortunately Schut had sharpened the saw. The woodshed is getting full now that the wood from M[r.] Stratenus has been added. Snitselaar is here sawing the wood by hand (for 15 guilders). It's forbidden to use gasoline for sawing, and because of the neighbours Dientje didn't want the regulation to be broken on her property.[47]

---

47 Presumably Dientje was afraid that neighbours might report its illegal use to the German authorities. The cottage was on her family's estate, so it was up to her to set the rules.

Marietje and I clambered to the loft in the barn and with a rope we lowered your military trunk and a suitcase, dusted them off, and lugged them upstairs in the house. In the trunk we put all your boots and shoes. In the suitcase we put all your suits and coats. Marietje found it "creepy" work, but I told her that she had better not think too much about it. Why did I do all this? Well, if there is a fire or if suddenly there is looting, then I can quickly throw the trunk and suitcase out of the window; the clothing is after all expensive stuff. Christie did the same with her own winter clothes, but I haven't got to that yet.

I received a letter from Oom Willy, saying that he can arrange to get a letter from me to you via Kristiansen.[48] I'll write it this afternoon and send it to O.W. I'll have to consider quietly what I can write.

The Red Cross wrote that no parcels can be sent yet. Are you very hungry, my dearest? Are you becoming very thin? Are you cold? Are you sleeping all right? Today was your exam. I think about it constantly.

Evening. This afternoon de heer Bentinck came again. He says that he'll drop by regularly. He and de heer Koolemans Beijnen are my regular gentleman visitors! They are both so elderly that you don't have to be jealous!

Friday, 12 June, afternoon. Moeder Iete is coming over in a little while. It's raining today for the first time in more than three weeks and we can certainly use it—the garden was nothing but dust.

With Marietje I tidied up the mess behind the water heater and found some more oats. I also found oats in your tool cupboard.

---

48 It's not clear why Madzy still needed to use this covert channel of communication even though she now knew Wim's address in Nuremberg. Possibly she hoped that a letter sent via Willy would not be censored.

That should be fed to the pullets which, if I remember correctly, should arrive one of these days.[49]

From London there are warnings against traveling in dangerous places in this country.[50] We're pretty safe then, aren't we? All the same, I packed a rucksack, and your air gun stands beside my bed.

Evening: This evening Dick and Charlotte suddenly came to visit. And that was a good thing because Moeder's visit—though well-meant, as always—left me very depressed. She said things like "Wim will find it delightful to be a POW," and "You'd better be glad that he's there," and "He would never want to come back even if he had the chance," etc. I'm too vulnerable for such remarks—they only hurt me. Moeder has no idea how much strength I have to find in order to be "ordinary" so that I have milk enough for feeding Gerard.

Because this—the feeding—is by far the most difficult problem. And Gerard is, at the moment, getting only barely enough. That wretched printed postcard pushed my spirits down. If only I could receive something personal from you now, so that I would know that you're really still somewhere on the planet! For you it's a help that you know where I am and in what surroundings, but for me it is as though what is dearest to me on earth has suddenly and completely disappeared and all at once I have to stand on my own feet after having been so delightfully spoiled by you. I don't want to complain but I want to defend myself a little bit if I don't rejoice that you're gone.

Dick gave me good advice about the garden, and I realize that there's still a lot lacking. But it's a good distraction from all the worrying. Because worrying ... ach, dearest, I can't do anything about that. That will probably continue until you can

---

49 Evidently Wim had ordered them earlier in the spring.

50 Reports from the BBC in London were almost certainly the only reliable news the Dutch were getting, but they were not always up-to-date. See the entry for 13 June 1942.

again protect me from everything that threatens me, just as you always do. Will you then embrace me very, very tightly and love me very, very much? Because I need it so badly and I long for it so very much. Will you caress me much more than you have done in the past? I enjoy it much more than I showed, because I was still as shy as I was when I came to you on the *Statendam*[51] and hardly dared to look at you out of sheer bashfulness. I'm really still a bit like that, dearest, and therefore you will have to caress me more, because in my heart, now, I really long for it very much.

But Moeder says: "Be glad that Wim is *there*, because here you have hardly any food for him,[52] and he would only be bothered by that small baby. When Wim comes home Gerard will fortunately be a bit older and Wim will have more pleasure in him than now."

But I don't believe that. No, I really don't.

During the night. It's late but I just wanted to say that it's not you but I who am the guilty one if we are not affectionate enough. Sometimes I'm so "cold" outwardly, but not inside, and it won't happen again, when you're safely back with us. I've learned a lesson.

Saturday, 13 June. This morning I visited the de Jonghe's and was touched by the cordiality of de heer de Jonghe. A temporary estate manager for Broekhuisen is not to be found,[53] and now he's doing the work himself, even though he's too busy. But I pray to God that He doesn't allow you to remain away for too long because then you will lose the job at Broekhuisen. They will manage until the autumn, but not after that. What a pity it would

---

51 The *Statendam* was the ship by which Madzy travelled to New York in 1936 to marry Wim and that carried them back to the Netherlands two years later.

52 Iete was exaggerating; at that time food was, though rationed, not yet in *really* short supply.

53 This was probably, at least in part, because so many men were in camps (POW camps, or concentration camps, or labour camps) or in hiding.

be if you lost this too. But whatever happens you *must* and *shall* be an estate manager again when you return. On that we must set our minds, even though we have to skimp.[54] Because *that* is your calling in life. Let's hope that you don't have to remain in active military service for too long. We can easily keep on living here, and then we will together, quietly and diligently, start building things up again. That's also what you would like, isn't it, my boy? Will you always say precisely what you would most like to do?

Evening: After listening to the news I just walked to de Boerderij. After all, it's Saturday evening and another Sunday looms over me, which makes me depressed. A sister of Edward's was staying there. She told us that at the railway station in Utrecht she had seen Dutch officers in uniform; I pricked up my ears. They were coming from the direction of Arnhem.[55] It appeared that they were army doctors. And then my heart sank again. Yes, honestly, Dicks, with everything like that I think, "There now, maybe he will come back; there he is, coming home!" And then immediately I think again: "Yes, but here he wouldn't be safe. He's safer where he is."

Edward's sister also said: "They looked pathetic," and then hurried on to cover up this tactless remark.

Over the radio there are warnings to leave "dangerous places" or to demand bomb shelters from the occupying army. Don't they understand that there is no more cement to be had,[56] and that here it's dangerous everywhere? The food situation is also bad;

---

54 Madzy was probably saying that on his return from the camp he should leave the army and become a full-time estate manager; that was a career to which he was much better suited. This would mean a loss of income because the Broekhuisen position was at that point only part-time.

55 i.e., from east of us: Maarn is on the east-west transportation corridor between Arnhem and Utrecht.

56 Cement was being used for German defence installations like the Atlantic Wall, which (see Overy, p. 153) was being built at about this time.

in three weeks we've received a little bunch of carrots and two limp heads of lettuce, and 10 kg potatoes. Coupons have expired and I didn't even receive any. We're eating lots of brown beans.

This afternoon de heer Koolemans Beijnen again for a visit. There's a constant coming and going—you'd hate it. Dientje came at tea-time. For the rest of the afternoon I chopped and sawed firewood, two baskets and cardboard boxes full. I also thinned the beets. The goat happily eats the plants that I removed. That's why I do the thinning a bit at a time, so that every time she gets a fresh meal. Everywhere people are eating nettles—you can even buy them for 20 cents per kilo. You can also cook and eat the tops of radishes. But not all tops are edible, Dick says—some are even poisonous. When you have nothing, you do strange things.

Our little Gerard is a month old. If you had been here we would have celebrated.

Sunday, 14 June. This morning I had breakfast in bed. Gerard didn't wake up until 6:00 and now he will not get his next feeding until 10:00, which means that I couldn't go to seek my salvation in church.

It's 11:30 in the morning and the radio is on for once.[57] The weather is changeable, with much rain. Yesterday there was a downpour and I had to support the beans. They're very tall (too much fertilizer?).

To keep up my spirits I imagine how it will be on the first Sunday when we're together again. I can't picture to myself how

---

57 It would appear that Madzy rarely had the radio on in the daytime (though certainly she did in the evening to hear the news). At the top of this page, in the margin, she writes: "Oh! They're singing a Texas cowboy song over the radio! Now I have to turn it off. That makes me think too much about you and our happiness." The memory evoked would likely be of their time in the United States, and it's interesting that, at this point, she associates that with happiness. During most of that time she and Wim were far from happy, but at least they were together.

it feels to laugh from the heart, rather than to arrange my face in the required creases to indicate laughter.

The Oom Willy business is such a problem for me, and I don't know whether you would rather stay in the camp or how much you would sacrifice in order to come home. Moeder scolds me: I must not accept any favours from Oom Willy, not even to get a message to you to say that Gerard and I are still alive. It would get you into trouble, she says. So I also wrote that to Oom Willy, that it would be better if he did nothing more for us.

Oh, God, if only something were happening! But nothing at all is happening. Since the very bad bombing, things have turned around and now we have to wait until the new moon.[58] Besides, it's not going particularly well anywhere.

But what does England mean with "the second front"?[59]

Evening: I just went to the van Kekems to ask if they had heard anything about the army doctors. Ad would ask Dr. Gorter tomorrow. Who knows whether one of those officers might have seen you or might have a message from you? It's quite possible, isn't it?

This afternoon, out of pure loneliness, I tidied the barn and got out the ping pong table for Huis te Maarn, where there are again children evacuated from Rotterdam. I tidied your carpentry tools and did small carpentry jobs in the house and checked the feed for the goat and the chickens. I found lots more oats, which will be wonderful for the pullets, which still haven't come. This Sunday is, thank God, again almost over.

Today I again have such a strong feeling that you'll be back soon and that all of a sudden, with another group of fortunate

---

58 That was when the nights would be dark enough to give some protection to the overflying Allied bombers.

59 The Russians, who had since June 1941 been bearing the weight of the German assault, were demanding that the Western powers open a second front in Western Europe to divide the German forces (Overy, p. 101).

people (such as yesterday those doctors), you will just come home. When I go to bed I say to myself, "Maybe tomorrow? Tomorrow, maybe?"

This isn't such a crazy idea; of all the career officers who are now POWs, from all the countries, there are not many who have another career as well. Most of them are *only* career officers. Why would such a thing—your having another career—not lead to your liberation? After all, didn't you have to fill in an enormously long form? Who knows what you yourself have already been able to achieve, wherever you are? (Because that postcard from Nuremberg was dated 29 May, and I received it on 9 June.)[60]

Monday, 15 June. Evening. It was a turbulent day. This morning I heard that Dr. LeHeux's son had returned. I went right away but it was a false report, but Mevr. LeHeux had had a visit from one of the army doctors, Dr. Boer from Groningen, and told me everything. I wrote this report to everyone in the family.[61] I was very relieved. As far as physical comfort is concerned you don't have it too bad; so it is only the missing, and that I will have to bear bravely. Moreover we can now send parcels, which I immediately did today and will do regularly, using your coupons. We mustn't forget insecticide powder, they say![62]

I'll make this short because I have a headache. Bicycled a lot today and didn't have a rest. Had to go to Dr. van Kekem because my right breast is infected, and an infection in the breast can be very nasty. This one is very painful. Every feeding is a torture. This afternoon I attended to the parcel, where I

---

60 On this evening, 14 June, Madzy received a visit from one of the army doctors. She wrote down what he told her (typed, on onion-skin paper) and sent carbon copies to family members. At the beginning of the report she gave the name of the doctor, but before sending off the copies she blacked the name out so thoroughly that it is illegible. There are other signs of secrecy, such as the fact that she did not mention this very important visit in the diary. See Appendix A for the report.

61 For this second report, also see Appendix A.

62 Bill's note: "Not needed."

saw Mr. Koolemans Beijnen, and then visited Tante Betsy and Els, and this evening to Mevr. de Boer and Erna Goedhart in Maarsbergen. What a lot of lonely women there are on earth these days![63]

There is flying already. They say that something will happen before 21 June. I'd better get to sleep quickly. Good night, my very dearest brave boy; at some time we will have a beautiful future ahead of us here in the countryside with the children.

---

63 Betsy was one of them. Her husband, Ferd, was director of the Nederlandsche Bank in Amsterdam and was at this time not often in Maarn (information from Bill and from the interview with Greet Blijdenstein; see Bibliography). That is why he is almost never mentioned in the diary.

Chapter Four

16 June to 13 September 1942

Besides the reports from the army doctors, other information began to reach Madzy, including (at last) letters from Wim. On 17 June she received the first personal letter. But except for that and the doctors' reports, we don't know what information Madzy was receiving about his life in the camp. Probably, to judge by the correspondence between Henk and Coby de Pater,[1] she never received many details, not the kind of detail she would have liked to hear. To enable the reader to share something of what Madzy *did* know, however, I have put the documents that we have in Appendix A.

Many of Wim's letters would be a disappointment to Madzy. To pass censorship, he sometimes wrote in a code that he invented as he went along, which confused and worried her. The fact that not all the letters reached her, and that they often arrived in the wrong order, added to the confusion.

*****

Tuesday, 16 June, afternoon. From Oom Willy I received two medications containing Vitamin C. According to Moeder I shouldn't accept them but I'm going to do it anyway because it is already such an effort to produce enough milk for Gerard. I don't have nearly as much as I did for Pankie. Even real coffee and many glasses of whole milk don't help enough. And moments such as the one I had yesterday of agitation about you mean that

---

1   See Chapter Three headnote.

the milk immediately stops. The infection doesn't help. But you mustn't be angry later if I don't write those things to you in the letters. I plan, if it's at all possible, to send you only good and cheerful news. It doesn't help if you make yourself miserable; the Red Cross has let it be known that neither for the serious illness nor for the death of family members back home will POWs be allowed to leave the camp. Then it's better that you learn about our miseries only later, and that's why I'm writing this faithful, truthful book.[2]

Evening. I had wanted to do all kinds of things, but all of a sudden on the step stood Mevrouw de Beaufort from 't Stort and Ernestine;[3] they had come to tell me what Ernestine had heard from two of the army doctors. The whole thing agreed with what I had learned from Mevrouw LeHeux. Only that you have not much space for walking to get exercise, but that your food is reasonable, and that you'll be there for quite a while. And that we can send books through a bookstore, which I will immediately arrange. Also maybe *De Boerderij* [a farming periodical]. After that came Annetje Nahuys who had some amusing stories to tell about your sanitary arrangements (generals and cadets

---

2   The diary wasn't, and couldn't be, truthful in the most literal sense of the word, but it's significant that Madzy set this as her goal. As for "faithful," I think she meant that she regarded it as a faithful resource for herself, something that was always there. Her use of the word "book" is also important. She may not have been thinking of ultimate publication, but she certainly thought of the diary as a work of substantial proportions, and the fact that she was writing in a foolscap-sized hard-back notebook would lead her to think of it as a book. In the 1976 narrative, when she was rereading the diary, that was how she always referred to it.

3   'T Stort was one of the big houses in the neighbourhood, located close to the railway station. Willem de Beaufort, the owner, was the brother of Ferd de Beaufort of de Hoogt, and Ernestine was a daughter. Mr. and Mrs. de Beaufort's son-in-law, Willem van Tuyll (husband of another daughter, Cornelie), was in the camp with Wim (see Appendix A).

[all together—no privacy]⁴). Wendela visited this afternoon. Gerard is crying after having sucked his little tummy full from the broken breast and I spoke to him very seriously. He gave me his first dear little laugh.

My darling boy, now I have to go to sleep; sirens kept me from sleeping last night. I'm gradually coming to believe that we will see each other again only once there is peace.

Wednesday, 17 June. Today Gerard is five weeks old, and today I received a beautiful present, your first personal note, enclosed in a letter from someone in Doetinchem.⁵ When I opened the letter I was nursing Gerard. I thought, "What's that that fell out— some dirty little toffee-paper?" Then I understood it.⁶ I could read most of it, though ink-blots have obliterated some bits. Oh, Dicksy, my very, very own dearest, I'm so happy that the tears rise almost too high. With your dear words of support I can courageously go on with caring for our children and managing our lives here. I'm curious to hear what you thought when you heard that after all I planned to stay here in Maarn. Perhaps you hadn't expected that of me? You write: "Really, sweetheart, never doubt that I will come back, in any event before Christmas." That makes me so deeply happy. Now I'm going to count the days off on the calendar.

---

4   The words in square brackets were added by Bill when he was doing the translation, no doubt describing the actual conditions he was remembering.

5   A town east of Arnhem.

6   Bill's note: "It was a cigarette paper on which I had written very, very small. A military doctor put it in the cap of his fountain pen, hence the ink spots. This doctor must have lived in Doetinchem." This was the first personal communication that Madzy received, but it was the fourth Wim had written (he numbered them), so three had gone astray and in fact apparently never reached her. Madzy, not knowing at the time that he was numbering them, seems not to have seen the significance of the number 4 written on the top corner. See Appendix A, page 332, for the text of the letter.

The letter Wim wrote on a piece of cigarette paper, in the original size. For the text of the letter, see page 332.

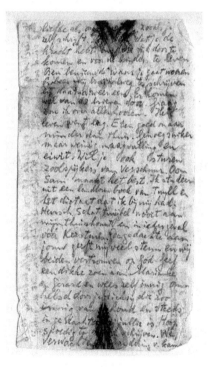

I can't express in words how very much I love you, my boy. In part it is a sort of maternal love. Every man is in a certain sense a child and every wife (or woman) a mother. But at this moment, with me, it becomes much more the love of a wife for a husband and inside me is growing a very close and fervent feeling for you. May you very soon be able to take me in your arms and embrace me very tenderly. Good night, my greatest treasure.

Thursday, 18 June. Afternoon. The whole village already knows about your message.

This afternoon I'm going to clean the chicken coop. That hasn't happened for a long time.

Gerard starts to smile so delightfully. He is a great treasure and I can rejoice in the prospect of how much pleasure you will have in him later. I would suggest that for the beginning we don't have any more children, but to live our lives with this dear twosome. What do you think about that?

Now I have to have my nap because I'm definitely getting very short of sleep these days. And even more so when there is artillery firing at night. We're also not getting enough fat in our diet, and are short of vitamins. There are no vegetables any more in the country. My hair breaks off, so that the hairdresser had to cut it quite short. My teeth are in very sad shape, so that on Monday I have to go to the dentist. And my eyes have become worse. But when I no longer have to nurse that will all come in order again.

Saturday, 20 June, afternoon. All of a sudden it's beautiful weather, and so we can again expect a lot of noise at night.[7] There's nothing to be done about that, and although on the one hand I like the idea that something is being done towards your return, on the other hand I find it dead scary to lie here upstairs

---

7   Bombing was, at that time, done mostly on clear nights. After January 1943, round-the-clock bombing began, by the British at night and the Americans by day (Bailey, p. 86).

under the shrieking artillery shells, with two children of whom one is terribly frightened, and an elderly nanny. But I can put up with the fear.

Meanwhile it goes dreadfully badly in Libya, and in Russia it stagnates, so that an invasion from England and the U.S. can be expected. Churchill is in the U.S. again.[8]

Sunday, 21 June. Thank God this Sunday is past and I have busy days ahead of me. The more I have to do the better because the war situation is very bad. Therefore my thoughts go constantly to a whole winter without you and I have to repeat to myself over and over again: "Really, dearest, have no doubts about my return home, certainly before Christmas." How can you be so sure of that?

The bad situation again gives rise to thoughts about the Second Front. And if that came about, then you would absolutely be safer where you are. But they're not doing anything. If only they did something! June is almost at an end and nothing is happening. There's only July and August and then the best chance is over and we head into a wretched winter of hunger. We have a ration of 1 kg of potatoes this week. Tomorrow a parcel will go off to you again. Mevr. van den Bent[9] said that the parcels will take 2 to 3 weeks. For that much longer you will have to go hungry, my dearest.[10] Fortunately I put this and that in the suitcase. If only I had put more food in! That jar of peanut butter is at least nourishing. But now I'm going to sleep because

---

8   On this day (20 June), Madzy wrote the report containing information she had received on 14 June from the army doctor (see Appendix A). That she made no reference to it here is part of the secrecy surrounding this incident.

9   It is never clear (because of Madzy's handwriting) whether the name is "van der Bent" or "van den Bent." The spelling used here is my best guess. Bill identified her as the wife or mother of an imprisoned officer but didn't give the correct spelling.

10 The assumption that he is suffering from hunger is rather illogical in view of the reports from the army doctors. See Appendix A.

I'm very tired and tomorrow, between feedings, I have to go to Amersfoort.

Tuesday, 23 June. This morning I put the goat into the pasture at de Boerderij with the mayor's horse. She's much better off there. It's a bother bringing her back and forth, but there she has company and the grass is better. Besides that, I cleaned the goat stall and the chicken coop, badly necessary. This afternoon I went to Joost,[11] and this evening watered the garden.

Wednesday, 24 June. Evening, while listening to the radio. Things are not going very well. The general opinion is that the worse it is, the sooner something will happen here. Everyone says, "If only something would happen!" We are constantly warned not to go into "danger" zones. But every beautiful evening nothing happens.[12] Says old de Bruin: "But when something happens, Mevrouw, then maybe we'll say, if only it hadn't happened."[13] We here are so dangerously in the middle of things. The tension in the country is increasing, becoming more threatening, and it really feels like the quiet before the storm. But where will that storm burst out?

I received another typed report from one of the army doctors, and it again showed you living in very primitive conditions.[14] That makes me very "down" again, but I just think to myself, you

---

11 Her older brother, Joost, who had Down syndrome (see Introduction), was living in Driebergen, about six kilometres (four miles) from Maarn, in the care of three unmarried women, Juffrouw Toos and her younger sisters, Anna and Dina. Madzy loved Joost dearly and had always mothered him, and she was his official guardian.

12 Good weather was suitable for bombing.

13 Bill's note: This was a labourer of Dientje's, who lived nearby. Marietje was also surnamed de Bruin, and later in the diary Madzy frequently mentions a helper called Willem (whose surname Bill gives as de Bruin). The entry of 1 October 1942 makes it likely that it was all the same family.

14 We don't have this report.

are after all officers, and it's better there than here in the camp in Amersfoort, about which the blacksmith told me stories when I was there to have the goat's chain mended. It's better to live in primitive conditions than to suffer torture.[15]

Thursday, 25 June, evening, 11:00. In a moment I'll feed Gerard but I just want to say good night to you. This morning I went to the dentist.[16] I have to go again on Monday, and after that I'll wait until Lies is here. I need a gold crown and had to give the gold for it: 5 links from a chain [a piece of jewellery?]. Curious to see whether the links will be subtracted from the bill. I have to be thrifty; I get only two-thirds of your salary. So unpleasant to be constantly asking Vader or Moeder. You become so dependent, and I want so much to remain free of their influence.

On the military scene everything is going very badly: the German army is 50 km [32 mi] into Egypt.

I heard that Boy Ruys[17] is in an extremely miserable situation, has just barely enough food to keep him alive: 4 slices of bread and a tiny bit of vegetables and 3 potatoes per day. They're not allowed to receive anything extra. Then *you* are, I think, better off, with the Red Cross parcels in addition to what you're being fed there, and much better still if you also get your weekly rations. Would you still be in Nuremberg? I have again

---

15 The camp near Amersfoort - actually a transit camp, not a concentration camp - was notorious for "anarchy, the lack of hygiene, the lack of food, lack of medical attention, and the cruelty of the guards" (Wikipedia, "Amersfoort concentration camp," accessed August 25, 2017).

16 Madzy's dentist seems to have been located in Doorn. It was only about four kilometres (two and a half miles) each way but included going over a hill, which is tiring on a bicycle.

17 Pierre Jean Baptiste ("Boy") Ruys de Perez was a Dutch military pilot who, on the night of 1 September, 1941, with two other men, tried to escape to England by crossing the North Sea in a small boat. They were captured and imprisoned (personal communication from Frank Steensma, May 22, 2017; his father was one of the other would-be escapees). See also entry for 22 August 1942.

such a strong feeling that you'll be back in the autumn, even if the war is not over by then. What do the Germans want with 2,000 officers, whom they have to guard? They're already getting so many prisoners. Ach, hope gives life.

Friday, 26 June, afternoon. I'm afraid that this book will be full—and how many more books?—before you return.[18] Or there will have to be a miracle. Today I'm very sad again; everything inside me hurts. And little Gerard comes short, however much I fight against it and however much trouble I take. I constantly pray to God for strength, but I'm gradually going to pieces.

Today I made jam with blueberries and strawberries from the garden. I'd love to be able to send some to you. But as long as we receive no news of you, I consider it a waste to send too much. If you actually get the Red Cross parcels twice a month, then you're getting more butter than we are.[19] And I imagine that you are also getting more than 1 kg potatoes per week.

This afternoon I'm at home alone with the children. Juus has gone to visit Joost.[20] Now it feels more as though you are with us, as though everything is as it used to be and as if, in a little while, towards 6:00, you will come home from Broekhuisen on the bicycle, in your business suit. But then I see your suitcase and your trunk and your stored-away bicycle, and gone is the delightful illusion.

Saturday, 27 June, evening. This morning I delivered 14 eggs. I'm swearing that one chicken has died—we'll eat it if you come home soon. This afternoon sawed wood and tidied the barn and raked the garden. Now everything looks neat for when Vader comes tomorrow to inspect.

---

18 At this point the book was half full.

19 Bill's note: "No, only a few parcels, never butter."

20 Juus, having been the nanny in the van Vollenhoven family, had of course looked after Joost when he was young.

Sunday, 28 June. Today I felt very miserable. After church, when I was walking to the station to meet Vader and Jet, I could hardly bear up and went into de Plattenberg [a café] for a cup of coffee to perk me up a bit. Fortunately Vader was more cheerful and we had a delightful day. Though we missed you every moment, we didn't say it.

I kiss you on my favourite place next to your ear.

Monday, 29 June. A very bad day. After my session with the dentist I dropped in to see Irma Pahud, who was in a bitterly somber mood. She said that she knew for certain that all of you would go to Poland, if you weren't there already. Oh, my dearest, so very far away! Or would this after all be safer and better for you? She also said that you weren't eating well and that the parcels probably weren't reaching you, nor the letters.

This has upset me greatly and this afternoon I lay in bed with dreadful heart palpitations. This evening I went to the doctor and asked him for some valerian for my heart. It's already better. When I crossed the railway tracks I thought, "If a train came now, would I want to throw myself in front of it?" But then I knew that I would never do such a thing, because of you and the children. Because, as Tante To writes, "You are now indispensable for your children," and therefore I have to keep going, no matter what awfulness is ahead of us. And there will be a lot of it; that I know well. Tonight there's a full moon and therefore no doubt this and that will happen, so let me try to get as much sleep as possible before that. The day before yesterday an airplane was shot down near Woudenberg;[21] the whole world was lit up, not to speak of the noise. I nearly fled downstairs with the children but it was already too late for that.

Tuesday, 30 June, afternoon, 2:30. I'm content today, insofar as I ever am these days. I have my little kingdom to myself, the two

---

21 A village just northwest of Maarn.

children, the house, the garden, the animals.[22] There is no one who wants to take the work out of my hands, no one who wants something else than what I want, no one who says that I have to go and rest. This sounds very unkind towards those who so much want to help me. Therefore I say it only to you. On days like this it is almost as it was formerly, and that we are at home waiting until you come home from your work. It's almost as though there is no awful nightmare lying between, and as though the world doesn't look quite so hopeless. Gerard lies in the cradle outdoors and is singing a little tune after his meal. Pankie is having her nap like a grown-up in the guestroom in the large bed. We've had our warm meal and Marietje is not coming until late this evening, just to sleep here. The flies are buzzing, it is sticky weather outside. We don't have to have tea now that Juus is away. That dear good person is ruinous for my food supply. Pank and I drink milk, and by way of a treat I ordered a "gevulde koek."[23] We will manage well with the coupons, thanks to your and Gerard's rations. It's surprising that all 2,000 officers can continue to get rationing coupons.

This morning I was in Maarsbergen, first with Mevr. de Boer and then with Erna Goedhart. Mevr. de Boer had talked with an army doctor, Dr. Brouwer, a friend of her husband. He said that he thought you would probably come home soon! This story, after the somber rumours about Poland, was quite a contrast.

Might this actually happen? Even the possibility makes me deeply happy. Only it seems too beautiful a prospect to be true. But ... in times like this you can expect anything. Maybe they are still making a selection; you had to fill in all those forms, and you have your job.[24] And then I constantly think about your own

---

22 Clearly Juus had left; earlier, Madzy had indicated that that would happen about July 1.

23 This is a large cookie with almond-paste filling, big enough to be divided into portions. "Ordered" probably means that she ordered it from the baker, to be included in the door-to-door delivery.

24 Bill's note: "I never filled in any forms."

words: "... and in any event before Christmas." Is that perhaps something more substantial rather than completely unfounded optimism? Did you hear something about their not keeping you past that date?

Just now I had to look after the goat, and then I noticed that a rabbit had been at the cabbage. The [garden] gates don't close properly anymore. Like a genuine dyed-in-the-wool carpenter I devoted all my skill to it and hope that when you come home you won't ridicule my pathetic attempts. Better a funny-looking gate and cabbage than rabbits and no cabbage.

On Friday we have to fetch the pullets. We'll receive white Leghorns because the red ones are not available any more. I will use my book-learning on them. People tease me about my farm. I have a whole library: about the goat, about the chickens, about the garden and seeds, and about the canning. The day after tomorrow I'm going with Mr Koolemans Beijnen to buy cherries for canning. That will provide me with some juice for Gerard for this winter.

Wednesday, 1 July. Yesterday I received in the evening mail your first letter (number five); I was very glad to get it but I don't understand why you have to write in German while we are allowed to write in Dutch. And I learned with a shock that in spite of the stories from the army doctors you're suffering from hunger. Because you ask for bread and then once more for bread, while people were saying that you were getting more of that than we were. Clearly they want to make you weak and unenergetic by starving you. Now I only hope that the parcels arrive. I'm going to sleep, have a terrible headache. Good night my dearest treasure; may God protect you for us and bring you back to us soon, in good health.

Thursday, 2 July. It was a busy day. This morning, after all the household chores and caring for Gerard, I took the goat to the pasture at de Boerderij and then worked in the garden and canned lettuce. Then it was lunch-time and after that, after Gerard had been fed, I went with de heer and Mevr. Koolemans Beijnen on the bicycle to Cothen[25] to a cherry orchard, where we sat happily gobbling, which is a disadvantage for Gerard who can't stand fresh vegetables and fruit. Came home with 13 pounds of cherries and 4 pounds for Mevr. de Boer, who can't ride a bicycle very well. Just in time for the 6:00 feeding. After dinner I cleaned mine and put them already in the canning jars, 7½ L. Then it was 9:30 and I could just relax a bit. Now Gerard is demanding attention. Pankie was reasonably quiet and easy in her bath. She was, I have to say, bothersome with Juusje, constantly crying. Now I'm going to help Gerard and then I'll fall over with tiredness.

De heer Koolemans Beijnen said that your parcels were sure to arrive, and I sent you 2 kg rye bread today and will do that regularly. That is a bit more than is covered by your coupons, but I also have Gerard's coupons. And he also said that the Poland story was not true but that you are probably somewhere in Austria. Well, time will tell. Moreover, General Zeeman[26] said that because of all the frightening rumours it was much worse for the people staying behind than for the POWs themselves who really didn't have it so bad and were nicely together, and if we would please think about that and not exaggerate our anxieties. Easily said! We wives live in constant anxiety and misery about you, and you can't just put something like that aside. Besides, life here doesn't become any nicer, with all the extra cares and worries.

Saturday, 4 July, evening, 11:30, and Gerard still has to be fed, but he's sleeping so nicely, already since 6 o'clock. He's very sweet

---

25 Bill's note: "Not far, just south of Doorn." It was about eight kilometres (five miles) each way, in de Betuwe, an area famous for fruit-growing.
26 I have been unable to identify this person and, because Madzy's handwriting is not clear, am not sure of the spelling of the name. What I give is my best guess.

today; he's sleeping a lot and has just discovered his fist, on which he smacks noisily when he's awake.

The pullets flourish; at least they walk cheerfully in their pen and greedily eat their oats and some lettuce and drink a lot. The goat also drinks a lot in this warm weather.[27]

There's a chance that I may be able to get a beautiful young dog, a golden retriever! Would that be a good idea? I really like the idea, and from the doctor I can get cod liver oil that is no longer fit for human consumption. I would find it such pleasant company, and at the same time it would be a watch-dog.[28]

Now I'll go and feed Gerard. He doesn't want to wake up. But if I don't wake him now it will cause problems during the night.

Wednesday, 8 July. Oh, my own, during the night something unfortunate happened. I've lost my self-confidence. I woke suddenly and thought that I heard someone walking on the gravel of the driveway. But there was no Dicksy lying next to me whom I could wake. I closed the windows, turned on the light then turned it off again so as not to wake Gerard. I lay tensely listening, for hours, and the consequence is that today I feel very wretched and exhausted and my milk is considerably less and Gerard has cried a lot.

Friday, 10 July. I'm already losing contact with you. It is like *such* a terrible dream that I'm gradually becoming dulled. Now you're not allowed to receive magazines any more. I've re-directed the

---

27 This is the last time the goat is mentioned, and there is never any reference to its having its kid(s) or to Madzy milking it (or even learning to milk). In view of her various illnesses in the months to follow, and the general busyness of her life, she probably decided to return the goat to Vlastuin. She does mention, on 26 October, that the chickens ate all the seed she had saved to grow feed for the goat; her having fed it to them also suggests that by then the goat was gone.

28 Madzy loved dogs and in later years, in Canada, almost always had one or two.

subscriptions for all four of them[29]—will let them come here and then you'll be able to read them later.

Now and then it feels as though you've never been in my life and then I have to recall some very intimate moments so that I can in some sense feel how it was when you were still here with me. I imagine many things; how you might be lying in bed now, among only other men. An emptiness such as I'm feeling here is impossible for *you* to feel, surrounded by so many other men. But how is it with you? What are you thinking about now? It's all so strange and awful for me. I'll never be able to come even close to telling you how it hurts me inside. Is it possible for someone to endure this for very long? Would it become normal?

And how will it be when you are here again and I don't have to decide and do everything? What will our life be like? Will you have to remain in the army? Now and then my head nearly breaks because of the unbearable worrying all day long. Go to sleep, my dearest, with your hungry stomach and in an empty bed. Go to sleep and keep going. Will you be very much changed when you return? More coarse? Rougher? Strange? Or will you be able to remain my own gentle, dear Dicksy in spite of all the roughness around you? I'm so afraid of the first days, when we will both be so strange to each other, so changed. And how can we maintain our contact if you are only allowed to write sporadically, once every 7 weeks, and then in German![30]

Saturday, 11 July. Oh, Dicks, this evening I received a letter from ... Oom Sammie![31] I didn't know what I saw. When I talked

---

29 This indicates that the prisoners had at first been allowed to receive magazines.

30 Wim was writing much more frequently than that, but Madzy is drawing conclusions from the fact that so far she has apparently received only one official letter. She is forgetting that it was the fifth that he had written.

31 Sam and Kuuk van den Berg had been neighbours (but not relatives) of the van Vollenhoven family when Madzy was young, and they were good friends of Iete's. Bill explained that Sam was a colonel in the army.

to Moeder the day before yesterday I said, "Maybe Oom Sam will have a chance to come home."

"Oh, no," Moeder said brusquely, "that's not his kind of thing. He wouldn't want it himself." That's typical of Moeder, with her notions!

Oom Sam wrote that I should make all possible efforts for you. Speed is needed. There I sat with two children and no one else in the house. I on the bicycle to Marietje, who came at once to babysit. I went to de Boerderij, from where I telephoned de heer Stratenus; he was very lukewarm and unenthusiastic. Then I requested a long-distance call to Oom Sam and in the meantime phoned Emiel de Jonghe. He was more enthusiastic but still doubtful. Then I asked Oom Willy (another phone call) whether he would still come tomorrow, in spite of the beastly weather (storm, cold, spells of heavy rain). Yes, he is coming. And now I don't care but I'm going to beg him to help us and maybe he can write a request to Kristiansen or something like that. I'll discuss it with him. You understand that I was in a state. I had actually, from the beginning, hoped for such a chance but everyone ridiculed me or called me naïve.

Then I got Oom Sam on the phone, and he said that we should apply to the Ministry of Economic Affairs. He will come here himself soon with Tante Kuuk. But, oh my darling, he said that you have lost weight. Oh my dear, I hope you don't get sick. Now I'm making myself still more worried. I'll try to send more bread.[32] But that's not so easy and I still don't know whether my parcels are reaching you. I'm sending them and sending them and hear

---

He had been in the same camp as Wim but, because he was elderly and ill, he and a group of other officers who were in poor health were sent home.

32 Bill's note: "Actually I cannot remember that the food was so bad, although of course there was not enough, but we were not starved like the people in concentration camps. It was really stupid to tell those stories to wives in Holland. In the camp there were rumours that efforts should be made in Holland to request the return of prisoners, and a few officers were actually returned."

nothing. I spend a fortune and send carefully hoarded things, and who will eat them? If *you* eat them, I'll send everything, even from my own ration, but if it doesn't reach you? I prayed to God to give you this chance. You, who are so good and so brave and such a good worker, you would be able to use this opportunity so well. Ach, dearest, my heart beats in my throat.

Sunday, 12 July. This afternoon Oom Willy was here and I said that I would accept all the consequences and gave him full authority to do what he can. He said: "Wim is worth it. He has had many jobs and now at last he has found what he wants to do and now he is not so young anymore[33] so now it is really important that he be able to get on in this job." He will also try to send you German books about agriculture, and magazines, if that's allowed. I'm so happy that I was able to talk with him.

Annetje Nahuys had supper with us.

By means of VaVa I received a message that Mevr. de Boer had "very good news" for me and whether I would come as soon as possible. I got Marietje to babysit and bicycled to her. But she wasn't at home, so I just went on to Erna. So tomorrow morning I will go to Maarsbergen again to hear that news. It's now nearly 11:30 and I still have to feed kiddy[34] so I'll stop this. We are doing everything to help you, my own boy. Oh, if this good fortune be granted to us, I will always and always try to be a support to you and not a burden.

Monday, 13 July. Today little Gerard is 2 months old; these 2 months feel like at least 4. But today is an amazing day. Because when I went to Mevr. de Boer this morning she said exultantly: "They will all be home before August!"

"Oh, my dear woman," I said soberly, "please don't believe it."

---

33 Wim was thirty-one.
34 She uses the English word.

"But it's true!" she said. (I'm now allowed to call her "Suus."[35])

Can we believe something so wonderful? When I phoned Mevrouw van den Bent this evening, she also spoke along those lines about rumours that she had heard, but she also didn't dare to believe them. I don't know any more. I had better just trust in God, and wait and see.

I don't dare to believe in that miracle, and yet I imagine how it would be if at this moment you were to walk in. It's not good, and also I'm making no preparations whatsoever. I will leave your bicycle where it is; it can be put in order quickly enough, and until then you can use mine. Your bed is still made as it was when you last slept there, with the same sheets. I'm leaving them on it; they smell of you and I often bury my head in them to smell the scent of you. Your clothes and boots are in the suitcase and chest. I leave it; I leave it. It can all be put in order quickly enough.

Wednesday, 15 July. Today you've been gone for 2 months and I received your second (censored) letter marked Number 6. But what joy this letter brought! "Jean will certainly be there on your birthday."[36] Dicks, oh Dicks, can this be true? Would there be a chance for you to come home? Tomorrow Oom Sam comes here and I can talk about it with him.

Thursday, 16 July. Today Wia Kloppenburg and Oom Sam came to visit. Oom Sam gives you a 10% chance and says that all the stories about your coming home before 1 August are unfounded. It's now nearly midnight and I'm too tired to write.

Wednesday, 22 July, evening, about 11:00. Kiddy is demanding to be fed, but he has to wait for a bit. I've been writing less in the

---

35 Agreeing to use each other's Christian names marked a formal and distinct step forward in their friendship.

36 Wim was writing in code: "Jean" (the French man's name) was his own middle name, and Madzy's birthday was on 25 August.

diary because I'm now writing at length to you.[37] Moreover in the evenings I'm extremely tired, because the nights are disturbed, especially by the children. Pankie has a gall-bladder infection and is bothersome. Yesterday a very big group of planes flew over our heads, and Monica was restless all night long, and Gerard was also awake early.[38] Then you feel exhausted already in the morning, let alone in the evening at 11 o'clock.

Thijs de Stoppelaar is dead.[39] How terrible! I'm constantly thinking about it.

The weather is awful: rain and storm and damp. The garden isn't looking good. The small cabbage plants that I got from Schut have all been eaten, but not by a rabbit.

Now I'm going to sleep. Yesterday I received another postcard, in which you wrote about your speedy return.[40] Would it really be true? Aren't you "making yourself happy with a dead sparrow," and me too?[41] Every day I expect to see you standing in front of me, and over and over I think, "Now, maybe, with this train."

Bicycles have to be turned in.[42] I will hide yours still better.

Sunday, 26 July, evening, quarter to 12. I had the feeling today that I couldn't carry on. I went alone to walk in the woods for a bit, when the children were in bed, and spoke with myself. Then

---

37 This indicates that the system of forms was not yet in place, because they certainly did not allow her to write "at length." See entry for 10 February 1943. See page 151 for a depiction of one of the forms.

38 Monica was the two-year-old daughter of Lies, Madzy's sister-in-law, who (as Madzy wrote in an earlier entry) would come to stay from 15 July until 1 September.

39 Bill identified Thijs de Stoppelaar as a reserve cavalry officer. Being a reserve officer, he had not been in a POW camp, but perhaps he had been seized as a hostage and executed.

40 Bill's note: "In the camp there were the same optimistic rumours, but completely unfounded."

41 This is a Dutch expression about comforting yourself with false hopes.

42 In spite of edicts like this, many people were able to hold on to their bicycles. Madzy's was never taken. Sometimes, however, bicycles were confiscated right on the street and the owners left to walk home.

I went home, smoked a cigarette,[43] and drank three cups of very strong tea. All of it forbidden! Then I felt a bit better and could finish writing my letter to you, writing cheerfully as I hope to write all the letters. And now it's time to go to bed because last night it was again a din, much roaring of thundering bombers and artillery fire, the children awake, and then awake again at 6:30. Good night, my own.

Monday, 27 July. If the promise of Captain de Boer is to come true, then you will be here before Saturday! If *your* promise is to come true, you will be here within 4 weeks. Only 4 more weeks? That would be just a pea-shell compared to these past 11 awful, hopeless, long weeks. And even though Lies says, "If Wim says such a thing, it is true; he wouldn't make you happy with a dead sparrow," still I don't have complete faith in it. All the same, about half an hour after each train I listen for footsteps on the gravel and become more and more nervous. I am so tired—endlessly and bottomlessly tired—with all the worrying and cares, and fretting, and making decisions. I didn't have time to recover properly from giving birth, and in my heart I am so afraid that at some point I will just collapse. If you're away for a long time, then I don't know … *enfin*. Good night, my dearest. Are you still alive?

Tuesday, 28 July. I'm waiting until Lies has finished her shower. Then I will have mine; I'm so dirty from the work in the garden and want to be clean before feeding Gerard.

Today I received another letter from you. In it you say three times that Jean will be home by the autumn. This makes me so nervous, because no one knows what this is based on. At best on rumour, says Oom Sam, rumours which often contain truth but are also often false. If only you don't count on it too much. I would so much like to spare you a disappointment. I would be so glad to be able to save you from all sorrow and difficulty here on earth.

---

43 Madzy never smoked, but there would be cigarettes in the house to offer to guests.

Saturday, 1 August. I've been sick. It gave me a scare. High fever and an infection in my left breast. It's better now. But it shows that I'm gradually becoming exhausted. At some time all the unhappiness and misery will destroy me. Maybe before, maybe after your return, it depends how soon that happens. But would that be as soon as you wrote to me in your letter? Before my birthday?

Oh, my boy, I'm so unhappy, because just this evening arrived your postcard in which you ask for many woollen clothes. And that I should stop sending private parcels, but should not take things too seriously.[44] All of this is a sign that you yourself no longer believe that you will be coming home soon. I try not to cry because otherwise my milk, already not much, will become minimal.

Sunday, 2 August. 78 days you've already been gone. My milk has diminished since your postcard of yesterday and therefore I must not cry and worry any more. I packed a lot of warm clothes for you. It's an extremely hot Sunday, and the suitcase expedition was quite a trip.[45] Pankie helped me and recognized all your suits and said, "Mamma, you remember, those trousers Pappie wore when he worked in the garden and those when he went on the bicycle." And then she said, "But listen, Pappie is coming home the day after tomorrow, to comfort me." The darling!

Wednesday, 5 August. If I had still had some hope, it's all gone now that I received, this evening, your postcard in which you tell about your camp being moved.[46] Where are you now on this

---

44 Perhaps this means that she could still send parcels through the Red Cross.

45 We don't know where she had to bring it.

46 In the first days of August the prisoners were moved to Stanislau, which was then part of Poland but was occupied by Germany. (It is now in Ukraine.) Apparently Wim didn't yet know that that was their destination; when the prisoners were moved, they were not told where they were going.

earth? What are you doing? How is it with you? Are you ever coming home? They say: Lemberg in Poland. Oh, my God, my God, how can I bear this?

I will probably now have to stop breast-feeding Gerard.

Last night bombing at de Hoogt. It was as though our house here collapsed. At 't Stort considerable damage, but none at de Hoogt. What is still ahead of us?

Pankie is now sleeping every night with me. There's too much disturbance.

Sunday, 9 August. Sunday morning and in my imagination I see you sitting in the church service [in the camp]. I've looked after the children, washed diapers, washed the dishes, fed Gerard, made coffee, and now I can at last relax for a moment. We were already awake at 5 o'clock because of Monica but fortunately all of us went to sleep again. The nights are disturbed either by activity over our heads or by the children.

It's true that you've been moved to Poland. To Poland! We officers' wives have been constantly afraid of that. On Friday another group of officers came home, but no Dicksy. And would you still, now that you are so far away, have a chance? Oom Willy said yes, but that it could still be several weeks until his request was granted.[47] Every four weeks groups come home, so perhaps there will be another one in four weeks? But certainly not before my birthday. I now know for sure that I won't be able to endure spending a whole winter here alone. I'm frightened when it gets dark. I can bear less and less. If you only knew what tension exists here, how we expect an invasion every day, how we go into every night with anxiety, how frightened we were when the bombs dropped on de Hoogt!

Sunday, 16 August. I'm too tired these days to write late in the evening. I have constant pain in my head and back and am very

---

47 This indicates that Willy did indeed send an appeal. See entry for 12 July 1942.

quick to catch infections, in my breasts, or from wasp stings. The feeding goes better again.

I'm now going to fetch Pankske, who sleeps in your bed at night. It's quarter past 11, and there's a lot of flying. What sort of night will we have? It sounds as though they are shooting with machine guns very nearby.

Saturday, 22 August. I don't often get to writing; everything is so strange. We've heard that you are in a Heimatslager,[48] which means that from there you would be gradually sent home. I constantly think, "Might he come today? Or tomorrow?" Oom Willy's request should be reaching its destination.

Boy Ruys has been executed.[49] Poor May, poor Tante Anna. Five hostages executed, all young men. The husband of Kathy Telders and two brothers-in-law of Flos Telders. We're all shattered. Then I ask myself whether it would be safe here for you all. But there in Poland it's also not so wonderful.

Life is gradually reaching its saddest point. And with each passing train, with every passer-by, I think, "Dicks maybe?" I'm getting so tired, so tired.

And then still the [Allied] invasion![50]

---

48 Bill explained that this was a camp for those being returned home gradually, but apparently the rumour was unfounded.

49 See footnote for entry of 25 June 1942. May was his wife (personal communication from Frank Steensma, May 23, 2017). "Tante Anna" was probably Anna de Gijselaar, a distant relative of Madzy's and someone Madzy knew from her years of living in Leiden. Ruys's parents were old friends of Nicholaas and Anna de Gijselaar, and Ruys was like a son to them (personal communication from Hansje). Information about Jhr. Nicholaas and Anna de Gijselaar is given in *Frontiers and Sanctuaries*, p. 48. The next sentence implies that Ruys was a hostage, but my understanding is that he was imprisoned as punishment for having attempted to escape to England.

50 The Allied invasion would, Madzy knew, mean serious, perhaps devastating, on-the-ground fighting.

Monday, 24 August. Tomorrow my birthday.[51] "Jean will certainly be home for your birthday." If only the day were over.

Sunday, 6 September. It looks as though Pankie is getting sick. She has a temperature of 38.7° [101.6° F.] this evening. I'm alone, it's Sunday evening, I have just written my usual "cheerful" letter to you, but I'm anything but cheerful because without a telephone I can't reach the doctor and I now carry all the responsibility myself. What could ail Pankske? I don't know.[52]

My visit yesterday to Dr. Tellegen gave me a blow; he talked so definitely about the coming winter, saying that there was no possibility of your returning.[53] There is still a group coming this month, they say. If you're not with them, I give up hope. Then I will hire someone to stay in the house with me, and will hope for next year. But how will I get through the winter?

I'd better not think about it.

Thursday, 10 September. I'm sick; I have a high fever, something which I seldom have. It began yesterday but then that passed so that today I canned applesauce (very necessary) and then suddenly this evening I have fever again.

But there is one thing that keeps my courage up, one sentence in your postcard of 28 August, that arrived yesterday morning:

---

51 She turned thirty-two.

52 Evidently Lies had left; she was a nurse so, had she still been there, Madzy would have had company and also someone knowledgeable to consult.

53 Dr. A. O. H. Tellegen had just returned from the camp. He lived in Zeist, about eight kilometres (five miles) from Maarn. "When in May 1942 the Dutch career officers were sent as POWs to Germany, [Dr. Tellegen] went with them to organize their health care. He did this as a volunteer 'because according to the Geneva Convention he should not be sent to a POW camp.' He returned to the Netherlands at the end of August 1942" (http://eindhovenfotos.nl/TELLEGEN.htm, accessed April 7, 2017). The material on the website (see also Appendix A) gives an indication of what he would have told Madzy. Dr. Tellegen was executed by the Germans in October 1943.

"If Willy would pass his exam in the middle of September, this is not official, but just ask him" ....[54]

This last I can't do, because I'm sick. But that sentence makes my heart beat longingly in my throat, and I listen to all the trains that race past Maarn through the dark, clear September night.

I know that I must not get my hopes up too much, so that I don't have a bitter disappointment if the next group arrives without you. I know that I have to keep my common sense because of our children. But I can't help it that my heart—free as a bird—beats, and beats, and beats ....

I tidied your drawer in the dresser ....

I set your slippers at the front in the cupboard ....

I wanted to put your shaving soap on the washbasin ....

Then I didn't dare to do any more.

Because even though you would not write such a thing without a good foundation ....

Although you never "cheer me up with a dead sparrow" ....

Even though I know that a group is expected home about the middle of September, and Oom Willy's help was very drastic ...,[55] so much can happen: invasion, the Germans changing their plans, and especially the unexpected, which nowadays plays such a large role in our lives.

But ... deep inside me I can't help hoping for this miracle ....[56]

Saturday, 12 September. The fever was gone this morning, only I feel dreadfully weak and tired and painful. Again we had a

---

54 Again this is in code, and it's impossible to know from this small fragment who "Willy" might be. My guess is that the real information in such messages has to do with the date when Wim thinks he might be returning. However, the next sentence suggests that she interpreted this to mean that she should ask someone for information.

55 This shows that Madzy realized by then how dangerous it had been for her to ask for Willy Schüffner's help in pulling (official German) strings to try to get Wim released.

56 All the ellipsis marks in this passage are Madzy's—her way of capturing the workings of her own mind and emotions.

muggy day, but now there's a thunderstorm and the weather will probably change.

I'm worrying about the garden. Now that I'm so weak and still have lots of apples to dry and sauerkraut to can, I need someone to help me in the garden.

The heavy thunder is getting close and Panks is frightened, because "now the invasion is coming and those are bombs." I laugh her anxiety away and now she's lying next to me in your bed and will probably not go to sleep until late; but children in this time have to be handled in one way more strictly but in another way much more gently.

Sunday, 13 September. Gerard is 4 months old today.

The fever came back again. It will be a long business, I'm afraid. Because I'm as weak as wax and getting even thinner, and have pain everywhere especially in my breast. Tomorrow Ad [van Kekem] is coming again.

Now I'm going to sleep. What will this week bring us? Nothing? Emptiness? Because everyone says that that's what I have to count on.

Madzy with the children, probably in autumn 1942, in front of the house. This is one of a group of eleven photos of us that were bound into a small coil booklet and sent to Wim in the camp. Each photo is, on the back, stamped "Geprüft," indicating that it had passed censorship.

Chapter Five

14 September to 29 November 1942

On 14 September Madzy marked her and Wim's sixth wedding anniversary. As I wrote in the Introduction, they were married in the United States, where Madzy had gone to join him, and American regulations required that the wedding take place within ten days of her arrival. None of her or Wim's family attended the ceremony, but on the ship (the *Statendam*) she made the acquaintance of colleagues of her prospective father-in-law, Gerard Brender à Brandis, who were on their way to a conference in New York. Several of these people attended the wedding, and one of them was the best man. Wim had invited a few acquaintances from New York. He had also arranged that Madzy, before the wedding, would stay with Cornelius and Mimi Kolff, a father and daughter (originally Dutch) whom he had come to know well and who lived on Staten Island.[1] He himself was living in a boarding house in Montclair, New Jersey, and commuting to his office in Manhattan; he had arranged for a Presbyterian minister in Montclair to perform the ceremony, and he had rented a small apartment there for them to return to after the honeymoon.

Because no family members were present—it's poignant to realize that on this important day she was surrounded by strangers and near-strangers—Madzy typed a detailed account of the wedding and honeymoon on onion-skin paper with multiple carbon copies to send to family members. It was a "public" narrative, very cheerful, and there are significant differences between it and what she was to write in the war diary (see below) when she looked back to that day. I have

---

1   I have not discovered whether they were related to Dick Kolff.

included a portion of that earlier narrative in Appendix B to show the difference between Madzy's public and private voices (letter and diary) and between the comparatively carefree pre-war Madzy and the one who, six years later, wrote about her difficult wartime life. The two narratives illuminate each other.

Six years after the wedding, therefore, in Maarn, during the war, Madzy remembers. Had Wim been at home, she would certainly have made it a festive occasion, but in his absence she did the best she could, which was to write about it. More than ever, we see that, for her, writing was one of very few outlets, a space where she could create something for herself, *of* herself. This is not only a diary entry; it is an essay, a memoir, and a love letter. The "memory" part of it is written in the third person: she looks back at her younger self from where and who she is now.

*****

Monday, 14 September. Our day. The day that belongs just to the two of us, and no one knows how many and what memories this day awakes in us. Because don't you also see them in front of you, my dearest, all those moments that, for us, make this day forever unforgettable? When I think of this day I always have to smile, smile with the knowing, understanding smile of the old married woman about two ignorant young people—children.

And I'm not smiling because of the minister, or about Pappie,[2] or about your dirty laundry or about the minister's wife and the black verger, but I'm smiling about the things that no one knows except you and me.

I think of how, with a deep sigh of relief—"at last we are alone!"—you loaded my extensive wedding baggage in the back of the Ford which we borrowed from Mimi [Kolff],[3] put the bride herself in and yourself took the wheel and sped off so as to get

---

2   This was apparently a Mr. Bakker; he was one of the group on the *Statendam* and was the best man.

3   Actually the baggage had been loaded into the car at the Kolffs' house that morning.

away as quickly as possible. And I think about the drive to the north, and about the things that we *didn't* say on the way, and about the little hotel where we finally arrived.[4] How must you have felt then, Dicks, young and ignorant as you yourself were, with a young girl beside you who was so dazed that she was barely aware of what she was doing?[5] What were you thinking when you went (discreetly) to look for a bathroom and left her alone in the bedroom, too bewildered to think or feel?[6] Were you aware that she knew nothing—nothing *at all*—about what was awaiting her and was deathly afraid, so terrified that she sat there with chattering teeth? Did you know that?

And weren't you also afraid?

And did you realize that it was only when we arrived in the Shenandoah Valley that she came to herself?[7]

And that her life passed in a haze until [after the honeymoon, back in Montclair] she woke, as out of a wonderful dream, in a miserable dark, frightening night, when she went every evening in the dark to the bridge at the Lackawanna railway station to see if you were coming?

Oh, those lonely evenings in the dark, when everyone else walked together and she walked alone, waiting for the next, always the next train ....[8]

Six years have passed.

In those six years much more has happened than in many a marriage of twenty years. Through everything, our love has become more closely-knit and more beautiful. We have two children.

---

4 They apparently reached a small town called Greenwood Lake.

5 Madzy was twenty-six.

6 Presumably he left her alone so that she could undress in privacy.

7 They had struck very cold weather, so on the following day they turned south and, that evening, reached the Shenandoah Valley in Virginia. See Bill's note on these events, in Appendix B.

8 It was at this time that she developed her intensely unhappy reaction to trains passing in the night: see entry for 21 May 1942.

We both have changed. We've learned a great deal, learned much about each other and about living together.[9] But one thing has remained the same: we still stand pure and unspoiled in our relationship with each other. There has never been anything ugly or frivolous between us, not one moment. Nothing has damaged so much as a hair of our love.

And there is one more thing that has remained the same: again I am waiting in the dark for the train that will bring you to me. You did say the middle of September, didn't you? And again my heart beats in my throat and chokes my breath, and it feels again as though I'm just married and am walking along Montclair Avenue through the darkness, and hang over the railing of the bridge peering in the dark for the one eye of the Lackawanna train in which you might be sitting. And I wait and wait, with beating heart and bated breath and I beg God: "Oh, bring him, bring him, bring my Dicks in this train, in this train, oh God, please, God. Do what you will, oh God." Again I feel just as young as I did then, again longing just as much, again just as lonely ....

Oh, Dicksy-Dicks, I can't do without you any longer. It is as though my heart will break entirely if I have to live any longer without you. I know very well that I have to look for my support in God, but after all God gave you to me because I wasn't strong enough to bear everything in this frightening life. Why, then, does He take you away from me again? I would so much like to be brave, but how? It's so difficult with everything that rests on my shoulders, when I'm so miserably weak now with this

---

9   At the time of their wedding, the acquaintance between Madzy and
     Wim consisted of a casual school-time contact (they had briefly played
     on the same field-hockey team), a correspondence of about two years
     while Wim was in New York, a few days at Christmas 1935 when they
     became engaged, and the nine days after her arrival in New York—a
     skimpy acquaintance on which to base a marriage. It's obvious how
     important that two-year correspondence was. Both of them were good
     letter-writers; it was through correspondence that they got to know
     each other well enough to decide to marry.

flu so that I can't take a step, have difficulty breathing, have a constantly pounding heart, and can barely think rationally. What will become of the three of us without you, Dicks?

Tuesday, 15 September. For the first time I was actually up again, but oh how glad I am when I'm in bed once more![10] My back is breaking, I feel nauseated, I have no appetite, and my head is spinning. My clothes droop on me and my little corset flaps around my middle. But it will get better. Because today I received another letter from you, and after your previous postcard I was tense with anxiety to see what you might have written to me now. I was so wretched that today I had spells of heart palpitations again. "Because," I thought, "if he doesn't write anything about when he is coming home, or he writes negatively, then I don't know whether I can keep going today." But ... it turned out to be the opposite: "I am studying just as hard as Willy so we will probably both pass our exams," and "Jean had better congratulate Pankie for me."[11] Am I an idiot or can I interpret this to mean that I can mark off the days only until 5 October? Oh if only it might be true! They do say that you are safer there, that here you would have to report regularly to the German authorities, that all kinds of dangers would threaten you here, etc., but even though I would be anxious for you every day I would still rather have you near me before the winter.

Oh, Dicksy-Dicks, I won't know what to do if, this month, you walk in. I don't know why, but this evening I feel so warm inside, so rich, so intensely happy. Might it really work out like that?

Thursday, 17 September. I don't know why, but I feel so strange inside, as if something very wonderful is happening! Might you come back tomorrow? I always count on it happening on a Friday or Saturday. Up to now all the groups have come home on those

---

10 Probably she had someone to help with the housework and children, but that is the kind of detail that she would have written in a letter to Wim.
11 My birthday would be on October 5.

days. I feel as though I will, at any moment, burst out into some happy song. How have I come by this?

I am again out of bed, and today I even tidied the barn with Marietje in case "Meneer unexpectedly stands in front of us."[12] But oh, I'm still so weak and tired. In the morning I have breakfast in bed, in the afternoon I have a long rest, and in the evening I'm in bed by 9:45. And I delight in all that rest. It's as though I am finding peace. Mevr. de Boer wrote to me that she had received a letter from the Captain, "cheerful and hopeful." That also gives me a feeling of happiness. Oh if only all the officers might be home before the winter, as everyone is always saying will happen.

Actually I should be very "down" because I just received a letter from de heer van Mierop.[13] You overestimated your indispensability a bit, my dearest. We are going to work hard together to make sure that you *really* become indispensable. I'm going to work with you. I'm already busily learning bookkeeping.[14]

Friday, 18 September. Today arrived your intensely loving postcard that was meant for our wedding anniversary and with which you made me so deeply happy, my darling. You write that you are grateful for everything that I did for you and the courage with which I came to Montclair to marry you. But I did so little for you. In these 4 months I've become aware what I can *really* do for you. And it took no courage to go to Montclair, it was an

---

12 "Meneer" is how Madzy and her helpers would refer to Wim. It's not clear why the barn needed tidying so often. There would be some mess connected with the goat and the chickens, but perhaps she did it compulsively because it was something that connected her with Wim. It's possible, however, that the barn was sometimes used by divers and that she was removing any sign of their presence.

13 Bill's note: "Head of provincial forestry department where I did some minor part-time work." Evidently Madzy had asked him to put in an appeal for Wim's return.

14 We don't know when she began this bookkeeping course.

inward compulsion and I'm convinced that it was God's hand that brought me to it.

I have a lot of faults, especially that I am egotistical and that I find myself a very important little person. That will change now; that has already changed. I have changed inwardly in these 4 months, just as you also will have changed, at least that is what I read in your letters.

Monday, 21 September. Autumn. A whole summer has passed, a summer to which I had been looking forward so intensely, for the four of us to enjoy, after a winter of cold and of discomfort because of the baby coming. Gone is this summer that, in place of pleasure, taught us a hard, heavy lesson.

Today I had dinner at de Hoogt. It was very companionable. Coming home I had to struggle through the darkness—my bicycle lamp was broken but there was moonlight. Tante Betsy asked whether I wanted to take piano lessons together with her.[15] I'd love to but don't know whether I have the time or the money. I would like to be able to play a bit better, to give you pleasure. I'm considering it carefully. I told Tante Betsy about my bookkeeping course; I thought she would laugh at me but she told me that she herself had learned it from de heer Huizinga.[16] I get along very well with Tante Betsy.

I received a report about Stanislau via Mevrouw LeHeux, almost exactly the same as what I had heard from Dr. Tellegen.

Thursday, 24 September. It is evening and I'm alone. The shutters are closed, the animals and children in bed, I took out my bookkeeping assignment and am now going to stifle the loneliness with a difficult interest calculation. It's odd that *you*

---

15 We had an upright piano; Madzy had had piano lessons when she was a girl.

16 Mr. Huizinga was the bookkeeper at the estate management office (owned by Willem de Beaufort, Betsy's brother-in-law) where Wim would work after the end of the war (see Conclusion).

have too much human company and that I have to put up with too much loneliness.

Moeder Hans stayed until today.[17] When I saw her, I had a dreadful shock: she is thin, old, and weak. Really in bad shape, with feverish red cheeks and burning hot hands that shook. Walked with a stick, stooped.[18] But she improved visibly, a sign that much of it is psychological. She slept well, her legs were becoming less swollen, the high colour disappeared and her eyes were calmer, her hands no longer trembled and the hoarseness in her voice disappeared. She even hummed, and played the piano, and enjoyed it enormously. Her doctor didn't want her to be away for too long because he was afraid that she might have an infection in one artery in her leg, otherwise I would have kept her here. She enjoyed it so much and was so grateful for the eggs, the porridge, the grapes, etc. I brought her breakfast in bed, which gave her great pleasure. And she found the children sweet. She might come back next month. Your return would do her an enormous amount of good; the fact that you're away really hurts her and is the main cause of her illness.

And now I'm waiting again for "Jean." Because the group of mid-September is not yet home.[19] I expect it tomorrow or the day after. But Jet had heard that that group would contain only the sick. And so we hear only rumours.

Friday, 25 September. I'm again alone this evening. Just now both electric fuses blew. What an awful feeling, to be alone in a pitch-dark house and have to go upstairs, entirely by touch, to get the flashlight. Really scary.

---

17 We don't know when Wim's mother had arrived; presumably Madzy had mentioned it to Wim in a letter.

18 Hans was fifty-nine.

19 Madzy was projecting on the basis of the pattern that she and others had noticed, but there was no assurance that there would be a group returning in mid-September.

Saturday, 26 September. The last train has passed; you weren't on it. Today your postcard, in which you wrote: "I hear that Willy's exam has been postponed for a few weeks." Although this postponement is a heavy blow, still this is the most positive expression that you've ever given. You're sure, therefore, that you are coming home, and that it has only been delayed. But now I'm being childish, eating myself up with nervousness. I am so afraid that you are not coming, or that I will collapse at a bad moment. I've become very thin: with clothes and shoes, I weigh less than 67 kg.[20]

Just then Piet and Christie [van Notten] came and interrupted my plan to wash my hair. So I will still do it now, even though it's already almost 11:00, because tomorrow morning I'm going to church and tomorrow afternoon to VaVa for tea with Gerard and Pankie. This afternoon we were at the van Kekems' where Mevrouw[21] was half giving birth but was still up and in the garden, so she was glad of the distraction. (I found two packages of tobacco [for Wim] from Charlotte in the scullery, which she had tossed in through the window while I was away. I'm sorry to have missed her.)

Sunday, 27 September, evening. Alone with the children; the loneliness here in this small house among the high, dark woods weighs heavily on me.[22] I believe that this loneliness is gradually making me melancholy; only the hope for your speedy return gives me the strength to keep going.

---

20 Sixty-seven kilograms is 147 pounds imperial. She was about six feet in height and always slender.

21 This is a joking reference to Mrs. van Kekem, whom Madzy normally called Dick.

22 She had no "media" entertainment except the German-controlled radio and the BBC, no source of music except the radio and her own piano-playing, no reliable newspapers except such underground ones as reached her. She had no telephone to allow her just to call someone for a chat. She had books and magazines to read, and she could write letters or knit or sew, and she could write in the diary.

Today a beautiful sermon by Ds. Koolhaas about which I wrote to you.[23] I came home really feeling cheerful. But being alone with the children is so deadening to one's spirits; you have no exchange of thoughts with someone else. Might I get help tomorrow? Hans van Ketwich Verschuur would gladly have sent someone to stay but I haven't heard anything more about it.[24] At night, because I'm alone, I am again so terribly frightened and sleep badly, and I don't have a rest in the afternoon, so I'm short of sleep.[25] I can't carry on like that for very long and I hope very much that *if* you're going to come home it will be soon. On Tuesday perhaps another letter? Why weren't you allowed to write on 11 September? Punishment?[26] There are rumours again that you will all come home together, but would this be true? However ... no fire without a spark, as they say. It would make everything easier.

I have to be careful about the garden work because of the nursing. It goes moderately well but G. gained only 70 gr this week, which isn't overly much, and yet I would like to nurse him for at least three more months because it's so difficult to get additional food for him [on the rations] that would be comparable to the mother's milk. He gets only ¾ L per day of low-fat milk, Pankie (starting on 5 October) only ½ L, and I myself ½ L of skim milk or buttermilk.

---

23 Bernhard Cornelis Koolhaas (1875–1956) had retired as predikant in 1939 and was listed in 1941 as "assistant preacher" in Maarn (private communication from Gijs van Roekel).

24 Bill's note: Probably someone who had gone underground and needed a hiding place. Warmbrunn (p. 190) wrote that the placing of divers with host families involved issues of compatibility and of security for both the host and the diver. There was a Resistance organization that specialized in this.

25 According to the entry for 9 October, Marietje was sleeping there; "alone" means that Madzy was the (solitary) head of the little household of servant and children.

26 Bill's note on a similar entry (deleted) was "We were never punished for anything."

It's cold this evening but I haven't lit the stove just for me. To comfort myself I'm drinking some warmed-up tea and now I'll work on knitting your sweater and listen to the radio. How I will delight in every evening in the future when you're here! It will be all one interlocking chain of happy moments.

Thursday, 1 October. I've had 3 awful days with carpentry work going on indoors and painting outdoors,[27] and with a strange girl in the house (dug up by Hans van K. V.) who got terribly on my nerves, didn't like it here, ate far too much, did not bring her own butter, sugar, jam, etc., and then still had complaints. I sent her on her way today. I hope intensely, however, that I don't get into trouble because of it. Result is that I'm dead tired, I still have to do the homework for my bookkeeping course, and the house is a terrible mess.

The delivery (to Germany) of labourers is becoming a tense business: three of the de Bruin family were tested, even girls, including Marietje.[28]

Tuesday, 6 October. Yesterday Pank's birthday, our little Pankepoek already 4 years old, and can you still see her in her cradle, or in the playpen, or in the car?[29] And today your letter, in which you wrote: "You should try to remain at home until the end of October. Jean will soon be coming to look after Pankie." My heart beats in my throat, and my stomach is doing funny things. Nerves! I will go to pieces yet from the pent-up nervousness! Dead tired in bed with an infection in my gums. But tomorrow Marietje and I are going to do the autumn

---

27 Bill's note: The work would have been ordered by Dientje.

28 Olson (pp. 218–219) writes that the conscription of men from the occupied countries became worse after the enormous loss of German troops on the eastern front.

29 Bill's note: "During the mobilization, a few years earlier, Marianne often travelled with Madzy in the car."

housecleaning and change the rooms around in honour of your return. And—although hesitantly—I got your business suit out of the mothballs. You never know ....

Wednesday, 7 October, 11:30 p.m. Today I moved to the guest room and converted our room into the children's room. It was an enormous job but it went well. I couldn't get any help because half the village will be emptied in the direction of Germany tomorrow and on Thursday of next week [because of the labour draft]. I'm very tired. It's as warm as in summer.

Thursday, 8 October. It's high, high time that you come back, my dearest, because little Gerard is hungry because of your continued absence after all the promises about returning! Because you can't do anything about it, you don't have to feel guilty! But today Gerard was crying with hunger, and when I weighed his 6 o'clock feeding it turned out to be only 100 gr, so that I had to give him the other breast as well, and now as the very, very last resort I have to open our tin of coffee. I'm drinking a lot of it, eat lots of porridge, and by 11 o'clock I will try to cobble something more together. Because in spite of everything that has happened, Gerard hasn't yet been hungry and must not be. And I wish so very much that he can get his mother's milk for 7 months, just as Marianneke had hers. And I would also like it so very much if you could still see him drinking at my breast.

Friday, 9 October. I'm alone again, and it becomes easier and easier to be alone. Because then I can listen better to the trains and to the noises in the dark forest that shuts in our little house. I'm alone with my thoughts, my children, my memories, my work. I listen for the postman's footsteps.[30] When he has been, it's quiet until Marietje comes running. She always runs

---

30 The postman, Gerrit Heerikhuizen, would die in a bombing raid in September 1944 (van der Donck, *Vrijheid geef je door*—"Freedom: you pass it on," p. 10).

because she's afraid of the dark. The 8:00 train is just passing. If you're not here in half an hour you're again not coming today. Maybe tomorrow? That hope lifts my heart again, and although I know that a black night full of frightening images threatens me, there'll be another day with new expectation, new hope for the miracle. So the days pass, so the nights come, in one unbroken monotonous row.

Monday, 12 October, evening, alone. This morning shopping in Doorn, this afternoon Marianke played with the van Nottens [Jim and Bem] and Gerard and I went along.

This evening your letter of 28 September. I just went upstairs to pass on your "happy birthday" kiss to Pankie.

Shall I tell you how I read your letters? When I receive them from the postman, my heart flies into my throat but I say cheerfully, "Oh, a letter from Meneer!" (because that letter always lies on top, that's what the postman always does). Then I slam the door closed and run to the couch, where I read the letter very, very quickly, holding my breath and with a heavily beating heart, to see as soon as possible whether there's something awful in it. When there is some awful moment—as for example in this letter where you ask for winter clothes[31]—it is as though everything in me cracks open with the pain. Then I see the winter long and lonely in front of me—don't know how I will ever survive it.

Wednesday, 14 October. Today Moeder Iete was here. They say that Paul and his family are safely in Australia. That would be too good to be true in these times.[32] Letters came from you with the message regarding the sending of winter clothes and your

---

31 She had sent winter clothes a few weeks earlier; evidently that parcel had not reached Wim by the time he was writing this latest letter.

32 It was in fact not true. Madzy's half-brother, Paul, and his wife, Mita, and their four young daughters were in two different Japanese prison camps in the Dutch East Indies, where they would stay until the war in the Far East ended.

message that if you don't come home with the next group I have no reason to hope any more. And with that I had wretched heart palpitations, that won't go away. Silly of me, eh?

Monday, 26 October. Haven't written for a while, extremely busy with the harvest. Today prepared the little suitcase with winter clothes, but don't know whether I should send it because I haven't heard anything from you in 15 days, and in your last letter you wrote: "If Jean doesn't come at the earliest opportunity ...," and this first opportunity hasn't happened yet. No "next group" has come yet, and it looks as though none will come before 1943. Yesterday Oom Willy here; he is still optimistic and told me not to lose hope. About his country [Germany] he doesn't say much.

I'm writing badly because I hurt my hands with taking apart the stakes of the climbing beans. The garden helper won't be able to come until next week, probably, so on Friday I'll harvest the beets myself. Then only the strawberries will have to be done. The chickens ate all the seeds that I had intended to use to grow feed for the goat!

Sunday, 1 November. Yesterday I went to Pahud.[33] And this is the beginning of a very difficult time: awaiting the next 100, and accepting it calmly if you are not among them. When will those 100 come? That can be in hours, days, weeks. On the previous occasions the groups came on Friday or Saturday, but Pahud came on Tuesday. So it can be any day, and it may not be for a long time.

This week Annetje [Nahuys] is coming, and that's a good thing because the days and especially the nights are now one breath-clenching struggle.

---

33 Bill identifies this person as a cavalry officer he had known in Amersfoort and who had been in the same camp as Wim, but he doesn't give the first name. Mr. Pahud had evidently come home very recently.

Wednesday, 11 November, Armistice Day. The Germans are invading France without opposition. The Americans and English occupied North Africa on 8 November. Life is full of storm and upheavals: evacuation, executions, anxiety about invasion, reduced rations.

Both children have terrible colds. Panks has a nasty cough that looks like whooping cough and Gerard has dreadfully infected eyes with pus coming from them, while I myself have cramps in my stomach because of a stomach flu. I should keep myself on a diet, but meanwhile I still have to produce enough milk. The two can't be made to rhyme together! It's already dark so early, now that the winter time began on 2 November; we close the shutters at 5:00 and then I sit with electric light until the following day. Still 40 days before the days start to get longer again.

Friday, 13 November. Gerard is half a year old, but on this occasion I don't miss you so intensely because you have had no part whatsoever in him, no contact between you and him. You also hardly ever write about him, and that is so understandable because you can't picture him to yourself. He is still so entirely mine, my son. But when you come home I will give him to you.

Wednesday, 18 November. We are all sick: I now have bronchitis.[34] But there is no Dicksy to look after me. Therefore I've been digging in the garden.

---

34 Sometime about now, Iete sent Juus to us again. I don't know the exact date, only that (as Madzy recorded in the 1976 taped narrative) it occurred in November 1942 when we were all sick. Juus would stay with us until the end of the war.

Juus Egner as she was in 1945.

Saturday 21 November. This is a heavy day; in the first place I'm basically sick and during the night lay fighting a fever, and this evening your postcard of 8 November, that kills all hope of seeing you again soon. So now all I can do is look towards the far future, when the war is over and all the prisoners of war are back. When will that be? Oh, I'm not such an optimist as to think that it will be before Christmas. And I'm anxious about the time when it *is* over, when we will have had no contact for a long time. What is waiting for us then? I held my little Gerard close to me and begged for God's mercy on him: what still hangs over the heads of our two little scraps of humanity?

My darling, my heart is flying again like a mad thing, I'd better go and read a book to distract myself. Because I have to continue to have milk for sick little Gerard, who is already crying so pathetically because his little nose has such a bad cold in it.

Sunday, 29 November. The day before yesterday Toulon was occupied, the French navy scuttled itself. General mourning in England for the men who drowned.

Today I miss you dreadfully, my darling. I don't know what brings on these spells, but when they happen I feel so broken inside in the evening that I don't know where to find comfort. A good book is then my only salvation and distraction. My dear, I'm losing the contact with you so much, and because of that I feel so awfully lonely and lost in the world. Last night I dreamed that I stood with the two children somewhere in the middle of an empty open space and the wind beat against me. I feel that way now. How does it feel to you? Are you still with us? At least you can picture how we are living here, but I can't picture anything about you,[35] and therefore everything around me is so dark and lonely and lost, because it's as though you don't actually exist but are only a vague fantasy. I'm so deeply unhappy....

---

35 This shows how scanty the communication was. Wim, aware that his letters would be censored, would probably be cautious about describing life in the camp in case the censors regarded that as potentially dangerous to the Germans.

Chapter Six

10 February to 28 December 1943

As Madzy writes in the first entry, it has been a long time since she wrote in the diary—nearly two and a half months. In fact, from now on for the next fifteen months the diary entries are much less frequent than they had been before or were again later. On 29 April 1943, she indicates that this was a way of saving paper. As well as writing less often, she used abbreviations and wrote as compactly as she could. She omitted paragraph breaks almost completely; I have inserted them to make the text more readable.

*

In the entry for 18 March 1943, Madzy mentions that her sister Hansje's friend Dick (his surname is never given) might go underground with our family in Maarn—i.e., become a "diver." He would have joined a large and rapidly growing group that included Jewish families and men who were evading the labour draft. There were also downed Allied airmen and, later, the Allied soldiers who, after the Battle of Arnhem, had not managed to escape to Allied-held territory; these soldiers and airmen were hidden by the Dutch Resistance and, when possible, smuggled back to safety.[1]

As noted in Chapter Five, Resistance organizations found hiding places for divers and helped the host families to look after them.[2]

---

1   See headnote to Chapter Ten.
2   The Wikipedia article "Dutch Resistance" (accessed Jan. 24, 2018) indicates that in the Netherlands there has been a debate about exactly what constituted "resistance," and a distinction is made between actual resistance and illegality. I am using the term "resistance" to refer to both categories.

Divers received no food coupons so the host families had to be given additional ones, which the Resistance forged or stole from German administrative offices. False identity papers had to be provided. Divers had to be moved if their hiding places were no longer safe or if friction developed between them and the host family. The same people who distributed clandestine newspapers might carry forged or stolen food coupons or escort a Jewish family to a different hiding place.[3]

"Diving" could consist of moving to a different address and taking a false identity, but for many (especially Jews) it meant staying out of sight. For all divers, hiding was a way to survive and also a form of resistance. Helping them was certainly a form of resistance. Large numbers of Dutch people were involved in this caring work, and it was dangerous. Those who were caught were either executed on the spot or sent to concentration camps.[4] Local people sometimes knew—and sometimes did not know—whether their neighbours were harbouring divers; the host family could not always be sure which of their townsfolk they could trust and who might report them to the occupying authorities.

I have found no statistics for the number of people in hiding in the winter of 1942–1943, but in 1944 there were probably about 300,000, and during the winter of 1944–1945 that number may have doubled.[5]

Madzy certainly knew—and knew about—divers in our area. Some of her friends went underground. Divers sometimes came to the door to ask for food or other help. Different divers made for her, no doubt in gratitude for help received, a leather shoulder-bag, a small

---

3   Janet Keith, *A Friend among Enemies: The Incredible Story of Arie van Mansum in the Holocaust*, passim. Van Mansum's story illustrates the extent and danger of this work.
4   The Wikipedia article "Dutch Resistance" refers to "the hundreds of thousands of Dutch men and women who performed illegal tasks at any moment during the war."
5   Van der Zee (p. 129). The entry "Onderduiken ['Diving']" in the Dutch Wikipedia (accessed Jan. 24, 2018) says that at the end of September 1944, when the railway personnel had gone on strike (see headnote for Chapter Seven) and had, almost automatically, gone underground, there were more than 350,000 people in hiding.

tabletop weaving loom, and a handsome wooden sewing kit, all of which we still have.

As for resistance in general, it could take many forms. An incident that Madzy did not mention in the diary but of which she later wrote a wryly amusing account was the confiscation of the radios. In May 1943, the period covered by this chapter, the Germans attempted to confiscate all Dutch radios to prevent the Dutch from listening to the BBC. Madzy, like many others, was determined to keep her radio, so someone gave her a huge, old-fashioned radio to turn in. She concealed her "working" radio in a small closet behind the chimney, where she could listen to it secretly.[6]

*****

Wednesday, 10 February 1943. What a long time it is since I wrote! But we've all been sick, whooping cough and jaundice, and this book was left lying.[7] Also I didn't have such a need to write because I could write to you, my dearest, in more detail. But now that we have to use those wretched forms and write telegram-fashion I again need an outlet in this book. I'm again so nervous, and now I wish with my whole heart that you would either come home very soon or write to me that your return is definitely off. If I'm out for the whole day, as I was today, then I race home for the last stretch to see if you're back or not.

Tomorrow Moeder Hans is coming. On Saturday I want to bring in my firewood. It's lying close by and I have to saw it and bring it in with Dientje's donkey cart. Tomorrow I have to have the saw sharpened. I'm busy, fortunately, because then I forget the stress.

Sunday, 14 February, evening. Last night I had an experience: first I dreamed a nasty dream about intense poverty; I was in

---

6 The story is told in detail in *Frontiers and Sanctuaries* (p. 103ff).

7 In the 1976 narrative Madzy mentions there were no longer any medications to deal with such illnesses, and that we were indeed very sick. Gerard and I had whooping cough, and Madzy had jaundice.

the middle of it but I don't remember the precise details. When I woke for a moment I turned over and thought, "Now I'll have a nice dream." And then I dreamed about you. But "nice" it was *not*! I dreamed that you were on a boat that was moored alongside a wharf, and that you were going to go away again, and I had come to show you the children for a moment so that you could say good-bye to them. You were in your cavalry dress uniform and looked very lean and attractive. I wanted to cry but didn't, but I felt wretched when I woke up. On the way to church I had a heavy, upset feeling and I have had it the whole day, such a tired, hopeless feeling, as though you want to cry all the time but you're too tired to do so, as though you've wept all your tears and now your heart is crying, but the eye remains dull and tired.

We heard a beautiful sermon from Ds. Koolhaas charging us to be aware of the danger for our children (the older ones) and very well expressed, and that we had to trust only in God: "Do not put your trust in princes ...."[8]

This afternoon Hansje came to lunch and stayed until Els came to fetch her to have a drink with the Hoogeweegens. I went to Mevr. Everwijn Lange. He (Mr Everwijn Lange) is very nice and talks a lot.

Darling, where are you? I need you so badly. But everyone says that you are so much safer where you are now. Maybe you could escape via Hungary, people say, or the Russians will liberate you and send you to England. All monstrous imaginings. But what is ahead of us?

Wednesday, 17 February. The day before yesterday I received your letter of 5 February, number 11, so that 9 and 10 are still

---

8　During the war, children of an age to be learning right from wrong were living in a lawless and brutalizing world. Even "good" people, who might otherwise have been moral examples for the children, were doing subversive and illegal things. "Schoolchildren are often sent into the streets with orders to steal" (van der Zee, p. 156). Madzy refers to this in a letter of 22 November 1945 to Virginia Donaldson.

missing and I live with riddles, and naturally I worry, even though you say twice that I mustn't do so. Sentences such as: "Will you really not worry about what I wrote about Paul and Mita?" (about which I still know nothing) and: "regardless of Willy,[9] I know an excellent solution. In that case Jean won't want to leave you." These words don't bring me peace of mind nor cheer me up. "I could chop off one of my fingers—then I'm of no use as an officer ...."[10] If only the missing letters come I might be a bit less worried.

Saturday, 20 February. I still haven't received the missing letters, just now when I'm longing so much for more news because your letter #11 was such a riddle. Today beautiful spring weather and I worked in the garden. Hansje and her friend Dick are staying here. They eat their meals at de Hoogt. When they arrived Dick gave me a kiss, the first kiss that I've had from a man since 15 May 1942! Not at all nice—I blushed deeply. I find him so-so. Juus

---

9 Bill's note, made in his old age, explained that in this passage "Willy" was code for "the German situation." We can understand Madzy's confusion and frustration.

10 When I discussed this passage with Bill during the work on *Frontiers and Sanctuaries*, he explained that after the war he, as a career officer, would have had to go to the Dutch East Indies to serve in the war for Indonesian independence. Indeed, in the summer of 1945, after his return from the camp, he was sent to a location in the Netherlands to take part in a training program for work in tanks. After two weeks he was declared unfit for active service on account of the colitis he had contracted in the POW camp, and he received a medical discharge. But this discharge did not mean an end to his military career: he could have been re-tested later and, if fit by then, still been forced to return to active service. By this time, however, both he and Madzy hated the fact of his being in the army, and after his discharge in 1945 the possibility of his being returned to active service hung over their heads until they emigrated to Canada in 1947. When he was in the camp and writing this letter, these events were still more than two years in the future, but clearly he was already considering how he could get out of the army after the war: chopping off a finger would have meant an end to his army career, but fortunately it didn't come to that.

said, kindly, "A sweet little boy." Whether there's much to him? Hansje thinks there is.

Monday, March 1. The following conversation took place this afternoon between Pank, who in her warm winter clothes sat playing in the sandbox, and Mamma.

Mamma comes out and asks: "Pank, what did Pappie do last year about the apple tree? Do you remember? How did he clean it?"[11]

"With those brushes, you know, Mammie, those steel brushes."

"Do you know where they are?"

"Have a look in Pappie's tool cupboard." Pank carries on making a mud-pie.

"Come along," Mamma says, "and then you can show me."

We nose around in the cupboard. "They're black, and hard," says Pank. But we don't find them. Mamma looks round and sees them on the high shelf in the barn.

"Good for you," says Pank. "Yes, yes, that's them."

"And how did Pappie cut off the dead branches?"

"Oh, gee," says Pank, "with those scissors that you sent back to Tante To."

"Well, then I'll have to do it with a knife. Do you happen to know how Tante Dientje's gardeners do it?"

"Oh, yes, Mammie, with a saw."

What do you say to such a helper?

Monday, 2 March. Today I received a letter and postcard from you, from which I make out that someone else (Dus?) is already on the way home and is bringing all kinds of things from you.[12] You write: "I'm sorry that I asked you for testimonials," but you

---

11 Bill's note: "Probably she means cleaning the moss off the bark, something which is necessary in Holland."

12 Dus Fabius, one of Wim's fellow cavalry officers, was sent home from the camp at this time for health reasons.

didn't ask me for any in the letters that I received. I'm missing one letter and one card and everything is very mysterious. If only you understood how anxious those vague, unintelligible remarks make me. They disturb the tiny bit of peace that I still have.[13]

Sunday, 7 March. Today I went to the [Remonstrant] church in Amersfoort, and that I will also definitely do with you because I got a great deal out of it. During the night there had been a hard frost and it was beautifully clear weather. I did it in ¾ hour on the bicycle, and on the way back I dropped in on Charlotte. The sermon was beautiful, and I felt that a Remonstrant sermon is something different than a Reformed one and I felt more at home. After a late lunch I knitted busily on your scarf and then all of a sudden a friend of Charlotte came to photograph us. I think that this is a really nice birthday present for you.[14]

Thursday, 18 March. Today Jolien Blom told me that her mother had spoken yesterday to Dus Fabius on the [railway] station at Amersfoort, on his way to The Hague, where he had to sign out. He had been traveling from Friday evening to Tuesday afternoon. I had to keep a stiff upper lip because it was an enormous disappointment—Dus *did* come home but not you. Jolien didn't know much more, but this evening I phoned Dr. Fabius [Dus's father] in Arnhem and by good luck found Dus there. He said that you were well, and when I asked him about your possible return he said that he would write a detailed letter to me about that. I'm very curious and tense. What will it be this time?

---

13 Bill told me that he had meant well in writing to her in this kind of code, but he was (at the time of doing the translation) very sorry about it. He had not foreseen that the letters would not all arrive or would arrive out of order, and that the obscurity of his remarks would make Madzy nervous.

14 Wim's birthday was on 20 April.

Hansje's Dick has not been reporting to his job since Monday, and will probably go underground here. That will make the little house very crowded, but he'll have to work hard at sawing wood and sowing seeds in the garden.[15]

Monday, 22 March. Nothing further from Dus. Today to Wolfheze with Pank for Tante To's birthday.

The photos of us, taken for you, are exceptionally good.

Friday, 27 March. My dear, your Mappeke has had wretched days since Dus's return. At first waiting for his letter, then hearing that he actually *was* in Arnhem [last?] Friday (he had said that he wouldn't be), that Wia had visited him and already had the photo (I don't have it yet, and this coming Wednesday Dus will have been home for 2 weeks already) and then a short note from Dus in which he said that you were "more than well but longed very much for home." That there was a chance for you to come home as "selected or individual" and what my opinion was, and whether I would write as soon as possible.[16] From his remark on the phone that he had come home with three "selected" officers "among whom Wim *fortunately* wasn't included" I understood that that was something degrading. My opinion—if your future career would suffer? .... I've worried like anything. Couldn't sleep. But after having, first, written to you yesterday in hesitant terms that we [two or three illegible words, presumably indicating that he should come home if he had a chance], today I recklessly used my last letter-form and said that you shouldn't do it. You will never know how much this cost me. When I mailed the letter I had the feeling that the world sank away under me, and near the post office I felt nauseated. Coming home I had difficulty

---

15 There is no further word about him in the diary; he never came to live with us, but he could have gone underground somewhere else in the neighbourhood.

16 It's not clear to whom Madzy was supposed to write. She apparently interpreted it to mean that she should write to Wim.

concealing my tears. And yet I know, deep in my heart, that it's best that you return after the war with the others.

A group of officers in the POW camp in the Stanislau period. Wim is the fourth from the left in the back row. Bill told me that photos like this—we have several similar ones—were taken by local photographers and sold to the prisoners. This one was printed as a postcard and mailed to Madzy.

Saturday, 10 April. This evening for the first time since November I'm alone,[17] but now it's light and that's less lonesome; besides, I'm waiting for Tini [Sandberg], who can arrive at any moment. Her meal is keeping warm on the stove and I think about the many, many times that I waited for you while *your* little pot stood simmering: Montclair, Amersfoort, here. I worked all day today in the garden, and for a little while that gave me satisfaction, but I can't get rid of the heavy sadness; it is as though my whole soul is shrouded, as though a terrible calamity is approaching.

---

17 This indicates that Juus had been with us since November.

Sunday, 25 April. Easter. Cold, stormy, and lonesome. In your postcard of yesterday you write for the first time that you will stay with Klop to the end, because that would be better, and that your eyes are getting worse.[18] That about your eyes I had also already thought of but didn't think I should mention it.

I've been down, there is constantly the threat of an invasion, there's the battle for Tunis .... It makes me miserable.

Saturday, 1 May. The whole country is, as of today, under police rule. We aren't allowed outdoors between 8 p.m. and 6 a.m. There's a strike. The whole army has been made prisoners of war, and all the army personnel—NCOs, mostly—summoned to report, taking clothes.[19] Consternation everywhere. Does this mean that something is at last going to happen?

This morning I went to fetch my own milk and bread.[20] There's no more butter. I slogged around for 1½ hours to get the day's food. Unfortunately the trains are still running.[21] But the

---

18 Bill translated this as "stay with the others to the end": "Klop" is his good friend Wim Kloppenburg, husband of Madzy's friend Wia. In his memoir (see Appendix A) he writes about going to an optometrist.

19 See Introduction. The Dutch army had been demobilized in May 1940 and just sent home. (It was not until two years later that the career officers like Wim were taken prisoner). In those two years, a number of officers had escaped to England, and others had gone underground in the Netherlands. As we've seen, the possibility of imprisonment had been hanging over the heads of the reserve officers. The strike Madzy mentions here was provoked by a proclamation by General Christiansen, Commander of the German Armed Forces in the Netherlands (the Wehrmacht), ordering Dutch army veterans to report for re-internment in Germany (Warmbrunn, p. 133). I'm not clear why Warmbrunn uses the term "re-internment," because my understanding is that these men had not yet been interned. The wording of Christiansen's title comes from Warmbrunn, p. 33.

20 This suggests that up to now it had still been delivered to the door, as was customary.

21 This is a wry comment; during the occupation the railways were extremely useful to the Germans as well as to the Dutch people. See headnote to Chapter Seven.

feeling is that after all something is about to happen; people are more hopeful instead of that constant waiting.

Saturday, 15 May. The day before yesterday our son was one year old. I was deeply thankful that this most dangerous year of his life has passed safely.

Maybe, later on, you'll be interested to hear how I spent this day.[22] Up at 7:00 and quickly pull on a dress and open the shutters. Nowadays Pank does this with me, after she has got into her slippers and dressing gown. We go to the bathroom, and then Pank gets a slice of bread. Geert sits enthroned on his potty for the first time of the day. Juus makes tea and Geert's porridge. When the shutters are open and we have assessed the weather, pulled up the weight of the clock, and finished the slice of bread, we take our tea upstairs. I feed Geert his porridge, and we finish dressing ourselves.

This morning we had breakfast at 7:45 already, because the new food ration coupons became valid today and the food provider (me) had to be on her way.[23] Quickly check the finances and discuss the menu with Juus and at 8:15 on the bike and away. De Greef [greengrocer] fortunately had 3 heads of lettuce and … a bunch of carrots! At Steenbeek [general groceries] only coffee substitute, but also 1 kg of sugar and 2 jars of jam. My letter to you into the post, and then on to Driebergen. At Kraal [books and stationery] got labels for the 7 jars of spinach I canned yesterday; at Haagedoorn calcium peppermints[24] for you and pectin for canning fruit. Macaroni, barley, oatmeal, children's flour, and rusks at the grocer, but no sugar. Dropped off something at Joost's and then quickly back home and here found Moeder Iete,

---

22 It was a significant day, the anniversary of Wim's imprisonment.

23 People had to be at the shops early, while there was still something to be obtained with the new ration coupons.

24 The website www.eindhovenfotos.nl/levensloop_frans_de_waal.htm, which contains photos and documents about the POW camps, says that families had been asked to send this form of vitamin D to the prisoners.

who is staying at Hotel Stameren.[25] Put away all the purchases, then replied to the letters for Geert's birthday, and wrote a letter to the head of the agricultural school in Scherpenzeel.[26] Then lunch and children to bed. Made a parcel for you and, having changed my clothes and freshened up, on the bike to Suus de Boer to remember this day together[27]—taking her 3 turnips (which she can't get) and flowers. On the way home stopped in to get milk for Geert from the farmer.[28] Came home, had dinner and washed up, kids to bed. Read to Pank. Watered the lettuce and mowed the lawn. At 9:00 listened to the radio [probably the Radio Oranje program] and then had a shower and washed my hair (I get so dirty from that garden work).

And, see—now I'm sitting in my dressing gown writing, and in my thoughts all the Saturday evenings with you pass before me, especially those in Leeuwarden with the portable bathtub in front of the living-room stove, and raisin bread afterwards. Do you remember, my boy? Oh, how glad I would be now to wash your back, how much more, and more fully, would I give myself to you, how I would like to attune myself much more to your feelings and wishes and longings. And still I am constantly, even at this moment, so grateful for what I received. But on my side there was much lacking, very much. I constantly focused on myself. I have learned in this year to forget myself to some extent and to put my "important" little person in the background.

And for that hard and bitter lesson I am grateful to God, although a year is a bitterly long time to learn this, and although there is still not nearly any end in sight.

---

25 A very small hotel in Maarn of which Annetje Nahuys was manager. Later it was requisitioned by the Germans.

26 Possibly this letter was written at Wim's request.

27 Suus's husband, Captain de Boer, had been taken prisoner on the same day.

28 This may have been goat milk; at some point it was discovered that Gerard couldn't digest cow's milk. By now "our" goat was permanently at Vlastuin's farm, but Gerard remembers Madzy telling him she was able to obtain goat milk for him sometimes (regularly? often?).

My heart is heavy with a burden of sorrow and with fear for the future.

Wednesday, 19 May. Today the brown beans will be planted. On Monday I checked over the maize; birds had eaten much of it. In future I will immediately set up scarecrows with the maize.

Wednesday, 2 June. We've acquired a new housemate, Keesje, a puppy of about 9 weeks old, a dwarf-keeshond by breed, and adorable. I've already become completely attached to him. Both of the children are a bit frightened, so it's good that they start getting used to a dog when they are still young.

For the rest, what a day! First to the post office and shopping, then piano lesson, then to Charlotte where I had lunch and fetched vegetables (there are no vegetables to be found here in the village). I brought two heavy full bags to Maarsbergen through a thunderstorm and downpour.[29] These I delivered to Erna Goedhart, then spent 1½ hours at the funeral service for Ds. Schuurman Stekhoven (who died 21 days after his wedding). Then home through the rain, looked after the children and the dog,[30] had dinner, Pank in the bath, fetched milk, went to Piet van Notten for radio and bank business. And now I'm at home exhausted, because I'm actually seriously unwell [menstruating]. What a nuisance that we women have to struggle with that too!

---

29 It's not quite clear from the punctuation and capitalization whether the two heavy bags were what Madzy brought from Amersfoort or whether that's what she took to Maarsbergen. Two such bags would be an enormous load to transport on a bicycle for such a distance (the trip to Leusden, where the Kolffs lived, was nine kilometres or six miles each way, and Maarsbergen an additional three kilometres) in bad weather, and it's unlikely that she would take *everything* that she had obtained from Charlotte to someone else.

30 This is the last reference to the dog. When I was working on *Frontiers and Sanctuaries*, Bill remarked that as the food situation became worse, she would have had trouble finding food for a pet.

Wednesday, 16 June. It's becoming empty here. The reserve officers have to report on Monday. Also the sick officers who had been sent home [and are now well again] have to report. Where is it going to end? Are the English never coming? Are the Russians also not going to start something against Germany?[31] Rumours that the camp in Stanislau will soon be closed down or the inhabitants moved to Dresden don't cheer us up. Everything that is superfluous I've sent away.[32]

And now we have to say goodbye to Piet and Dick.[33] For how long? Weeks, months, years?

Iete van Vollenhoven, Madzy's mother. We have no photo of Iete as she was during the war; this one was taken about ten years earlier.

---

31 The Battle of Stalingrad had taken place during the previous winter, and the Battle of Kursk would begin a couple of weeks after this entry.

32 This would refer to valuables. German raids on private houses ("razzias"), which were common, frequently involved looting or destruction of the house, or both.

33 Piet van Notten and Dick Kolff, as reserve officers, were summoned for internment in POW camps. Bill told me that, instead of reporting, Piet went underground and remained in hiding for a time but was eventually captured and, as it happened, ended up in the same camp as Wim. Dick Kolff went underground and never did leave home. The latter information comes from an e-mail from Carel Beynen, Charlotte's nephew.

Friday, 30 July. Today Pank and I made a little outing to The Hague. We took the nine o'clock train. Near Voorburg we saw many people lying sunbathing on the bomb shelters, and the streets were empty because of an air-raid alarm. When we left the station we immediately crossed the street.[34] You press yourself against the houses. We tried to catch a bus but it was packed so we walked to Moeder Iete's house. In the morning we shopped in the neighbourhood; in the afternoon, after lunch, into the city, to the Bijenkorf [a department store] where we bought a little scooter that we had to lug around with us. There was a second air-raid warning just before we ran into the Bijenkorf. In the roof garden we ate some watery ice cream. Pank thought everything beautiful. We looked around for a long time in the toy department and admired everything. Then back to Moeder Iete where we ate a sandwich and cookies and then we got home safely (train crowded so that I had Pankie constantly on my lap, whenever I could get a seat at all).

Sunday, 3 October. There are still stubborn rumours going around that the camp in Stanislau is going to be moved, and now they're saying perhaps to Innsbruck. And with this my heart is in my throat again and is beating hard and unevenly. The comparative rest that calmed our nerves a bit is broken again and is replaced by an anxious tension. Too bad that this is happening just before Panks' 5th birthday. I had bravely resolved to make something nice of it and now I've lost all desire to do so and will have to create a birthday mood with the courage of despair.

Tonight "summer" time ends. Autumn is coming and the annual melancholy falls on me, now a degree worse. How will I ever get through this second winter without Dicks?

Friday, 8 October. I haven't heard anything from you in weeks; my last message was of 5 September. Other people had letters of

---

34 As there was an air raid in progress, it was sensible to get away from the railway station as quickly as possible in case the tracks were bombed.

18, 20, even of 23 September. And now I eat myself up inside with awful anxiety. What can be the trouble? Are you sick, perhaps already dead and buried? Will I receive, tomorrow in the mail, a cold death-notice such as some wives and mothers have already had?[35] What has happened? I pray that tomorrow there will be a letter from you, and I'm irritable with the children and sit for hours on the bicycle rushing around, yesterday morning to Woudenberg, then to Scherpenzeel, then to Renswoude,[36] and back home via the small roads, in the afternoon to Driebergen— had a flat tire coming home so had to walk. After that to de Hoogt.[37]

Yesterday Moeder Hans visited, and unexpectedly we got along *very* well. She asked me pressingly to look after Lies and to support her.[38] I promised to do everything that was in my power. All of a sudden I feel so old, because I feel that I'm also partially supporting Moeder Iete, also Hansje, also Joost, quite apart from the children. It's a heavy task because I feel so inexperienced and weak myself, but I think that God has laid this charge on me so that I become stronger myself.

Tuesday, 28 December. The Christmas days are past.

There is a miasma that hangs around me like a thick fog and that I have difficulty penetrating so that I can draw close to people. It is as it was before my wedding, before my engagement. A longing creeps through my body and constantly causes a vague yearning for something unattainable; it's such a strange feeling. If Dicks were now here I would have only one longing; to creep

---

35 Bill's note: "Not from our camp. Only one officer died, after an operation."

36 A woman named Rika, who had been Madzy's maidservant in Amersfoort, lived on a small farm near Renswoude, twelve kilometres (seven miles) from Maarn. Madzy probably went to her in search of food, as she would do a number of times in the coming years.

37 Bill's note: "All are long distances for anyone, certainly for someone who is underfed."

38 Lies was Hans's daughter. They would be talking about moral support, not financial.

into his arms and be absorbed in him, body and soul. And, just as before my engagement, that is now also impossible. And so that feeling creeps like hopelessness through me and can't find an outlet. It is an irritating, restless feeling that brings me almost constantly close to tears. When I'm alone, on the bicycle or walking alone in the dark, the tears pour over my cheeks, and it costs me an effort to keep my patience with the children.

The last days of a wretched year. Moeder says, "I wouldn't like to re-live one single day of 1943."[39] I don't dare to be so ungrateful to God. There have been beautiful moments with the children, but every beautiful moment has had a deep melancholy. There has not been one moment in this whole year from which I've been able to take complete enjoyment.

My God, what have You planned for us in 1944?

*****

Madzy had, as usual, set up a Christmas tree. When she put away the decorations again, she included a note with them:

While I am putting all these Christmas things away, my thoughts go to Christmas 1944, when I will unpack them again. Many thoughts go through my head: will it be Peace? Will my Dicks be back? Will I still be in this Tuinmanshuisje?[40] Our destiny lies in the hands of God. And I pray: Oh, God, let 1944 be a true peace on earth. May Christmas 1944 find the four of us together, wherever in the world that is. But above all, Thy will be done.

Madzy

*

Our only two surviving postcards from Wim were written in November and December 1943, so Madzy would probably have received them during this time. Both are stamped "Geprüft,"

---

39 It's not clear which mother this is, but it sounds like Iete.
40 The name of our house, "the gardener's cottage."

meaning they had been passed by the censor. On neither of them, so far as I can see, is there the "number" that Wim was putting on each of his letters, but the dates are clearly given.

18 Nov. '43
Dear Mammie, Marianke, Geert, Juus and Bear, Minet, and the chickens.[41] I wish you a very happy Christmas. You will have to make it cheerful. I hope that you still have a candle for the Christmas tree. Marianke will have to show this card to Bear and read it aloud to the animals. I gave some tea and prunes to "het Kerstmannetje" ["Santa Claus"] and maybe he will have a small piece of chocolate.[42] At Christmas there is just as much snow as in the picture and then I will also celebrate Christmas with my friends here. Next time we will celebrate it again with all of us [together], what a feast that will be. The father of Bear is doing fine. Mammy will certainly read a beautiful Christmas story aloud, and I am thinking extra much about you. A big kiss from Pappa."

2 December 1943.
Dear Mamma, Pankie, and Geert. I come to wish you a very happy and prosperous new year and hope very much that in the new year your wishes may come true. In the new year Pankie has to be a good and obedient little girl, and Geert had better grow well. I also hope that we may all remain healthy. To Grootmoeder, Oma Iete, Grootvader, Oma Jet, Tante Hansje, Tante Lies, Monica, Juus,

---

41 "Bear" and "Minet" were my toys. The card was evidently directed mainly to me, which explains the absurdity of wasting precious space by including my toys and the chickens in his Christmas greetings. In the top right-hand corner, he drew a small picture of a winter scene—logs being moved with a horse and sleigh, an adult and a child carrying a Christmas tree, some evergreen woods, and a small house. Footprints indicate deep snow.

42 This seems to suggest that he was able to send a parcel to us, but (if so) this is the only reference we have to such a thing, and in the diary Madzy never mentions receiving this or any other parcel from him.

and Marietje I also send wishes for a good 1944. I had hoped to send them together 2 of the 3 Christmas cards which were here in Stanislau printed from our design but they are not ready yet. If we look back on 1943 then after all we also have to be grateful that we are all making out so well in comparison with so many other people and we can go towards 1944 cheerful and hopeful. Many warm greetings to all of you from your Willem.

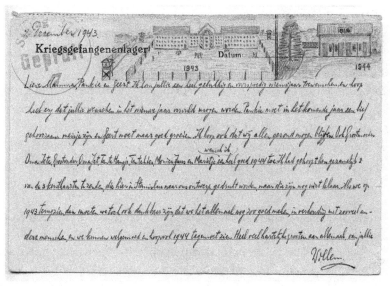

This is one of the forms that were in use during most of the period of Wim's imprisonment. This letter is dated December 2, 1943. The drawing on the left is of the Stanislau camp; the one to the right is of our house in Maarn. The dates send a message: "1943 in Stanislau, 1944 in Maarn." For the text of the message, see pp. 149-150.

Chapter Seven

3 January to 23 September 1944

During this period, there are still sometimes long gaps between entries, but Madzy recorded important events. In January 1944 the prisoners in the Stanislau camp, including Wim, were moved to Neubrandenburg, north of Berlin. In June she reported the D-Day landings, the all-important event that, along with the Allied progress in the Mediterranean, put the Allies on the mainland of western Europe and led to their ultimate victory.

On 6 September she recorded a rumour, based on a mistaken report in the Radio Oranje program, that the Allies, who had been moving eastward from Normandy, had crossed the border from Belgium into the Netherlands. The rumour caused jubilation in the Netherlands but proved to be false. However, as liberation did appear to be drawing nearer, Madzy resolved to record the progress of the war in more detail. She became, consciously, a chronicler of events.[1] She followed the news closely, and evidently she was listening to English-language BBC broadcasts as well as the Radio Oranje programs because in the diary she frequently used English phrases.

However, Madzy's radio was silenced in October 1944 because the electricity was cut off. Electricity and gas were generated by coal, most of which came from the southern province of Limburg. "Coal

---

1   I have not included all of those passages about war news, which are mostly brief items from BBC newscasts, but kept enough to reveal how they affected Madzy's moods and thoughts. The news she heard was not always correct, but it was what she was hearing. As indicated in the Preface, I have made no attempt to correct any mistakes in her reports of the war news, though I occasionally draw attention to discrepancies.

was at that time almost the only energy source in the Netherlands. ...
It was essential for the pumping and purification of drinking water,
for the proper functioning of the sewage system, and for the [ongoing]
draining of the polders [the land below sea-level]." But Limburg was
by then in the hands of the Allies,[2] and the front divided it from the
German-held northern provinces, which included us. No coal crossed
the front. The occupying forces used Ruhr coal for their own purposes
but provided little if any to the civilian population.[3]

From the moment when her radio was silenced, Madzy depended
for news on what happened in the neighbourhood, what was passed on
by people who had battery-operated radios, and what she read in the
underground press. It is noticeable that news about large-scale "war"
events appeared in the diary when she had just had contact with other
people—for instance, at church.

*

During this time, the estuary of the rivers Rhine, Maas, and Scheldt,
which separate the southern Netherlands from the northern provinces,
was of crucial military significance. We lived just a few kilometres
north of it. Operation Market Garden was the Allied attempt in
September 1944 to cross the rivers northward, from Belgium through
the Dutch cities of Eindhoven and Nijmegen to Arnhem,[4] and it failed.
During the winter of 1944–1945 the provinces south of the rivers were
liberated but we were still occupied. Moreover, living conditions north
of the rivers became much worse. "In the days immediately after their
victory at Arnhem, the Germans blew up the ports of Rotterdam and
other cities and flooded thousands of acres of farmland."[5]

Nevertheless, the Allies were making progress, moving eastward
through the territory south of the rivers. With the fighting coming
closer, there was more danger in Maarn, and there would be some bad
air raids, though there were comparatively few deaths. However, even
fairly slight damage to buildings caused hardship because workmen
and construction materials for repairs were almost unavailable.

---

2   Van der Zee, pp. 36, 189.
3   Kaufman & Horn, pp. 52–53.
4   Arnhem was forty kilometres (twenty-five miles) east of us.
5   Olson, p. 399.

Broken windows were a disaster because there was no glass to replace them. And the winter of 1944–1945 was an extremely cold one.

On the evening of 17 September 1944, a few hours after the first parachute landings in the Arnhem area, the Dutch railway workers were asked by Supreme Headquarters, Allied Expeditionary Force (SHAEF) to go on strike in order to hinder German shipments of V-1 and V-2 weapons to the coastal launching sites from which they were fired at Britain.[6] Since the beginning of the occupation, the Dutch railways had been running more or less as usual and had, as noted earlier, served the Germans as well as the Dutch. Now the Dutch workers were being asked to go on strike. "It was the most important act of defiance to the Nazis [that] the Dutch were ever asked to make. More than 30,000 railway workers had to ... go into hiding, all connections in the country would be broken, and not only enemy transport, but also the supply of food and coal to the crowded cities in the west and easy communication between the Resistance groups would stop."[7]

Almost all the workers obeyed the order to strike. The Germans retaliated savagely, and this enormously increased the hardships of the "Hunger Winter" of 1944–1945.[8] "In an attempt to break the railroad strike, the Germans in October imposed an embargo on movements of foodstuffs from the eastern Netherlands to the western section of the country. Partly as a result of the embargo, food rations decreased to starvation levels during the winter and spring."[9] Moreover, van der Zee writes that in September 1944 the Germans were systematically looting the Netherlands for food. They took meat, tinned vegetables, sugar, and hundreds of thousands of pigs, horses, and cows.[10]

*****

6   "The V-1 was a jet-powered flying bomb, and the V-2 a liquid-fueled rocket" (Bailey, p. 132).

7   Van der Zee, p. 29.

8   Van der Zee, p. 28ff. Olson writes: "The leaders of the railway strike were imprisoned [by the Germans] and several were killed. From then on, every act of Dutch rebellion, however small, was met with mass executions" (p. 399).

9   Warmbrunn, p. 16.

10 Van der Zee, p. 308.

Monday, 3 January 1944. Already for a long time I've been wondering whether this book will be big enough to last me until Dicks' return, and I'm gradually writing more thriftily. Because there are still long, lonely months ahead of us. Today I had my French conversation lesson, and although my tutor, Atrice (who is old and blind), and I spoke in general terms, she said suddenly with such conviction, "When you pray, pray with all your soul, God will help us. But one has to have confidence, one hundred percent."[11] That gives me some support, and I will pray with my whole soul that Dicks will soon and for ever return to me.

Monday, 27 March. Wim[12] is sick, and my heart beats in my throat and I worry the whole day long.

Saturday, 29 April, evening. Is there still a chance that Dicks will come back earlier because of ill health? I don't know, and I don't know what I should hope for, so I leave it to God, but my heart is restless. Or could that be because everyone expects an invasion to take place this weekend? Have we ever lived so much on our nerves?

Tuesday, 6 June. And last night the invasion did indeed begin[13] ... and yesterday Rome fell to the Allies .... Memorable events.

This morning I was down. Moeder oppresses me more and more, and the possibility of her coming to live here in the house because of the invasion appeared to me the worst of nightmares.[14] I worried. I bicycled to Driebergen after lunch

---

11 Madzy gives the words in French.
12 Bill's note: "She never called me Wim. That must have been when I had colitis and was for two weeks in the sick bay. From then on I got only porridge of various grains instead of other food 1 time per day."
13 Madzy is referring to the D-Day landings in Normandy.
14 As noted elsewhere, during the period covered by the diary Iete was moving back and forth between The Hague and Maarn, though some of those moves may have been just visits rather than evacuation. It was evidently expected that, because of the D-Day landings, she might have

and there heard the first news of the invasion. I didn't believe it. Now, since this evening, I know for sure. What is there ahead of us? Thousands of questions press on us.

When I was home again, and laid the clothes ready for the children, and my fur coat and purse and shoes,[15] I suddenly became afraid. There are so many planes flying, and all of a sudden there was a big bang close by. I took Pankie and Geert close against me. Their quiet breathing calms me and so I will also try to go to sleep.

Wednesday, 26 July. Hitler nearly murdered! How lucky that God prevented this, because he must not become a martyr. No, for Hitler God certainly has something different in mind!

Tuesday, 15 August. Second invasion in France, now close to Tante Zus.[16] When will *we* see an Englishman? Today as many as 5,000 planes flew over to bomb all the airfields used for the night-time bombing raids. That nearly cost the life of Pankske, because while we were swimming in de Venen,[17] and I was getting dressed after swimming, she went (against all orders) on the raft. Chris and the Mackays were looking up at the overflying planes, and they didn't notice that Pankske slid from the raft into the deep water and went under. Only when she had come up and grabbed the raft (everything happened in seconds) did Chris see her and dive in fully dressed, and I too! This day, the day of the second invasion of France, I will long remember.[18]

Wednesday, 6 September. Since the day before yesterday the Allies are in our country but there has been no further news

---

to leave The Hague (again). Madzy would have given details about such moves in her letters to Wim.

15   These were preparations in case we had to flee.
16   Zus van Vollenhoven was Madzy's aunt by marriage and lived in St. Tropez, France.
17   Bill's note: A pond on the Blijdenstein property near our house.
18   I remember being in the water under the raft.

for at least 30 hours except that they are near Breda.[19] The wildest rumours circulate, that they are near Culemborg, that parachutists have landed near Rotterdam, but the BBC said only: "Near Breda, 10 miles over the Dutch border."

These will be important days and I am planning to chronicle them carefully.[20]

Yesterday morning I went out for the last time, to do the last grocery shopping in Doorn.[21] Everyone stood on the street as though the Tommies were there already, watching for them.[22] Some people had laid a tree across the main highway but it had already been removed. There was also an attempt to damage the railway track here in Maarn but it misfired because of inefficiency—the trains are still running.

All German citizens in Holland have to leave, and the NSB [Dutch supporters of the Nazis] are allowed to go along. A train was seen with white flags and soldiers with bayonets and machine guns, and in the train a large number of our political prisoners, probably from the camp in Leusden or somewhere else, being taken to Germany.[23] They say that prisoners from Vught have

---

19 This was the false report referred to in the headnote. The day following that on which the incorrect report was broadcast came to be called "Dolle Dinsdag" (Mad Tuesday) because the Dutch went wild with excitement.

20 She does. The almost-daily entries for the next nine months make up about half the length of the diary. This also explains her including so much war news. By now she is certainly thinking of a wider readership for the diary than just Wim.

21 Presumably she thought of this as the last trip to Doorn before the expected invasion/liberation.

22 The term "Tommy" was first coined in the eighteenth century [Tim Cook, *The Secret History of Soldiers* (2018), p. 94] and originally referred only to the English, but Madzy (as she explains in the entry of 18 September 1944) uses it to refer to all the Allied armed forces.

23 As the Allies advanced, the Germans were apparently moving their prisoners and hostages from camps in the Netherlands to camps in Germany. Bill identifies "Leusden" as "the camp near Amersfoort." It was a particularly dreadful camp (see entry for 24 June 1942).

also been sent to Germany.[24] When I bicycled home from Doorn (people warned me that my bicycle might be confiscated) I saw an NSB man with wife departing in a beautiful car, much luggage in the back, a rifle, a bicycle, and followed by a big German truck.

When I went to have a rest after lunch and was half undressed, suddenly many airplanes came and began to do a lot of firing in this neighbourhood. It appeared that they were firing on a locomotive at the Maarn railway station, and besides that the railway track near Bunnik [south-west of Maarn] is broken, so that since then we haven't heard a train passing. There has also been no mail. Moeder Iete came for a chat and after the shooting ended she left again. In the evening came Annetje Nahuys.

There was no news. Tonight peaceful and dead-silent because no trains are running. Now and then a German truck races past. Moeder came to see how we were making out; I was busy unpacking Wim's clothes and hanging them up to air, and what did I suddenly see? That a mouse had eaten my *whole fur coat*.[25] I would have wept, if I hadn't been aware of worse things happening around me.

A man came to the door asking if someone here could give a message from him to his wife. Moeder took it, saying, "I would

---

24　Van der Zee characterizes the camp at Vucht, located near 's Hertogenbosch (Den Bosch) in the southern part of the Netherlands, as "the worst and most lethal camp" (p. 125). From Wikipedia: "When the allied forces were approaching ..., the camp was evacuated [by the Germans] and the prisoners were transferred to concentration camps farther east. ..." When the Canadians liberated the camp, "there were around 500–600 live prisoners left, who had been set up for execution that afternoon. ... About 500 inmates were also discovered dead in piles near the gates, who had been executed the very morning of the day that the camp was liberated" (Wikipedia, "Herzogenbusch concentration camp [Vucht]," accessed Sept. 1, 2017).

25　She must have had two fur coats: a day or two earlier she mentions having laid "her" fur coat ready in case we had to flee.

never want to work in a Dutch secret organization, they are so careless."[26]

She had just gone when I heard a voice ... Oom Willy! "Haven't you left yet?" I asked, astonished.[27] He came to ask if I would buy (in a fake transaction) all his belongings, for 500 guilders that he himself would give me, and then Tante To and Tante Rietie would have the use of them as long as they lived. I suddenly felt that I must *not* do that. Oom Willy's belongings are German so at the very last moment [of the war] I would receive money that belonged to the enemy. For us it might be a loss of 12,000 guilders, so *not* a small matter, but I do *not* want to do business with German citizens. I hope with all my heart that Wim will understand this. That money will be confiscated and go to the state. Well, that's where it belongs. So much has already been taken away from the state. Oom Willy didn't agree with me but did understand. It was a deeply tragic visit and I'm still broken up about it but I know that my decision was the right one.[28]

And now it is nearly 3:00 and there are again many Tommies flying over and shooting. There is still no news—perhaps at 6

---

26 The man was no doubt a diver or someone in the Resistance.

27 She was astonished because she had expected that Willy, a German citizen, would have left the Netherlands a day or two earlier along with other German citizens.

28 This is an obscure passage. It appears that the property of the German citizens who departed was to be confiscated by "the state"—by which, to judge by the context, she seems to mean the Dutch state, not the occupying forces. Her reasoning is not clear, and she doesn't give any more details, so we have no way of understanding the arithmetic. Bill translated it so as to include not only Willy's movable possessions but his house as well.

Tante To and Tante Rietie were Willy's sisters-in-law and Madzy's aunts. By complying with Willy's request, Madzy would therefore have benefited her aunts as well as herself and Wim.

This is the last reference in the diary to Willy Schüffner; either he left the country, or perhaps there was an estrangement between him and Madzy. But they corresponded after the war, and when he died in 1949 he was (still, or again) living in Hilversum.

o'clock. I'm very curious how far Holland has been liberated. Prince Bernard is certainly already on Dutch soil and the underground troops are hard at work;[29] near Woudenberg the railway track is also completely destroyed.

9:30 p.m.: Breda is no longer being mentioned in the communiqué, but the Belgian coast (Ostend) is, and Boulogne and Calais. Some people are saying that neither Breda nor Maastricht has seen an Ally. That may be true, but they are not far from there.

In the distance I hear shooting and the house is trembling. They say that the electricity will be cut off; that would be awful for the canary bird [the hidden radio]. The factories aren't operating any more, not even the milk-processing plant; is it possible that we will get only whole milk?

Thursday, 7 September. And again nothing is happening. During the night there seems to have been some noise but I heard nothing. The 8 o'clock news said nothing about Belgium and Holland but did report that the Russians are at the Yugoslav border. The 1:00 report said that from 17 September on England no longer has to do the blackout, and that the Allies are near Ostend and Zeebruggen and Ypres, but nothing about Holland. They did say that the Dutch government was ready to move from England back to Holland, and Professor Gerbrandy had given a leave-taking speech, and an English Minister had given a speech full of praise for our Queen.[30]

The families of NSB members have all had to move to a camp in Drente—the former camp for Jews.[31] The weather has been bad but is clearing; I actually see blue sky. In the village

---

29 For Prince Bernhard, see headnote to Chapter Three.
30 Professor P. S. Gerbrandy was prime minister in the Dutch government-in-exile. As it turned out, Queen Wilhelmina did not return to the Netherlands until 26 April 1945 (Olson, p. 417).
31 This was the notorious camp at Westerbork (van der Zee, p. 23).

it's impossible to buy anything. During the night two freight trains passed, but for the rest there is no traffic.[32] It is quiet, empty, oppressively still, so that you hear your heart beating in your throat. I think I prefer the noise of shooting to this heavy quiet-before-the-storm.

It's now 8 o'clock and everyone has to be indoors. Here the electricity went out slowly, like a night-candle, and so there is no news any more. I had thought that this was the predicted end of the electricity because of lack of fuel, but now Annetje Nahuys arrives saying that she still heard the news at 7:00. (She came to bring a suitcase full of clothes, out of fear that she might have to flee, because suddenly 2,000 Germans have arrived in Doorn.)

The electric pump is working again! Hooray, we have light again! Probably the power failure was caused by this afternoon's storm having blown a tree down over the power line, and they've fixed it. How much longer will we be able to enjoy it?

Friday, 8 September. Today didn't bring us any further. It's now widely known that there is no Ally on Dutch soil. But in the meantime we're in a situation! No transportation, therefore no vegetables, etc.[33] No food (meat, rusks, yoghurt) for Gerard. The schools are closed, there is not a single train running except occasionally one to Maarsbergen, the mail comes occasionally, including a newspaper four days old. Meanwhile the Germans are reinforcing their position: 2,000 in Doorn, who requisitioned all the houses, etc. The Allies did cross the Albert Canal, 25 miles [40 km] from the German border (but the word "Holland" isn't

---

32 Caspers (p. 190) writes that trains manned by German personnel were sometimes using such tracks as had not been bombed by the Allies.

33 This was not the result of the major strike of railway workers mentioned in the headnote, which would begin about ten days later: Madzy seems to be referring to a general deterioration of communications and food supply and the destruction of railway tracks.

spoken any more).[34] Is it possible that we could be shut off and become a "pocket of resistance"?

Saturday, 9 September, 9:00 in the evening. The Allies are in Ostend and already a bit past Liège and a good distance into the Ardennes and past Namur. Moreover they have two bridgeheads over the Albert Canal and they are holding Gheel and Bourg-Leopold.[35] That does bring them in our direction but they say themselves that it is hard fighting and that the Germans have stripped Holland of all their troops to reinforce the armies there. I hope the Allies know that many new troops have arrived here.[36] I don't believe any more that there will be a speedy end, even though Christie still trusts firmly in a "cease-fire on 19 September."

Dr. Noordam, the doctor at Valkenheide, was murdered by the Germans because it was said that he concealed military divers. In fact, he was sick and knew nothing about it.[37]

---

34 Her using the English measurement shows that this news came from the BBC. The Allies were pushing eastward, south of the rivers.

35 Towns in northern Belgium.

36 This is one of those instances where the BBC news doesn't seem to reflect the situation on the ground.

37 Valkenheide, in Maarsbergen, was a vocational school for boys. What Madzy had heard was not quite correct. The whole complicated story can be found in Caspers (pp. 110–119). It is, however, a fact that on 8 September Dr. Noordam, the director of the school, who was sick in bed, was ordered to get up, tied to a chair, placed in front of his house, and shot.

The people of Maarn have been told to guard the highway against the scattering of nails, and felled trees. Whole groups of Maarn people![38] Willem was trembling with fear.[39]

Sunday, 10 September. There's not much news. In northern Belgium tremendous resistance. There have been troops brought even from Denmark, and that's why the roads and railway lines here are being bombed.

I'm sitting outside for the first time since the end of August, because the weather has been abominable, and I hear airplanes, and shooting in the distance. Along our railway line there's again a train now and then, and they are not yet getting bombed. It's again fearsomely quiet. The Allies are 12 miles [17 km] from Aix-la-Chapelle and 4 miles [6 km] from Limburg.

4 p.m.[40] Dearest, very dearest, darling dear. I'm sitting in front of our little house in the September sun on the white bench. It's quiet, very, very quiet around me; I hear nothing except a barking dog in the distance, and from time to time a cackling hen, and the breeze that comes blowing through the trees. The sun repeatedly defeats a thick, white, cotton-wool cloud. Silence, solitude. Juus and the children have gone to look at the 13 foals that got stranded on the pasture of 't Stort after the locomotive

---

38 Nails on the pavement would cause flat tires; felled trees would slow German traffic. (By now, almost the only vehicles on the roads were German.) The implication of what Madzy is saying here is that local people were forced to work *for* the Germans and *against* the Resistance groups, which would have included their family and neighbours. In the event of sabotage, whole groups of residents (guilty or not) would be executed in reprisal.

39 This is the first mention of Willem de Bruin, but Madzy's casual reference suggests that he was already a well-established helper. He assisted Madzy with many chores. It is from Bill's translation of the diary that we know his last name. See entry for 24 June 1942.

40 This is a special entry. Madzy writes in ink, which she practically never did, and she makes no effort to write compactly so as to save paper.

of their train here in Maarn was fired on.[41] I'm therefore alone, entirely alone, and that is something which hasn't happened to me in a very long time, something which hasn't happened to you in two-and-a-half years. Solitude: what a treasure. But then comes also, with all its overwhelming storm of feeling, my longing for you, my love for you. Dearest, this is a love-letter, an expression of my overflowing heart, full of love that I can't give to you. I miss you, I miss you so dreadfully. I try to imagine how it will be when I can again touch your arm, and it makes me tremble. In my spirit I try to summon up your eyes, and it is as though their glance cuts through me.

Dearest, do you know how every fibre in my being is bound to you, how deeply I have grown into you? Dearest, dearest, I mumble the words to myself because I have no other outlet for my feelings and like a one-note song it whispers through the woods. Dearest ... dearest ....

I've been sitting reading this book, the beginning, to find you back, to reach your spirit properly. But I haven't succeeded, and my heart is empty ....

Evening.[42] The nine o'clock news has cheered me up again. Frank Gillard explained to us that the Albert Canal is a strong zone of fighting; the Germans want to stand fast there at any cost because it is actually their last line, since the Siegfried Line is absolutely not strong enough. But meanwhile the Allies have received their supplies[43] and it is again fine weather (the barometer is high, and the evenings are cold and clear). They fly a lot and bomb all the transportation routes in Holland. I presume that here north

---

41 Horses were vitally important to the German army, which, in 1944, was still using one and a quarter million of them (Overy, p. 5).

42 Here she again writes very compactly and with many abbreviations and elliptical expressions. For some time now she has been cramming at least twice as many words on each page as she did in the beginning.

43 Their supply lines had been overextended.

of the rivers there will be no real fighting, but that south of the rivers there will be.

Monday, 11 September. Luxemburg is free. The national anthem rang out [over the radio] "as a salute to our smallest gallant ally." When will it be the "Wilhelmus" [the Dutch national anthem]? The Princess has arrived in England,[44] Zeebrugge is in the hands of the Canadians. The Allies have expanded the two bridgeheads over the Albert Canal. They are already firing from Belgium at targets on German soil.

Evening after 9:00. The Allies broke through the front at the Albert Canal! They are on Dutch soil, heading for Eindhoven! They are getting close to Maastricht! Dutchmen are fighting side by side with the Allies. Oh, how our hearts are beating! And outside it is so peaceful, except that twice there was firing at trains on the railway line here. Because there are still trains running! Now again the tension is much worse. And this morning I still received a card from you, my Dicks, the one from 24 August. Oh, how happy it makes me.

Tuesday, 12 September. All day today there was flying and shooting, and our little house still trembles now and then. We wait. The roads have to be guarded, sometimes for 6 hours at night, (and it is already so cold at night, and by day it is beautifully clear weather). The armies are advancing. Yesterday at ten to six p.m. the Allies came for the first time on German soil, to the north of Trier. In our direction they haven't advanced very far, at least there is no news about it, but Le Havre has fallen (Brest, Boulogne, Calais, and Dunkirk are still besieged). The whole Belgian coast is in the hands of the Canadians.

---

44 Presumably Crown Princess Juliana had returned from Canada to London to be closer to home at this critical time.

This afternoon I took our "large" laundry on the bicycle behind me to Doorn—I can get it back in a week.[45]

Wednesday, 13 September. Today comparatively little news. At 6 o'clock they said that the Canadians, who are moving along the coast, are now near Zeeuws Vlaanderen.[46] Bruges has fallen, they say. In Holland: Wassenaar[47] has to be emptied this afternoon: 16,000 people have to leave, and they have no vehicles and no roof to go to. It's because of the V-2 launching site, they say.

They [the Germans] set fire to the house of the former mayor of Leersum [a small town near Maarn] because nails lay on the road in front of the house. They went into the house and said, "In half an hour your house will be burned down; you may only take some clothes." No winter clothes, and what they managed to bring to the neighbours was taken away, and a few pieces of furniture that they wanted to keep as souvenirs were thrown back into the burning house, on which the Germans had liberally poured gasoline to make it burn well![48]

Four Tommies flew over our house, one of them so low that we thought that the chimney was gone. Gerard was scared to death. There is more firing on trains here, and there is regular firing on automobiles, columns of vehicles, etc.

Thursday, 14 September. Our eighth wedding anniversary! For five of them we've been together and this is the third one apart.

---

45 It was usual to have the "large" laundry done by a commercial laundry (see headnote to Chapter Two). I still have a bath towel with the laundry number 2284 on it, printed on a tiny piece of cloth tape stitched to a corner. In normal times the large laundry would have been picked up at the house.

46 The southernmost part of the Dutch province of Zeeland.

47 The northern part of The Hague, close to the coast.

48 Caspers also describes this incident (pp. 123–124). Following it, the family went underground.

Moeder was here to celebrate her birthday;[49] the children were bothersome, as always on such occasions.

And as for the war business? It's *dead silent*, frighteningly silent. But the Canadians and the 2nd British Army are pushing towards the Dutch border.

Discussed with Moeder after lunch what we should do with Joost after the war.[50] If we [Madzy herself and Wim] had a big house, should we take Juus and Joost to live with us? I myself would gladly take on that task, but what would Wim say?

Friday, 15 September. It's so warm today that we sat outside in summer dresses until 8 p.m. Then we had to go indoors because of the curfew.

Saturday, 16 September. There has been much flying and shooting today. Even so the children and I got on "the family bus"[51] and went to Landeck, Zonnekanje, TWED.[52]

---

49 Iete's sixty-eighth birthday was on the same day.

50 The three ladies with whom Joost lived were elderly, and perhaps there had been discussions about making other arrangements. In fact, this issue would come to a head in the next few months.

51 This is her wry description of her bicycle. With the two of us on board, it must have been very heavy pedaling.

52 Landeck was the house of the Bentincks (Lägers & Veenland-Heineman, p. 107), Zonnekanje that of the Everwijn Langes (Lägers & Veenland-Heineman, p. 98), and TWED that of the Koolemans Beijnens. "TWED stands for 'Tegen Wil En Dank', a proverb meaning 'against our will.' Mr. and Mrs. Koolemans Beijnen who had been living in The Hague, had bought the house in 1920 to start a hotel. Their two daughters [would have] preferred to stay in [The Hague] but had to move to Maarn and work with their parents in the hotel... against their will. In all probability they invented the name TWED" (e-mail of September 9, 2017, from Gijs van Roekel).

The "family bus." The photo was probably taken in the summer of 1944. The building in the background is the barn.

Sunday, 17 September. They're here! They're coming! Yesterday we were still saying, "It can easily last for quite a while still." This morning to church. But during the service hundreds and hundreds of planes roared over us, which was actually bothersome because although I said, "God, in Your hands I lay my children," you still can't be at peace.[53]

When I got home Juus and the children were in a very excited state; they had counted 600 aircraft and then they stopped

---

53 This was the beginning of Operation Market Garden, the Allied attempt to capture the bridges that would allow them to move northward across the huge estuary and from there into Germany. The bridge in Arnhem. about forty kilometres (twenty-five miles) east of us, came to be the best-known. Van der Zee writes: "Like an enormous cloud the planes swept over the Low Countries" (p. 28). "Market, the airborne phase of the operation, was monumental: it involved almost five thousand fighters, bombers, transports, and more than 2,500 gliders. That Sunday afternoon, at exactly 1:30 p.m., an entire Allied airborne army, complete with vehicles and equipment, began dropping behind German lines. ... [it was] the greatest armada of troop-carrying aircraft ever assembled for a single operation" (Cornelius Ryan, *A Bridge Too Far*, p. 11).

counting.[54] Lunch at 12:30, Gerard to bed. And then I wanted to surprise Chris and Dien, because their little cabinet [radio] has broken down. Therefore I went with mine through the woods to them. I was barely on the way when much shooting and flying began. But I arrived safely there. Meanwhile there was still a lot of noise, so much that at about 2:30 I wanted to go home. I was just in the woods with the cabinet on the bicycle when a plane flew *so* close by that I plunked down on the ground, bicycle and all. Then my stomach shook with laughter at the ridiculous situation, but still I hurried on. The Schuts [neighbours] looked at me wonderingly but I arrived safely home, with my heart beating hard.

The worst shooting was over by then. Later we heard that a train at Maarsbergen station was shot to pieces, along with automobiles, that a labourers' camp[55] was on fire, etc. Meanwhile German cars raced and roared past us here,[56] and at 5:30 suddenly the little doctor came by.[57] "An army has landed south of the Lek and Maas! They are near Nijmegen! Arnhem is black with Americans!"[58] She went on to spread the news further. Then came Moeder, who had heard the same news. We quickly had our meal and then I went to tell Chris and Dien. They were in a state. I home again. They say that we mustn't leave our houses. Moeder then went off. Dien came at 7 o'clock with

---

54 I remember the three of us standing on the driveway counting. The armada of aircraft filled all of the sky visible between the trees surrounding our house.

55 Madzy is no doubt referring to a camp accommodating forced labourers. The Grebbe Line, a line of defence (formerly Dutch, now German) which was being reinforced, was only a few kilometres to the east of us.

56 Bill notes that our road was a secondary German evacuation route; it would be heavily used because the Allies were bombing major transportation sites and corridors to hinder the German movement of troops and *matériel*.

57 The next sentences indicate that this was a woman doctor, evidently with a practice in the area, but I haven't been able to identify her.

58 This last statement was not correct.

pencil and paper [to write down details from the radio news report]. And now at 8 o'clock we've shut up the house because heavily laden cars are racing past and they would fire on us if we hadn't done the blackout. At this moment it's quiet. Now and then the house trembles. The clothes and shoes are ready. Also the knapsack on the little wagon, and the bicycle with the children's seats. If I get too frightened I will go to Dien or ask Willem to come and sleep here. Now I'll go back to reading.

10 p.m. [The radio broadcast] brought not much news, for security reasons. Just now an enormous column of heavy trucks came past. Juus and I, on our knees in front of the bedroom window, watched it. They shouted abuse, and sometimes turned on lights, and moved slowly. Fortunately there were just then no Allied planes in the air, otherwise we would have been under fire. Now the planes are flying constantly. It's bed-time. However, I'm so afraid that I will sleep too heavily—I've been doing that lately and then I hear nothing.

Monday, 18 September. Well, I had a wonderful sleep except for a few spells when there was some flying. This morning it was at first eerily silent: have they left? have they been repulsed? The news report didn't say much—"for security reasons," because the Germans still don't know precisely where the Tommies (American, British, Polish, Dutch) have landed.[59] But towards midday all hell broke loose, and from then on it was one unbroken roaring of gunfire in the distance (direction of Arnhem and Doorn), and flying. Now it appears that they have landed troops again, and they talk about Arnhem, Nijmegen and Eindhoven. Also the Second British Army is only 6 km [4 mi] from Eindhoven (*was*, yesterday evening; the BBC news is behind what we ourselves are experiencing). While we were eating lunch, again a silence suddenly fell, and at this moment

---

59 This was also not correct; the Germans did know.

we are more frightened by silence than by noise. But now they're flying again. What a strange experience: to sit outdoors knitting a sock and drinking a cup of tea, while the war is so close by. The tension is very high. Moeder, who dared to go out, said that people were sure that Den Bosch and Breda had been taken. She wants to go to Doorn tomorrow "because," she said, "the Tommies are coming and I still have to have my hair washed and set for the occasion."

The railways are on strike.[60]

10:30. "The Battle of Holland is going well."[61] An excited young Dutchman from Valkenswaard who spoke English was able to talk about his experience into the radio microphone.[62] Our hearts stand still and then beat faster than before! And still I won't be able to enjoy the liberation until you are safely home, my boy.

Tuesday, 19 September. Today exceptionally quiet. And yet it's going well. Eindhoven has been liberated and General Dempsey [British 2nd Army[63]] moves forward towards Nijmegen and Arnhem to join other airborne troops. Although the roads there are full of Allied troops, transports, etc., apparently everything is orderly. More troops, *matériel*, etc. were brought in today. In Denmark the Gestapo has taken the lead; poor people. In Finland today they signed an armistice. France and Belgium have been almost liberated (except Brest, Boulogne, Calais and Dunkirk, all

---

60 See the headnote of this chapter.
61 She uses the English words, quoting either the BBC newscaster or "the excited young Dutchman."
62 Valkenswaard, which is close to the Belgian-Dutch border, was liberated by the (Dutch) Princess Irene Brigade, fighting alongside the other Allies; this meant that Dutch troops had set foot on Dutch soil. Van der Zee (p. 64) writes that the town was liberated on Wednesday, 20 September; Madzy wrote this on Monday, 18 September. I can't explain the discrepancy.
63 Time-Life, *WWII*, p. 295.

of them almost completely bombed flat and destroyed). There have been many advances on the Siegfried Line and in one place they are entirely through it. Probably the Allies are trying to move in a more northerly direction from the Line, hence Arnhem.

Ede has been bombed, 60 people dead including Juffrouw Schut's half-brother and his wife, and one of their children wounded; nothing is known about the other one.[64] Stameren is empty, deserted by the Germans except that much cognac was left behind, as I could tell from Annetje and Floris when they were here for a moment.[65]

A few retreating Germans came through Doorn without guns or caps. They had had enough of it. Here also the universal opinion among the Germans is, "The war is lost, we're going home." It's now again eerily silent; I don't even hear an airplane. Only the house shakes from time to time, apparently for no reason.

Because of pure excitement we're all very hungry. There's no meat, but we can get cheese with the meat coupons. Do you know what I'm longing for now? A large plate of steak with rice.

There are many German vehicles parked behind de Halm [neighbouring farm] and on the Ruiterberg. I hope the Tommies see them and hit them hard.

Wednesday, 20 September. Today a "quiet" day except for a few explosions nearby, but in the late afternoon all of a sudden many high-flying bombers, making no sound. Off and on Germans drove past. That was all. There is fighting in and around Nijmegen, a fight for bridges along the "corridor" from Eindhoven to Nijmegen. Airborne [Allied] troops have dug themselves in around Arnhem and have taken many bridges. In West Brabant and Zeeland, it is calculated, there are still about 100,000 German soldiers, not fully equipped but still offering serious resistance. From Wassenaar flying bombs [V-1s] are apparently still being fired at

---

64 Ede is about halfway between Maarn and Arnhem.

65 Floris Kool went underground at Stameren; later he and Annetje Nahuys married. Stameren would later be again occupied by Germans.

England. The Germans here are of the opinion: "We're waiting for the Tommies and will then surrender." The Nazis are planning to evacuate all the German citizens to the other side of the Rhine.

Many people in this area are still thinking about building a bomb shelter. At de Halm there is a very fine one with electric light! Willem is also making one at his house. I don't feel much like it. Chris says that her cellar is OK. But mine isn't. I don't know what I will do.

Thursday, 21 September. Autumn. A beautiful day; we sat outdoors. The Allies now hold the bridge over the Waal near Nijmegen and are moving north to try to join with the airborne troops who have dug themselves in round Arnhem. All that fighting has therefore taken place at about 40–45 km [25–27 mi] from us; we notice nothing except now and then a vague rumbling this afternoon from some planes bringing supplies.

A girl here in the village was molested and now all women, especially the younger ones, have been warned.

We can use only 30% of the electricity because it's almost finished ([coal]-gas in the cities is available for heat and light for only a couple of hours per day). Bicycles are still constantly being confiscated.

Today I saw a long row of covered carts, each with two horses in front and two behind, traveling in the direction of Amersfoort.

Friday, 22 September. I had so hoped that this book would last until Wim's return, but is doesn't look as though it will.

The Tommies haven't advanced more than 2 miles [3 km] north of Nijmegen, and it is tough going. We hear and notice nothing except that there is no delivery of supplies, therefore no food. We're managing all right so far but there is no butter and little milk and no vegetables or potatoes.[66] In a village this is not very serious. But we are very sparing with electric light.

---

66 She rarely mentions her own garden produce anymore; probably she takes it for granted. The entry of 22 October (below) indicates that

This morning I walked (armed with a sharp pocket knife) through the woods with the little wagon to Doorn, to fetch the clean washing. It had actually been done (many other people's was still dirty): the laundry was not operating, awaiting the delivery of coal. I plodded up the hill again with my burden and at the top I just had to take a rest, sitting on the load of clean washing! Yes, we're getting run down, but after all it is a trip, and that on a breakfast of a couple of pieces of toast without butter and some imitation tea without sugar. It is again dead silent and we'd better go to sleep.

Saturday, 23 September. Yesterday was a critical day and although there are points of light the anxiety isn't over yet. "The Battle of Holland is raging ferociously"—those were the words used at 2 o'clock, and Hitler has sent his best troops here because it's now all about the bridge at Arnhem. If it falls intact into the hands of the Allies, Westphalia stands open to them.[67] It rained today, and only towards the late afternoon did it clear up and the barometer is rising. Now the sky is clear, and since 5:00 there has been quite a lot of flying. The Tommy fighters sometimes shear low over the beech trees here and the children look out longingly to see if there are any gasoline drums falling.[68] (Two fell near Huis te Maarn and one in Chris's garden.) "The Battle of

---

Willem was doing most of the garden work. As usual, when she talks about the food supply, she doesn't indicate whether "we" refers to the Dutch population as a whole, the residents of Maarn, or our family. The next sentence suggests there was food available locally.

67 Westphalia includes the industrial and coal-producing area of the Ruhr, which was vital to the German economy and war effort (Wikipedia, "Ruhr," accessed July 4, 2018).

68 This may be a reference to the additional fuel tanks that the Allies used to extend the range of their fighter aircraft and that were jettisoned when empty (Overy, p. 123).

Holland." It's again just as it was in May 1940,[69] and yet we feel differently even though the tension is still severe.

This afternoon all of a sudden there was a German soldier walking on my property. Did I have anything with which he could make a roof over his car—he was getting so wet. I pretended to search hard for something but wasn't finding anything. Fortunately another car came by and an officer ordered the man to drive on.

I heard a train just now! Have they repaired the track?[70]

Every vehicle that drives past is German (and there are many of them) and that is the only traffic, except for a couple of brave cyclists.

10:30 p.m. While I was listening to the radio dozens of Tommies flew over our heads, probably bombers. Tough fighting, but they sound more optimistic. The war report made me wonder how the people who live there can possibly survive. St. Oedenrode, Oisterwijk, I saw it before me and the people we know there.[71] And what is awaiting us still? Better maintain our courage and faith.

---

69 That was when, in five days of fighting, the Germans defeated the Dutch armed forces and the occupation began.

70 If so, it would be a German-operated train.

71 These are two towns in the south of the Netherlands, near Eindhoven. In April–May 1940, just before the German invasion, Wim was stationed in both of these places, and Madzy sometimes joined him there, though it was strictly against army regulations.

Chapter Eight

24 September to 22 October 1944

By this time, food was distinctly running short. Madzy referred to Iete buying some on the black market and to Annetje Nahuys filching things from the Germans who occupied Stameren.

In spite of the hardships, however—or rather, because of them—Madzy and her friends arranged little festivities in an effort to counteract the damage their children were suffering. Later, in Canada, when she was writing columns for a Dutch-Canadian newspaper, *De Nederlandse Courant in Canada*,[1] she addressed readers who, she knew, would include many women who had been in the Netherlands during the war. "I know for certain that [our young children] were deprived of something that for children of that age is very important, and that is the sense of safety, of security. Young though they were, the [wartime] events shook them, and many of them will spend their entire lives searching for something that will again give them the security they need to be able to live their lives."[2]

This chapter begins with a bombing attack on Maarn. Madzy's close-up view of what happened on the ground during such an event brings to life the statistics and the large picture that historians provide.

*****

---

1   See Conclusion, p. 316.
2   See *Frontiers and Sanctuaries*, p. 303. The columns appeared from 1962 to 1964.

Sunday, 24 September. Now I have to write quietly and in detail. It is Sunday evening, after many emotions. This morning at 8:00 there was little news from the front and we had breakfast in bed, made a cozy party of it because it was bad weather and I wasn't going to church. Then [I gave] a little Bible class and then, in spite of the rain, went to look for some chanterelles and other mushrooms.[3] So far it was just like a Sunday in peace-time. We did, though, while we were still in bed, see the Tommies flying over us, but after that the weather was "wicked," to use their own word. After lunch it cleared up. I read aloud to Pank while Gerard slept and we made a ragout with the mushrooms. At 3:30 Juus went out to visit the Schuts.

I dressed the children and myself neatly to go to de Hoogt and congratulate Nando on his second birthday.[4] On the road near Schut's house, with an enormous bang, my bicycle tire burst. We walked on to Chris and borrowed Dien's bicycle.[5] And so onward, until we arrived safely at de Hoogt at about 4:30. After the felicitations and greetings we sat down and had tea, and we were just eating our cake[6] when a fighter sheared over the house. And right after that ... an indescribable bang, and then another, and another. We saw the fighters circling in the direction of our little house.[7] I thought that they were aiming at the German vehicles along here. One after another came 7 bombs;

---

3 Edible mushrooms and beechnuts were "wild food" that we gathered in the woods beside the house. Nettles were also eaten; in fact, they were sold in stores.

4 Nando was the son of Els and Hans van Ketwich Verschuur.

5 Madzy would need to borrow a bicycle that, like her own, had two children's seats.

6 This cake would have been made with carefully saved-up ingredients and using substitutes for ingredients that were unobtainable even on the black market. What Madzy referred to as "tea" and "coffee" were almost always substitutes except on the rare occasions when the real thing was bought on the black market, and then she usually called them *real* tea or coffee.

7 De Hoogt, being on high ground, had an extensive view.

I saw 2 of them falling, and then we saw clouds of smoke. I feared that our house would be going up in flames. Then there was silence. We finished eating our cake and put on our coats again but meanwhile the phone rang a couple of times. At 't Stort the ceilings had collapsed on the furniture, and could they come and stay at de Hoogt.[8] The police phoned to ask whether any bombs had fallen on the German gasoline depot near het Berghuisje.[9]

Then I rode carefully home with the little ones, who had had a serious scare. At Rijnsoever's store the two display windows were lying in splinters, and people said that the house of Pastor Wolf had been hit. Further on I heard that the post office and Heerikhuizen's house had been hit.[10] At Steenbeek's shop a couple of windows were broken, also at de Greef's shop, and the roof. Beyond that it was less. At Chris's house there was no damage, and with my broken-down bicycle we walked quickly home. There also no damage.

It appears now that only Heerikhuizen ['s shop and house] was actually hit. Gerrit has been fatally wounded (lost a leg and an arm),[11] and the older man is limping. Also one of the people

---

8 'T Stort was the home of Willem de Beaufort, brother of Ferd, owner of de Hoogt. Mrs. de Beaufort and her daughter Ernestine were mentioned in the entry for 16 June, 1942.

9 A small country house not far from de Hoogt (Lägers & Veenland-Heineman, pp. 62, 134). Van der Donck (p. 11) writes that in this attack, sixteen bombs fell. Gijs van Roekel, in an e-mail of 11 March, 2019, gives the number as ten.

10 Jacob Heerikhuizen owned a bicycle shop (combined with their living quarters), where his (unmarried) brother Gerrit, the postman, also lived. According to an e-mail of March 2019 from Jacob's son, also called Jacob, the Nieuwenhuizen house and post office "didn't get any structural damage," but he was born in 1945 and was reporting what he had been told. Jacob Jr. writes that his sister, Dienie, "was buried under the rubble for hours" but was not badly hurt because she was lying in a doorframe. "The whole community came to find her (including German soldiers who lived at Plattenberg [a nearby house])."

11 Gerrit should apparently have reported for the labour draft on 7 May 1943 but hadn't, so he was then a diver. He was taken to hospital and

from Pastor Wolf's household. Bombs fell in front of and behind the house of Nieuwenhuizen and it is half tipped over.[12] At the other neighbours' houses all the windows are broken. People are guessing that the attack was aimed at Café Plattenberg, which is full of Germans and with many German cars, or at the house of van Ee, where there are always German vehicles. Alas, they missed, though by only a few metres. But I'm really very badly shaken, it was such a narrow escape for us all, and you ask yourself, "Today your turn, tomorrow mine?"[13]

Meanwhile the Allies have reached this side of the Rhine and we again hear the artillery thundering from time to time. Wolfheze also seems to have been hit hard, with 81 people dead at the mental institution.[14] What is still awaiting us? We here are certainly in a back corner.[15]

10:15 p.m. Patrols have crossed the Rhine and are helping the airborne troops around Arnhem, who have already been cut off for a week. The bridge has not been taken [by the Allies] yet. Yesterday 1,500 aircraft brought help to the 2nd [British] Army. Italy: Rimini fell [to the Allies] the day before yesterday and now the 8th Army is streaming into the Po valley. The Baltic: most of Estonia and Latvia are in Russian hands. Finland: the Finns are fighting German troops that were left behind. The Russians are over the border into Hungary. The weather is bad everywhere.[16]

---

died the same day (van der Donck, pp. 11–13).

12 This doesn't seem to agree with what Jacob Heerikhuisen wrote about there not having been any structural damage to the building. It is the kind of inconsistency that is often found in the historical record.

13 She uses the Latin expression: *"Hodie tibi cras mihi?"*

14 Wolfheze was just west of Arnhem. Madzy was no doubt hoping that her aunts To and Cor, who lived there, were safe.

15 She is referring to the fact that the front was actually to the south and east of us, instead of moving toward us from the west, as might have been expected after the Allied landings in Normandy. See headnote to this chapter.

16 It sounds as though she is writing this while listening to the news.

Monday, 25 September. A bad day. It's showery and chilly, and we all have terrible colds. I began the day with an old familiar attack of heart palpitations, which did not pass until close to lunch-time when I took valerian. Gerrit Heerikhuizen died of his wounds. One lady, Pastor Wolf's housekeeper, lay doubled over for an hour under the rubble but she is home again from the hospital. Three bombs fell at the pastor's house, one direct hit, and in that neighbourhood all the windows are broken.

Except that Heerikhuizen's and Nieuwenhuizen's houses are destroyed,[17] the worst damage is at 't Stort. There, not a single window is intact, there are lots of cracks in the walls, the sunroom is gone, the ceilings are coming down. The family is living in 3 bedrooms and one small sitting room. Four bombs fell, one in the pasture (the 13 foals had just, on Saturday, been taken to farms), one in the potato field, one in the rock garden in front of the house, and there is still one bomb unexploded. When the workman was looking for the broken electric cable he hit something hard with his shovel. "I'd better not go any further," he said. That was the bomb. I dropped by for a moment this afternoon. If I had gone that way yesterday with the children, I might have been in the middle of it.

At Arnhem it goes very well, much better, and the airborne troops are receiving reinforcements. Eisenhower has advised the foreign workers[18] in Germany to be ready to return to their homelands.

---

17 As noted above, Madzy's information about the Nieuwenhuizen house differs from what I received from Jacob Heerikhuisen. All the same, the post office (or a makeshift post office) was still operating—see entry of 27 September, below.

18 These were the men from the occupied countries who had been drafted for work in German factories and on farms.

Tuesday, 26 September. Little news. Arnhem has apparently been evacuated of civilians.[19] There are horrible things happening around us, too many to describe. At quarter past three it was apparently being said that the bridge in Arnhem was in German hands, but at 7 o'clock, for "security reasons," this was not reported. Everything is still confused and the fighting is "wild." The Canadians are now moving to the west of the corridor (which is 35 miles long and 25 miles wide) and are past Turnhout. They say that the Rotterdam harbours and the Amsterdam warehouses are on fire.[20]

10:30 p.m. Still "security," but everything sounded better. In the East[ern Netherlands] they are up to the Maas, in the West[ern Netherlands] the Canadians are making progress.

Wednesday, 27 September. After 2 days of "security silence" the sad news has come, that the [Allied] airborne troops in Arnhem have not been able to hold the north side of the Lower Rhine and have retreated to the south bank. Isn't this terrible? Will it prolong the war by a lot?

The weather here remains bad so I dared to go to the Bible group. But when I stopped by at the post office I found myself in the middle of a group of German vehicles and heard 2 Tommies roaring over my head. I got scared. How the fear sits unnoticed in you! Everything went well, Dicks, and fortunately now I have no appointments for 14 days, except that I would so much like to go to Joost. He was so deeply unhappy when Moeder last said good-bye to him, because it is now too dangerous for her to go there.

---

19 The Germans ordered the entire population of 100,000 civilians to evacuate; they were now all homeless (van der Zee, p. 47).

20 They were. The port of Amsterdam had been torched starting on 22 September and "[m]ore than 6,000 German explosives experts had been sent to destroy [Rotterdam] systematically" (van der Zee, pp. 38–39).

I've arranged with Juus and Willem: "When there is bombing go into the woods, when there is artillery fire into the hallway."[21]

10:30 p.m. "The Heroes of Arnhem!" People are talking about them (according to Johan Fabricius in London[22]). Of the 8,000, only 3,000 returned.[23] Ten days and nights of hard fighting, attacked from all sides, with one-sixth of the food ration, no water, constant rain. They rest in Dutch soil, with all the other heroes of this war.

Thursday, 28 September. 10:30 p.m. Received today a letter from Moeder Hans, 7 days old, but still good news. The V-1 launching site has been moved away and the people of Wassenaar are allowed to return home. There's a short rest in the fighting. The Allies are 10 miles from Den Bosch, and they've taken Elst. The Canadians are 3 miles over the Antwerp-Turnhout canal. General Dempsey's east flank (2nd British Army) comes closer along the Maas. In the Balkans: Russia is already fighting against the Germans in Hungary and at the same time in Yugoslavia; in the Baltic, Estonia is free and [the Allies] are now advancing towards

---

21 There was a tiny hallway in the centre of the cottage, and Madzy clearly felt that if the building collapsed it would be the safest place. At least it would be away from flying glass. There was a small cellar, but she was probably afraid that if we took shelter in it we risked having the entire house cave in on us.

22 Johan Fabricius was a writer who, during the war, worked for the Dutch news department of the BBC (Wikipedia, "Johan Fabricius," accessed Dec. 30, 2016).

23 These were apparently the figures that were broadcast at the time, but many modern sources say that about 17,000 Allied troops were killed, injured, or taken captive. (Beevor, *The Second World War*, p. 636, gives "nearly 15,000.") Fewer than 3,000 were successfully evacuated across the river to Allied-held territory. About 250 were left on the north bank but managed to go into hiding; some of these were smuggled to Allied territory by the Dutch Resistance (Time-Life, *WW II*, pp. 312–5; Ryan, p. 599ff; Hackett, *I Was a Stranger*, passim; van der Zee, p. 130). See headnote of Chapter Eleven.

Riga. In Italy they are gradually pushing into the Po Valley from Rimini. Against Japan everything is also progressing well. So we don't let ourselves be made down because of the setbacks at Arnhem, but encourage ourselves with the good news.

This morning, "under cover of the ground haze" (technical term!) I went to Joost. I brought him eggs and butter and he was so happy.[24] On the way I helped a couple walking, with a baby, who came from Zutphen; they had been brought part of the way by a Red Cross car and further by a cart with vegetables. The child had to be operated on in Utrecht.[25]

Friday, 29 September. 10:30 p.m. Today a very peaceful day; you'd almost forget that there was a war being fought 50 km [32 mi] from here, only for a short while shooting in the neighbourhood. Strange-looking Red Cross vehicles drawn by horses came past; Juus said, "German munitions," but I thought they were Dutch Red Cross.

Today worked on Pank's wardrobe until my back broke; she has outgrown everything.[26]

Monday, 2 October. I haven't written in 2 days, actually to save space. But I see now that this book won't last me until the end of the war and your homecoming, my dearest, so I will just be liberal. Moreover, little was happening, or at least what we nowadays call "little." In Brabant the [Allied] 2nd Army didn't make much progress but the impression we get is that they are preparing for a tremendous push. The Canadians north of Turnhout are over the border into Holland, and the last inhabitants of Zeeland have

---

24 This was probably food that Iete had bought for him on the black market.

25 The distance from Zutphen to Utrecht is over seventy kilometres [about forty-five miles] as the crow flies.

26 With no clothing available, keeping growing children supplied was a serious problem. Madzy was probably re-making some of her own and Wim's garments, using the sewing machine that she had brought back from the United States.

been warned to leave before the worst rain of bombs starts.[27] Amsterdam's warehouses and harbours have been destroyed (nearby, chunks of cheese showered down on the inhabitants!) and there has been more flooding.[28] At 6:00 this afternoon we got the news that the Americans had broken through the Siegfried Line near Cologne with 500 bombers, and now the armies are pouring through into the Ruhr. We saw all those airplanes flying over like silver birds against the hard blue sky. At first we thought they were parachutes, but they were bombers. Also Soesterberg [the nearby airbase] has been bombed this morning and there has been more shooting, probably near Maarsbergen.

Poor Suus de Boer has become a nervous wreck. In her front room there is now a German paymaster's office and she can't get over the fact that her hallway gets so filthy and that she—the wife of a captain!—has to clean the toilet. I—even though I'm only the wife of a lieutenant—would also refuse to do it.[29] Yesterday I was there for a short visit because it was such awful weather, but the shooting is nerve-racking. This morning I brought her some endives and valerian and heard that we are to receive refugees from Wageningen [a town about 23 km—15 mi—away]. I can accommodate a family upstairs; then we will live downstairs. I spoke with refugees from Wolfheze. What those people have experienced is indescribable.

Now it is a glass-clear night with full moon. They're flying again. I repacked the knapsack extra carefully, and the bicycle is loaded ready with clothing for the children.

You'll be startled to hear, Dicks, that Jeanne Pauw van Wieldrecht disappeared without a trace while she was bicycling from Leersum to Scherpenzeel [small towns near Maarn]. The last that's known about her is that a farm worker found her

---

27 This was the Battle of the Scheldt.
28 The Germans were breaching the dikes in order to flood the countryside—punishment for the Dutch and a handicap for Allied progress on land.
29 This probably has less to do with rank than with the resistance of the Dutch population.

sitting by the side of the road, and she told him that a German had just borrowed her bicycle but would bring it back shortly. People looked for her in both directions.[30]

Tuesday, 3 October. Marianke prayed: "Dear Father God, will You please look after Pappa and thank You very much that You have spared us and will You make sure that Pappa comes home soon. Amen." Gerard whispered in my ear: "Pappa is coming home soon, isn't he? And the Tommies are going to fetch Pappa." Oh, God, let it be so.

Wednesday, 4 October. My one diary book is full, dearest. Now I still have this.[31] It is the evening before the [6th] birthday of our big daughter. She is entering a new phase of her life; her infant phase is over; now she becomes a school-girl.

And this birthday is celebrated entirely under the "sign" of war. There are almost no presents: I couldn't leave Maarn to buy anything, and there is nothing to buy. The bakers are not allowed to make cakes or cookies. Guests have to be home at 7 o'clock. And yet we will make of it what we can. Months ago I bought little slippers of fur (for 18.57 guilders), which will be her present from both of us. Besides that I borrowed from the school a school-desk, and with a bookshelf and a little cupboard I've made a real little corner for her.[32] Juus and I have

---

30 Jeanne Pauw van Wieldrecht, who had been studying history at university, was working as a courier for the Resistance. The details now known about her disappearance are somewhat different from those that Madzy gave here. She actually disappeared on 23 September 1944. Her body was not found until 26 November 1946; she had been shot (Caspers, p. 178).

31 "This" is a slightly smaller book than the first one. It had previously been used for some other purpose, and the used pages had been removed.

32 The Germans closed the schools because they did not want to allocate coal to heat them. (According to what Madzy wrote in the entry for 29 March 1945, one of the school buildings in Maarn was being used by the NSB and the Landwacht.) However, education was very important

sewed clothes for the beloved doll Mimi. The excitement and anticipation are enormous. On the black market I bought a kilo of sugar for 16 guilders and half a pound of butter for 12 guilders (both bargains!) and made 3 cookie-tins of cookies and various candies, and for tomorrow evening 2 pancake-cakes,[33] each with 3 little Christmas-tree candles. Tomorrow afternoon Bem and Jim, Chris and Dien, and Annetje and Floris come, first to play games and then we end up in the kitchen with candles. Everyone brings a plate and spoon and we eat pea soup and the pancake-cakes, with water to drink. So a whole party has been put together. Juus remarked philosophically, "If only there's not too much shooting and bombing, it might even be a success!" And Pank said in her prayer, "Dear Lord, will You make sure that I have a fine birthday tomorrow?"

The Allies are preparing for an enormous offensive.

Thursday, 5 October. It has been such a strange, strange day, my Dicks, this birthday of our little mite. During the night there was constant flying and bombing in the distance. It was beautiful weather, and today also there was flying and we heard uninterrupted artillery fire, which seemed to get nearer. In between all of that we had to celebrate the birthday.

Meanwhile, refugees from Arnhem streamed into the village.[34] Everwijn Lange has 6 refugees, Tante Betsy 9 in the

---

to Madzy (note that she was taking lessons in French conversation, bookkeeping, and piano). During the coming winter she would help to organize a little class for four or five children (Jim and Bem van Notten, me, and one or two others) taught by the wife of the school principal. Madzy herself also taught me, and the borrowing of the school-desk was part of that.

33 Each "cake" consisted of a small stack of pancakes.

34 As we saw in the entry for 26 September, the evacuees had actually been forced to leave Arnhem on September 26–28. Presumably this group had been on the road ever since, looking for shelter.

two huts.[35] Christie has 6, plus 8 in Soria Moria [a cottage on the estate]. Someone came to me to borrow a bed. We also are waiting for refugees to be billeted here. Refugees passed by on bicycles, and one whole group came past with a loaded cart. Can you imagine how, then, you can be in a jolly mood? When you hear about all that suffering around us? When at every cannon shot we think, "Again many people dead, and wounded, and homeless"? When the sky is a hard, clear blue and the Tommies roar overhead in groups of 100 at a time?

But it went off all right; it was a wonderful day, according to Pank, and that's the main thing. The slippers of rabbit fur were beautiful, and the doll's clothes for Mimi still nicer, but when we sang "Lang zal ze leven,"[36] and the school-desk was delivered, then everything was perfect. She played in it for the whole day, and even ate her meal there.[37] The visitors were full of war stories, and in between that we played games. Finally, singing—each carrying a chair, plate, and spoon—we paraded to the candle-lit kitchen, where the pan of pea soup simmered on the stove, and the pancake-cakes stood on the table, each with three flickering candles. How I did miss you at that moment, my Dicks. You should have seen Pank's shining little phiz, and little Gerard happily tucking in, with his hand neatly on the table, although there was no room for it at the over-full table. The picture of our Queen hung decorated above us,[38] and all around us there is indescribable suffering and destruction. The harbours of Amsterdam and Rotterdam are entirely destroyed,

---

35 Madzy is referring to two camping huts in the woods on the estate. By then the Germans had taken over part of de Hoogt (the house), as Nando van Ketwich Verschuur told me during a telephone call on 8 August 2012. (At the liberation, Germans still occupied the entire ground floor, according to Briedé, p. 177.) Betsy and many refugees also lived in the house. Nando said that at one point it accommodated about one hundred people.

36 "Long will she live!" is the Dutch equivalent of "Happy birthday to you!"

37 I remember the desk vividly.

38 Displaying a picture of Queen Wilhelmina was a sign of resistance.

all the docks and warehouses. The building of the *Haagsche Courant*[39] and the Planetarium blown sky-high, all of Walcheren[40] under water.

Yes, Dicks, our country is in ruins and it will cost a lot to stick the debris back together again. And the people: broken, homeless, in rags.[41] Soon we'll have to eat from a soup kitchen because there is nothing to be had on our ration coupons. The electricity will soon be cut off—at first we will have some from 7 to 10 a.m. and 6 to 8:30 p.m., and then half-current from 8:30 to 7 during the night, and that also will stop after two weeks.

Moreover, we live constantly in "flight" mode, with the packed knapsack and bicycle and little wagon ready in the kitchen.[42] Also for you I'll pack a small suitcase. I have to admit that inside myself I'm nervous: all the uncertainty about you, the responsibility for the children, no contact with you anymore,[43] the knowledge that this month might bring the decisive outcome, the prospect of a winter coming that will be full of privations. "The final great battle of Holland is on!" May God spare us.

Friday, 6 October. Dearest, such a day as today I've never had before. Yesterday we were still, in spite of everything, having a nice party; today we have 8 refugees. I can't describe how we lugged and slogged to get everything in order. It's 2 families, butchers from Arnhem with wives and each family with 2

---

39 This was an important newspaper published in The Hague. Its presses were blown up because it refused to cooperate with the Germans (van der Zee, p. 31).

40 One of the islands in the southern Dutch province of Zeeland, it was the scene of savage fighting during the Battle of the Scheldt.

41 Van der Zee (p. 306) writes that when the war ended, 400,000 people had to be rehoused, and 8 percent of the whole country had been flooded.

42 The "little wagon" was the pulled-by-hand kind in which a couple of small children can sit. I believe she could hook it to the bicycle.

43 The latest recorded letter had arrived on 11 September but was dated 25 August.

children.[44] Juus is now sleeping in our bedroom, and hers is for one family (Molhuizen). The other family (West) is in the little room. The children are all sleeping in little beds or on mattresses on the floor, and one is even in the cradle. In the guest-bed sleeps one couple, and the sofa bed has been divided into a bed and a mattress, also for one of the couples. Sheets for everyone, blankets (they have some themselves), pillowcases, and towels. They are sitting now in the kitchen by the stove and are delighted, because last night they slept in a drafty hayloft, with a little ladder (and one of the women is expecting a baby), and they were icy cold and sick. What a situation![45]

---

44 When Madzy got to know the refugees better, it turned out that only one of the men, Mr. Molhuizen, was a butcher; the other, Mr. West, was a cigar dealer. Later the Molhuizen family left and were replaced by the elderly West parents and another West child.

45 Madzy here described the sleeping arrangements but didn't deal with other aspects of the crowding caused by three families living in one small house. Her entries for the coming months suggest that we and the refugees were living in more-or-less separate parts of the house, our family and Juus using the two downstairs front rooms, with Juus sleeping in one of the upstairs bedrooms and the refugees occupying the other two bedrooms and the squarish living-kitchen. In fact, however, the interaction was close and constant. As regards cooking, for instance, Bill told me there was a small wood stove in the kitchen. Madzy and Juus and the evacuee women all used it to cook meals and (when the electricity was cut off) to heat water. Opening off the kitchen were the bathroom and scullery (for washing dishes, clothes, etc.). They were also used by everyone; to reach them, we (our family) had to pass through the refugees' "living" space. As regards heat, in our living-room there was a small upright wood-burning heater, and in the other downstairs room, where Madzy and we children slept, was a small coal-burning fireplace, used only briefly in the coming winter because of the lack of coal. Water was normally pumped from a well by an electric pump, but the pump stopped working when the electricity was cut off. Fortunately, there was also a hand pump on the well. All the water for twelve people's needs, therefore, had to be pumped and carried in, and hot water had to be heated on the kitchen stove or the little heater in our room. When there was no more electricity, a "bath" would be a basin of (at best)

And while we were organizing all this, lugging things around, there was awful and steady artillery-firing, and the planes flew constantly over our heads so that my children trotted after me like chicks after the hen, too frightened to go out into the garden. Sometimes the house trembled so that I thought the windows would break.

I'm now sleeping with the children in what used to be the sitting room (Pank on the sofa), in a bed that Willem and I carried downstairs. Willem packed the glassware in a chest, and many suitcases, chairs, and little tables are being stored at his house. All the clothes that we can at all do without have been put away, because we now have only one hanging closet for the four of us. And then ... how long will we be able to stay here ourselves? When might *we* have to flee? Again the clothes for the children are lying ready to be quickly packed.

Moeder came this afternoon and has ordered a bomb shelter to be built here at her expense; everybody has one and it's becoming decidedly urgent. They will dig it in 2 days, close by the house. I've thought about it for a long time. If we come to be in the front line, our house offers absolutely no shelter with its half-brick walls.[46]

I can't tell you how exhausting it is to hear that constant artillery fire and bombing. It's still at a distance, to the south of the Rhine and Lek,[47] but they are moving forward step by step. The Germans don't let a foot of ground go without fighting for it. However dreadful it is, we have to recognize that this time [unlike in World War I] the battle will be fought on our soil.

---

lukewarm water. (I have assembled this information from memory and from various family sources.)

46 I don't believe the bomb shelter was ever built. Many able-bodied men had already been drafted by the Germans, and another draft took place two weeks after this (see entry for 22 October 1944). There were probably no building materials to be had; the Germans were using huge quantities to build and reinforce their defensive works.

47 The river was about twelve kilometres (eight miles) south of us.

11 p.m. "Mamma," says Pank (who woke up and was *so* hungry that in the end she had 2 thick slices of bread with honey and a thick slice of rye bread!)—"Mamma, there's a car tooting its horn." "No, dearest, that's one of the butchers, who is lying above our heads snoring, like this: ..." and then I do it to show her, because that's something she doesn't know about! Good-night, Dicksy.

Saturday, 7 October. Well, here we are like tea-leaves in a tea-caddy, fitted together in this house, and it is as though we have never lived here with fewer than 12 people. How empty and hollow it will feel when we are again by ourselves!

But oh! the bombing, artillery fire, etc. that there was in the neighbourhood today! And we have seen—*not* exaggerating—more than 1,000 bombers flying over our heads, and the droning was *so* penetrating that for a little while we didn't hear the artillery fire. Altogether 3,000 planes flew to Germany from England and Italy. It's the most there have been in this war.[48] However, we're still alive. Last night again a big bomb fell near Maarsbergen on the access to "'t Hazenpad" viaduct.[49] I thought our little house was going to collapse and all the refugees would fall on my head. Van Kleffens[50] has said over the radio that the dikes have been "mined" and that there is a chance that part of our country will be flooded under 6–7 metres [18-20 ft] of water. Yes, our day passes with one scare after another and

---

48 Actually, Operation Market Garden involved more aircraft than this, but Madzy would not have known that at the time.

49 "'t Hazenpad"—"the path of the hares"—was the local wartime (mocking) name for the east-west highway through Maarn, not yet completed. Construction on it had started just before the outbreak of war; after 1940 the Germans continued work on it because they needed a good road connection with Germany—as well as an escape route, hence the nickname. In 1944 work stopped again, to be resumed after the war (Lägers & Veenland-Heineman, p. 42).

50 Eelco van Kleffens was a member of the Dutch government-in-exile (Wikipedia, "Eelco van Kleffens," accessed Jan. 2, 2017).

constantly you say to yourself, "How amazing that I'm still alive! And still have an intact house!"[51] When you see the procession of refugees in pathetic little carts with white flags, you get a lump in your throat.

The food situation gets steadily worse. I've put away the sugar-bowl; there is only a little pot especially for the children, and Juus has her own little pot. I don't take sugar in anything; with porridge I take a bit of honey. Moeder treated us to 10 pounds of honey for 100 guilders! She dropped by; she has neuralgia again, very painful, and is going to receive 4 frightfully painful injections for it.

Sunday, 8 October. Today is for once a Sunday without military activities, no parachutes, no bombs, little artillery fire and only 2 airplanes! We felt disoriented and, out of habit, still didn't venture far from the house. Now my 2 refugee families and Juus are asleep upstairs, and my children here downstairs next to me, and I miss my own Dicks so frightfully that I'll just reread some old letters.

Wednesday, 11 October. I haven't written because things are difficult. When I was about to go to bed I was bitten by a wasp and now my whole arm and hand are swollen. Moreover there is little news. The war-scene is static, apparently preparing for the big onslaught. Aix-la-Chapelle is surrounded and is being bombed flat.

In our country things are very grim. The electricity is already shut off in many places, including Amsterdam, and it's said that tonight at midnight the PUEM[52] will stop. In The Hague, from tonight on, no gas [for cooking and heating]. Soup kitchens

---

51 This mood was reflected in the poem that Madzy would write for the upcoming Sinterklaas celebration; see Appendix B.
52 The local utilities service.

provide food.[53] Here we still more or less manage. Annetje filched meat for us from the Germans occupying Stameren, a whole canning jar full! Now we again have our stomachs nicely full. However, I am constantly hungry and am losing weight.

This afternoon there was a prayer meeting for peace in our chapel (now emptied of refugees). Mevr. Wendelaar told me that she had had a letter from her son dated 6 September, and Chris had news of Piet, also of 6 September. Will I also receive something? Oh, how I am longing for the mail.

Thursday, 12 October. No, no letter today, but tomorrow is a lucky day, for certain sure, the 13th and a Friday. I value the number 13 since Gerard was born on the 13th.

The Queen said almost a week ago that in 2 weeks the people would start suffering famine. Well, it begins to look like it, but now all of a sudden my refugee butcher came with probably 2 pounds of meat and an ounce of fat! And twice Annetje stole something for us from the Germans, so that we have never eaten as much meat as this week![54]

Today precious little news, only that in Hungary and the Balkans, and in Lithuania and Latvia, it's going well. Churchill is in Moscow, and also the Polish prime minister. When Churchill is home again perhaps something will start happening.

We still have electricity!

Today I saw 2 Tommies repeatedly diving and shooting, I think right near our railway station. There has been a lot of flying and shooting. This morning I had wanted to go to Doorn by bicycle but I hear that all the bicycles there are being requisitioned for

---

53 One of the responsibilities of Wim's father, as manager of the gas-producing facility for The Hague, was to decide how the very meagre supply of gas should be allocated.

54 We had no refrigerator, so the meat could not be kept.

the Landwacht.[55] That's also happening in Maarn. I'd better walk.

Sunday, 15 October. It's afternoon and I sent the children and Juus out. I needed for a little while to be alone. In this house with 12 people, where we with the four of us huddle together in one [day-time] room, there isn't one moment when I'm alone; in the evenings Juus sits here, and during the night the children also make demands on me. Now I'm coming to myself, a delicious feeling. Outside it's a grey autumn Sunday, and almost no one passes by on the street. It's dead silent; for a little while there was heavy shooting, and the English plane that had done the shooting came low over our house. Later many time-bombs exploded. The pressure on our land becomes worse, the emergency (the shortage of everything) increases. Meanwhile on Friday the 13th I received a letter from you, my Dicks, and even though it was from 27 August and therefore completely out of date I was intensely happy with it.

I walked with the children for 1½ hour in the woods. So peaceful and beautiful, but in the distance there were some airplanes flying and then the children are always frightened. When will we again be able to enjoy nature undisturbed?[56]

Riga has fallen, and also Athens. Budapest is threatened. Aix-la-Chapelle is being savagely attacked and there is fighting from house to house, from room to room. Here in our country nothing is happening except that the Canadians move very slowly forward to free the harbour at Antwerp: presumably nothing

---

55 The Landwacht had been set up by the German occupying forces in cooperation with Mussert, the head of the Dutch NSB, and was "of all [the enemy's] creations, … certainly the most contemptible." It was intended to be "a sort of auxiliary police," but in fact it was "a rabble of ruffians and desperadoes without discipline and proper training" (Maass, pp. 153–154).

56 During this walk we would again have gathered beechnuts, edible mushrooms, and kindling wood.

will happen before that, but then the Allies will be able to bring in more *matériel*.

Now that I see how unintelligently my refugees packed, I've learned how to do it properly and I constantly add something to the knapsack. Tomorrow I will ask Willem to check over the little wagon.

And how are you spending today, my Dicks? Is there anything cheerful there?

Tuesday, 17 October. Today I went to Suus de Boer for her birthday. Oh, how sad everything is, even though everyone does their best to keep a cheerful face. How longingly everyone looked at the pound of whole-milk cheese, the pound of bacon, and the meter-long loaf of white bread that she received for her birthday! At the exquisite grapes![57] And how afraid we all were in our hearts of the 500 men of the Organization Todt that have come with 4 trucks full of pick-axes and shovels to build fortifications here.[58]

This morning I first worked hard in the house, then went on the bicycle to Doorn, where fortunately I could manage to get 200 guilders from the bank, because I had not been in 2 weeks (we are allowed only 100 per week) and sugar (Gerard still receives ½ pound every two weeks, we [the rest of the family] 125 gr sugar or 200 gr jam) and apples (because I was so hungry, and you can't get cakes or pies anymore, only that awful bread that

---

57 All no doubt obtained on the black market.
58 The Organization Todt was a civil and military engineering group working in Germany and the occupied countries. The workers (almost all of whom were prisoners of war and labourers conscripted from occupied countries) were treated like slaves, and many did not survive the work or the war (Wikipedia, "Organization Todt," accessed September 20, 2016). Warmbrunn, in connection with what he writes about the labour draft (p. 72ff), mentions the building and reinforcing of fortifications during this time, including the Grebbe Line, which was only a few kilometres east of us.

contains sawdust[59]). Then to Joost to bring him something from Moeder. I had heard that he had no more potatoes so I gave him my coupons (we have some still) from these two weeks.[60]

At Suus's house the electricity is now being shut off at quarter to 12, so that will probably happen to us too. I have a swollen stomach from that awful bread, and the milk-delivery man hasn't been here so we have no porridge. We need a lot of courage and faith to get bravely through this time: no speedy prospect for liberation (the contrary, in fact), impending famine, cold, bad weather, poor clothing, primitive living conditions with many refugees, anxiety about perhaps having to leave our house because of the fortifications,[61] grief and misery everywhere, etc. etc.

Wednesday, 18 October. Dearest, today a letter and a postcard (from 7 and 11 September) from you. Mevr. Wendelaar even had a letter of 27 September! What service! But it's so peculiar (don't get angry) that I notice only now how much we have become strangers to each other. This letter shows that you have no understanding at all of our circumstances.[62] Your letter of 7 September was written in a hurry; not economically but widely-spaced. I see it before me: you want to write but you don't know what to write, and you are in haste because someone is waiting

---

59 The Germans prescribed and controlled the contents of bread baked in Dutch bakeries. Sometimes, especially in the last months of the war, it did indeed contain sawdust (Wikipedia, "Regeringsbrood," accessed June 28, 2018).

60 Joost, though living in the care of three elderly ladies, would receive his own coupons.

61 Along the coast, the building of fortifications had led to large numbers of residents having been forced to evacuate.

62 Because we have none of Madzy's letters to Wim, we don't know what she was writing, but if she held to her decision to write only the "good" things to him, then indeed he would have no understanding of how we were really living. Moreover, with the slow postal service, he could not yet have heard about the presence of the evacuees.

for you so that you can do something together. And so you write in a hit-and-miss way. I have probably also written in that way sometimes. And neither of us at that moment realized in what circumstances the other would receive the letter. At this moment my whole soul reaches out for support, for your comforting, safe, male arms. Instead of which I have to keep on worrying, with a load of misery and problems, with the whole weight of 11 housemates, of whom I am the "Head," whom I have to tow along, without support from anyone, because there is no one whom I can ask for support. So, through disappointment, we become wiser.

One of Mevr. Jos's[63] refugees has diphtheria![64] She was just here.

Saturday, 21 October. Today, and also yesterday, I worked hard to set up the little school for refugee children in the barn.[65] You would have laughed at me, Dicks. Three men worked under my orders, and today the little school has started with great

---

63 Mr. and Mrs. de Josselin de Jong had come to Maarn (evacuated from Bloemendaal, which is west of Amsterdam and close to the coast) in 1943 and had become part of Madzy's circle of friends (information received from their descendants). Madzy's informal abbreviation of the surname shows that she was saving paper and also that she was on friendly, but not first-name, terms with them.
64 "In 1944, diphtheria caused many deaths, since a virulent variety of the disease had been introduced from Germany" (Warmbrunn, p. 102).
65 Madzy was much concerned about disruptions in schooling and how far the children were falling behind—as well as about the lawlessness of their moral environment. Moreover, school was a way to keep them occupied. In "Memories for you and me," a tape she made for me in her old age, she recorded that she "set up a class with all kinds of children, also Jewish children who had to be hidden away and a Jewish woman, a beautiful and very intelligent woman, who took that in hand and made music and sang and gave little lessons and so on." This little class is never mentioned again, either because of self-censorship or because it was very short-lived. In the winter it certainly would not have been possible to continue holding it in the unheated barn.

enthusiasm and ended with singing. I had such a feeling of satisfaction.

But now it's evening and a great melancholy has come over me; again a precious Saturday evening without you. When I rode this afternoon through the beautiful autumn woods to get apples from the de Jonghes it came over me. After that I was busy with bathing the children, washing hair and cutting nails, but when in the half-dusk I went to do the blackout it descended on me again. And supper, however cozy, was one pain of longing for you. Now it's evening and the evacuees have friends to tea (who are braving the 8:00 curfew) and are sitting comfortably chatting. I sit with my eternal stocking to knit (Marian wears hers out so fast) and outside there is an enormous silence. Maybe tomorrow will bring us something? The weather is so beautiful and everything is waiting in such tension, and the present situation can't last. Everywhere there is famine and misery. We still have electricity but half of Maarn, Doorn, and Maarsbergen are in the dark.

Starting yesterday the news was a bit better. Aix-la-Chapelle and Belgrade have fallen to the Allies, the Russians are in East Prussia, the Canadians are north of Antwerp, and the offensive is moving in the direction of Breda and Roosendaal. There is something going on and it is again fine weather and the barometer is rising.

Sunday, 22 October, evening. This morning, before the high mass,[66] my refugees told me that all the men in Maarn from 17 to 50 years old had to report at 2:30 at 't Stort for the labour draft. At 10:00, also, a special messenger came personally from door to door to give the order. At 12:00 Willem stood on my doorstep, shaking, and asked whether I could put in a good word with the mayor.[67] I went to ask Christie's advice about doing

---

66 The evacuees were Roman Catholic.
67 The current mayor, J. P. A. de Monyé, was a member of the NSB, the Dutch Nazi party, appointed by the Germans (Caspers, p. 181). See entry for 23 May 1942.

that. She said, "No, because it won't help anyway." At 4:00 the conscripted men came past the house: Willem was with them, and also Mijnheer West but not Mijnheer Molhuizen because he is a butcher (an occupation that provides food)—and no one bothered to consider that he is now an evacuated butcher and unemployed. Great consternation! Who will do the hard work for us now? "I will be your gardener," said Mijnheer Molhuizen. If only he will saw firewood and help with cleaning out the rabbit cages,[68] and carry water when the electricity stops.

Besides this it was a quiet day, only with constant artillery fire from the direction of Rhenen.[69] They say that Rhenen and Bennekom [towns not far east of Maarn] have had to evacuate; more than 9,000 people are looking for a roof here and have been put up in churches for the time being. Breskens[70] has fallen to the Allies (the soldiers walk up to their waist in water) and the Canadians make progress in the direction of Breda and Roosendaal. It goes slowly, but at some time the front will roll over us. In view of the fact that they are now building up the Grebbe Line (hence the drafting of all those men) there will certainly be fighting here, and then we for our part will have to be brave.

---

68 This is the only time when rabbits are mentioned, but rabbit cages appear in one or two of the photos we have from this time. Presumably they were intended to provide meat.
69 Rhenen was the southern end of the Grebbe Line.
70 A town in the southwest corner of the Netherlands. The Breskens area was crucial to the liberation of the Scheldt River, along which the Allies would receive supplies through the port of Antwerp (Kaufman & Horn, p. 29).

Chapter Nine

23 October to 17 November 1944

One of my sources of information about living conditions during the latter part of the war is the correspondence, already mentioned,[1] that Madzy had soon after the war's end with Virginia Donaldson and her daughter, Rosalie Worthington. For instance, in the fall of 1945 Madzy reported that there was still a shortage of shoes, stockings, raincoats, and winter coats. We had two sets of underwear each, one on and one in the wash. Madzy had no winter coat. She wrote that we were using soap made of clay[2] and, in a letter of 22 November 1945, asks for one cake of toilet soap—such a modest request for a basic and inexpensive item.

*

The narrative of this last winter of the war[3] is a tale of danger and of ever more severe hardship, greatly increased by the cutting off of the electricity. Particularly it is a tale of hunger. The railway workers' strike stopped the movement of food from the eastern provinces to the western ones; in addition, the Germans, as punishment for the strike, "embargoed all shipping on Dutch waterways—the only other method of moving food and fuel."[4] Rations were reduced to famine levels.[5] Moreover, it was an unusually bitter winter, and the cold weather

---

1 See headnote to Chapter Two.
2 There was in fact a "soap" made of clay: it consisted of a clay base covered with sand (Dutch Wikipedia, "Surrogaat," accessed Sept. 8, 2017).
3 It came to be called the Hunger Winter.
4 Olson, p. 398.
5 Kaufman & Horn (pp. 52–53) reported that the official rations in August 1944 were 1,500 calories per day, on 1 November, 1,040 calories, at the

further intensified the miseries caused by the lack of electricity and gas. To provide some fuel, trees in parks were cut down, empty houses (many of them the former homes of deported Jewish families) were demolished for their burnable contents, and tram-line ties were dug up. People from the big cities trekked under desperate conditions to the farms, carrying their belongings to barter for food. Some of those trips took a week or longer. Aside from the deaths from warfare (bombing, reprisal killings, etc.), tens of thousands of people died of starvation and the diseases aggravated by the lack of heat and by insufficient and unnutritious food.[6]

Madzy also went on begging and scrounging expeditions, but she had the advantage of being able to go to friends like the Kolffs or her former maid Rika,[7] or to farmers in the neighbourhood. Because she refers to these farmers very casually, with no explanation, it is likely they were people Wim knew from his work as the Broekhuisen estate manager. All these trips were within a day's travel (on foot or by bicycle), but with her frail health, they were sometimes almost more than she could manage.

The details about what Madzy obtained during these trips and what she got on rationing coupons frequently do not correlate with what she reported about our actual meals. But, as she wrote, she was also supplying and feeding other people: "Everyone who comes to visit is hungry."[8] Some of the food she obtained was passed on to less mobile friends like Suus de Boer. No doubt some was given to divers, whose mobility was usually restricted and who officially did not receive rationing coupons. Some of the inconsistencies are therefore probably the result of self-censorship.

*****

end of January 1945 down to 520 calories, then in March slightly up to 770, and at the end of March down to 320.

6   This information is in all the sources: Kaufman & Horn, Maass, van der Zee, Beevor.

7   See entry of 10 December 1944.

8   Entry of 10 December 1944.

Monday, 23 October, evening. Well, this first sad day without the trusty Willem has passed. And we certainly did notice how much he has been doing for us! How we did miss him!

Our Meneer West came home full of stories. They worked near Oud Leusden,[9] so a considerable distance away. But he says he isn't going tomorrow. However, just now at 10:00, a personal card came for every evacuee saying that they must *definitely* report tomorrow, otherwise hostages will be taken from Maarn.

They say that Mijnheer Briedé, the town secretary, has already been taken.[10]

Tuesday, 24 October. Evening. A hectic day. First the baker came to tell me that bread deliveries are no longer permitted (also no milk, groceries, etc.) and we will have to fetch it ourselves. Then we had to do the ironing as quickly as possible because the electricity might be shut off. The rooms had to be done. With no Willem, all the gardening had to be done; Molhuizen wasn't there to help, and West had to go to the doctor. My evacuee ladies wanted to do a laundry and were busy with that all day.[11]

And then visitors: Floris and Annetje, telling us that Floris has gone underground because a German living at Stameren had

---

9 Bill's note: "This is an extension of the Grebbe Line near Amersfoort." Evidently some of the drafted men were living at home rather than in labourers' camps. Willem and Mr. West would probably walk back and forth to their place of work (six or seven kilometres, or about four miles, each way).

10 J. P. Briedé records (p. 170) that in the autumn of 1944 he was imprisoned in the camp in Amersfoort because, in his position as the Maarn town secretary, he had refused to cooperate with the German authorities in regard to the labour draft. When he was released from the camp, he went underground, and some local people attended to the office work. Also see Caspers, p. 181ff. His imprisonment was therefore, apparently, punishment; he was not a hostage, though Madzy's wording suggests that was what she thought.

11 As long as there was electricity, there was running hot and cold water; no doubt the imminent loss of electricity motivated them to do the laundry. With no washing machine, this was a major operation.

reported that he was still free. And in between there was the constant thunder of artillery, airplanes flying, bombing in the distance, etc., because it was a beautiful fall day.

This evening Willem was sitting here telling us about his experiences, and everything is uniformly ridiculous. The men achieve nothing[12] and the women slave themselves to death. It's time that there's an end to this because it can't go on any longer. We are more and more hungry.

But progress is being made.[13] Den Bosch is surrounded on three sides and there's fighting in the suburbs. Zuid Beveland is encircled.[14] A large [Allied] army is over the [Dutch] border in the direction of Roosendaal and Tilburg. And in Prussia it goes wonderfully well, also in the Balkans. And still …. Every day, every hour, is here a very heavy hour, a very heavy day.

Wednesday, 25 October. Evening. Yesterday so many people used our toilet that the septic tank overflowed and the toilet couldn't be used. Now you have to imagine our cigar-evacuee, West, who in his ordinary life also works at an undertaker's establishment. When he had to flee, he was dressed in his "funeral" suit (a sort of dinner jacket with striped trousers and a striped waistcoat and a shirt with a soft collar, and worn-out patent-leather shoes). Today (because, on account of his having kidney stones, he doesn't have to dig) he has—in this outfit, with his trouser-legs and sleeves rolled up—been emptying the septic tank a bit. I sometimes had to turn away because of the stench and the laughter. So there are also funny moments in this sad time.

The man who is supposed to shut off the electricity has been sick, but now alas he's better again. Many houses, including

---

12 "Achieving nothing" was sometimes a deliberate resistance tactic.

13 This entry shows how the large public picture and the smaller, private one interconnected. There would be no solution to the difficult local/family situation until the war ended, so Madzy's mind flew back and forth between the war news and the women doing the laundry.

14 Part of the southern Dutch province of Zeeland.

Willem's, have been shut off today, and this evening I enjoyed a shower for the last time and just quickly used the sewing machine to alter a sweater of mine to fit Marian.

Saturday, 28 October. Evening. I'm writing this with an almost-finished waxine light sitting on the corner of the book.[15] The electricity gave up yesterday at 8 o'clock. We can't flush the toilet, there is no shower, no hot water.[16] I went to bed at 9:00 yesterday and lay there worrying until 1:30, and then woke at 6:30. No, going to sleep early is something that I will have to learn still. Now it's quarter to 11, and I don't want to use a precious candle for me alone. I undressed and washed, and laid the table, with open shutters and a bit of faint moonlight. Indeed, until just now I sat by the window knitting underpants for Gerard and am cold through and through because the stove went out at 8:00. But now I know that in a little while I will go to sleep easily.

Because what a day! Up at 7 o'clock, stove on for tea and porridge, breakfast with porridge and 2 slices of bread each thinly spread, then did the rooms and arranged for today's and tomorrow's meals. We have to use the daylight to its utmost, you see, and we figure this out already in the morning. Made rye bread so that the other bread stretches further,[17] but Gerard

---

15 There is a small blank space on the top left-hand corner of the page where the little light stood. Lacking electricity, people invented all kinds of substitute sources of light. One consisted of a jar of water with some oil (whatever kind was available) floating on it. A string would be poked (with a needle) through a thin disc of cork that would float on the oil; the string served as a wick. I'm not sure whether that was what was called a waxine light, but I know that we used them because I remember poking the string through the cork disc.

16 The electric pump had stopped working, of course, and so had the hot-water heater. Having no running water, no flushing toilet, and no light was a serious problem in a small house with twelve people, including several small children, but there were other people worse off than we were.

17 In the 1976 narrative, Madzy described how she made rye bread. She would grind the rye (Bill explained that it was the grain that grew best

can't stand much of it and Marian also not well, though she eats it because she's hungry. After the meal and the dish-washing I set off with Marian on the little wagon: checked the list of coupons and bought this and that. Stood for about half an hour in the line-up outside in the cold for milk. At 4:00 home, quickly drank 2 cups of substitute tea without sugar and on the bicycle again to Dirksen's farm (halfway to Maarsbergen) to get buttermilk for Gerard. When I got home I found that Juus had surprised me by bathing the children already; I dressed them quickly and then changed my own clothes while stirring the porridge while Juus had her bath. We flew faster and faster to use the last bits of daylight, lay the table, lay everything ready so that at 5:30 we could eat in the dusk until we couldn't find our mouths any more. Blackout and one candle, finished eating and washed the dishes. Read aloud to children in pyjamas and then they to bed. Then unraveled a knitted baby blanket[18] and at 9:00 blew out the candle and continued by moonlight. But now I'm going to bed, tired but satisfied with my efforts, though very sad about all the misery.

The Hague has been entirely mined in case the British land. Den Bosch is liberated, there are landings and fighting on the

---

on the soil in that area) in the coffee grinder. She mixed the resulting coarse flour with a bit of water and salt, then formed the dough into loaves. Then a brick was placed in a saucepan, water was added to the level of the top of the brick, and the loaf set on the brick. Then it had to steam for four or five hours.

18 The yarn would be used to knit something else. Unraveled yarn was extremely kinky. It had to be wetted and then wound around a wooden board and allowed to dry. It never lost all its kinks but was at least somewhat easier to re-knit. I remember boards with drying yarn standing around. Besides things like this baby blanket, Madzy also unraveled her ski sweaters—remnants of a very different lifestyle—and anything outgrown or no longer needed that could be unraveled (and wasn't needed for barter). Worn-out socks had new feet knitted onto the tops. We children wore knitted underwear.

Zeeland islands. The bread ration has been reduced, no sugar, no flour, half jam.

Monday, 30 October. Slowly the news gets through to us.[19] Tilburg fell to the Allies several days ago and yesterday also Breda and Goes. It goes pretty well, but how can one be cheerful with so much suffering around us? 1,200 men picked up in Zeist. Our Maarn men work with 12,000 men on the Grebbe Line, which has to be ready on 8 November and then they will go on to other work. The food situation is wretched: the bread ration so reduced that we can only eat 4 slices each per day. And just now Pank said: "Mamma, I'm so hungry." Therefore: a slice of bread spread with fat, and tomorrow at breakfast I will satisfy my hunger a bit with oatmeal cooked in water with salt, because we don't get sugar any more. But we still have heat.[20] How is it in the cities, where there is also no fuel to be had? The miserable thing is that I absolutely cannot digest rye or brown beans, and not more than 4 potatoes per day, otherwise my innards go out of order; I already frequently have pain in my right side.[21] So now all four of us are plagued by intestinal problems, Dicks![22] Later on that will mean a diet of lots of rice and rusks and protein. Good night, darling, do you think of us often?

Tuesday, 31 October. This morning I tidied the rooms and was just tidying myself when a fat guy in German uniform came

---

19 No electricity also meant no radio reception, except for the people who had battery radios. I have no idea where, for the rest of the war, they found batteries; perhaps they were available on the black market.

20 We gathered fallen twigs and branches in the woods. Dientje Blijdenstein, in her diary, wrote on 12 October 1944, that two areas of forest on their estate were cut down to provide fuel for the local people.

21 She occasionally mentioned that she was eating rye bread, no doubt when there was little else.

22 Wim, by now, suffered from colitis (see entry for 27 March 1944).

riding up the driveway followed by a "veldwachter."[23] He stopped in front of my window and said, "How many men do you have in the house?" It was our rascal Bos.

I thought hard and, to win time, I said, "My husband isn't here, he is a prisoner of war. He is in Neubrandenburg."

"Yes, but how many evacuees—or are they retired?"

Now I've never been quick in such exchanges, and so I admitted that I had 2, but when he asked where they were I said that they were at de Halm [neighbouring farm], although I knew that one was sawing wood for me and one was pumping water for me.

"What are they doing at de Halm?"

"I don't know," I said, and then they went on to de Halm, and I to the garden [to warn the men], and Molhuizen disappeared into the woods and West went to the doctor.

Enfin, I dress and go with my milk can to get the milk and on my way back from the dairy store, weaving on the bicycle (because of carrying the milk can with one hand) I meet Bos and he turns around and bicycles after me and says, very loudly:

"Mevrouw, if your evacuees haven't reported tomorrow at 7:30 at the Woudenberg-Scherpenzeel railway station your house and furniture will be burned, and also Mevrouw van Notten's and Huis de Maarn."

"Very well, Meneer Bos," I said calmly and lurched on with my little milk can.

Meanwhile he had already delivered this message here at the house, and I went to tell Chris, and we agreed that we would rather risk it than let ourselves be bullied by such a scoundrel. As it happens, my evacuees have permits designating them as "freigestelt" [exempt], so they are not going. And at Chris's house a diver, who by accident was found, is also not going. So

---

23 A "veldwachter" was a sort of local police constable (Wikipedia, "Veldwachter," accessed Oct. 15, 2018). Apparently the man who spoke to Madzy, G. Bos, was in fact a member of the Landwacht and therefore someone to be feared. Caspers mentions him several times.

we have to be thankful that tonight we still sleep under a roof, and we've arranged that if we get kicked out of this house we will find refuge in the chicken houses at de Venen.[24] I'm taking everything very calmly. Except that I am annoyed about such a scoundrel, I don't consider it very important. Besides, the mayor says that Bos had absolutely no authority to say those things.

Wednesday, 1 November. Well, our house is still standing and nothing happened. De heer Bos was only giving us a scare. Chris had a wagon full of things taken to de Venen and I filled a dirty-laundry bag with many things, especially for Wim, and everything is standing ready. Because there is much flying again. At one moment an airplane flew over very low; just then three Germans were walking past our house and one, "as a joke," shot his gun at the plane. Tje! What a scare we had!

Pank complained about a sore throat and because there is a lot of diphtheria around I immediately asked the doctor's assistant to come. I had already kept her indoors and got her to gargle, and that was the right thing to do.

Besides that, there's no news, only a nice story: all of a sudden a strange man came up to the house with a loose goat following him. It was an evacuee who had been out walking, and the goat had suddenly attached itself to him. He didn't know where the animal came from: did I know? Well, I thought that it was Idenburg's goat,[25] and Pank thought so too, and so the goat and I climbed the hill. And, yes, the goat was greeted with delight; they had already been afraid because they had butchered its mate the day before and now it was lonely. The children loved the incident.

Pank is extremely bothersome and I don't know what to do with her. She doesn't want to do anything, is in a bad mood and disobedient and unmanageable. The circumstances have a lot to do with it.

---

24 Another property on the Blijdenstein estate.
25 Idenburg was the caretaker at Huis te Maarn and was very active in the Resistance (van der Zee, p. 141; Caspers, many references).

Saturday, 4 November. A confused day today. Moeder wanted very much to send a pound of butter to Joost, so I quickly tidied the bedroom and the sitting room and went out to do errands and go on to Joost. Everything should have gone speedily if only the Tommies hadn't just got it into their heads, when I was on the way home on the path along the railway, to bomb the broken-down locomotives once again. Oh my! I don't know how I got myself so quickly, bicycle and all, into a hollow in the heather. And the clouds of smoke rose about 50 metres further on. But you get used to everything and when the planes dove for the third time I already found it less frightening because I could see them diving.

For the rest, everything was all right, my house not yet burned down when I got home with the milk, 3 cabbages, and 5 kg of apples. Still the "pot" is becoming skimpy: 125 gr of butter every two weeks, and we'll get a bit of oil later. 1,600 gr of bread per week, that is 4 slices per day (two for breakfast and two for evening dinner), 2 kg potatoes per person per week (Gerard half that amount of bread, half the potatoes), 125 gr of jam every two weeks, no sugar except for Gerard who gets 250 gr every two weeks. No groceries,[26] oatmeal not available, Pank only skim milk. Whole milk only for Gerard. We more or less manage but it remains difficult and I will have to give some of your clothes to the man at the dairy. Do you mind, Dicks?

Sunday, 5 November. Evening. Another Sunday passed, but this time without anything eventful happening. During the night there was lots of bombing and shooting, but that's all that we heard. We had a beautiful walk, Pankie for the first time in her new ski suit,[27] and the weather was soft, with a strong south wind.

---

26 The term "groceries," at that time, did not include items from the butcher, baker, greengrocer, dairy store, and other specialized shops.
27 As there were no new clothes available for purchase, this would have been a garment outgrown by someone else's child.

Monday, 6 November. If I get old before my time, Dicks-darling, then you know that these years have counted double, just as in the Dutch East Indies.[28] The scare that I had on Saturday is still in my bones; and it was a narrow escape because two high-explosive bombs fell on the bicycle path a few moments after I had ridden along it! That they fell close to me I knew, but that they fell on the path itself I heard only today. The result is that I'm frightened, I've lost my nerve. Today there has been bombing and shooting everywhere nearby (the clouds of smoke blew over the vegetable garden). In Maarsbergen the stationmaster and wife and two children are dead. This afternoon I was just on the driveway on my way to Doorn to see if I could get my laundry done when they began to dive again, and artillery firing came from the woods. I turned around and fled back to the house. Juus had closed the shutters to protect the window-panes because everything shook so badly. When it was still again, she said, "Now you can go." And I didn't want to look like a coward so I went—but, oh Dicks, I was so scared, so scared ....[29]

The neurological hospital in Utrecht has apparently been hit—by mistake instead of the electricity plant. Unfortunately the Germans' aim is sometimes a bit off.

Oh, if only the fighting here is not as heavy as it has been in Brabant![30]—but it probably will be. I'm so dreadfully afraid. It will take a lot of prayer and trust before I stop being afraid.

Tuesday, 7 November. Evening. I heard just this morning that the tremendous bang of yesterday afternoon, that came when I

---

28 She referred to the fact that when her father worked in the Dutch East Indies before the First World War, the conditions there (weather, etc.) were considered so stressful for Europeans that, in calculating retirement age, each year of work counted as two.

29 It appears that when she reached Doorn, she found that the commercial laundry was no longer working, no doubt because of the lack of fuel, so this required adjustments in Madzy's housekeeping. See later entries.

30 The fighting south of the rivers was extremely severe.

was just setting out, was a large bomb that fell right next to the Knorrebuurt, next to Everts' house.[31] The only person hurt was one of Bouwmeester's sons, and not seriously. But that makes me realize that the Tommies also don't always aim well. I don't find it very safe anymore and had better stay home a lot.

Today just a few planes diving over the railway line, where they also missed their target and, instead of the station at Woudenberg, hit a farmhouse (all the inhabitants dead), but for the rest it was pretty quiet. Floris brought us a stolen loaf of bread, that sour bread, which tasted very good in comparison to our sticky, unleavened bread, and now suddenly our bread ration has risen to 3 instead of 2 slices. *Enfin*—at last a little piece of good luck.

If you miss 2 pairs of knee socks from your wardrobe, Dicks, we have ... drunk them up. Well, actually your son. Because I bartered them at the dairy for buttermilk. I have already given away all *our* clothes,[32] either given to the refugees or bartered for butter or rye or wheat.

Life is complicated, Dicks. To give you an example, right now I have my period. For one thing, it's *much* worse than usual, perhaps because of the nervous life, perhaps because of the inadequate food. Secondly I can no longer buy disposable sanitary napkins so have to make do with washable cloths. How do I wash them, and in what? All the pails are in use, containing water from the garden pump for us and for the evacuees, and there is almost no soap powder anymore except for the one weekly wash. So now, as soon as I take off one of the cloths, I immediately rinse it out, while it's still wet, in a special basin and throw away that dirty water. Then I have another basin in which all the rinsed cloths sit soaking in water in which I've dissolved some shampoo, of which Moeder had hoarded quite a bit. When they've soaked

---

31 This would have been quite near our house. See map.

32 Later she said she still had clothes of Wim's, so here she was clearly referring to her own and the children's. She doled Wim's out sparingly; clothes were important "currency" on the black market.

in that for a long time I lay them secretly over the hedge, some distance away, to bleach, and then I rinse them again and at night I hang them in the dining room to dry. (Why can't I do it by day?—because there are men everywhere.[33]) I still have 17 cloths, of which 5 are in the "flight" suitcase, and therefore if I need more than 12 I will have to get those 5 out and replace them as soon as I can. Do you see now what sorts of problems we have?

I bathe the children when it's still light, 3 times per week in the dining room in front of the stove, and I dry them on a tarpaulin that I've laid over the dining-room table, before we lay the table. And then we just hope that they don't make themselves dirty again!

Wednesday, 8 November. Evening. It's still a nervous business even just to go to the village for milk and bread, and it can happen that halfway we have to duck into someone's house or dash to the shoulder of the road, hugging our potatoes, can of milk, or loaf of bread.

Today I had a nice domestic moment. It's been probably 3 months or more since I was alone with the children, but today Juus went out for a short visit to admire Marietje's baby. And I can tell you, Dicks, that the three of us enjoyed the occasion like little kids, as though it were a party. Why? Not because of Juus herself. Her presence is a great help. But still, I need to be sometimes "among ourselves." I would *love* to have an evening to myself. That hasn't happened in a long time.

Juus's help can't be adequately paid for. She works the whole day and often in the evenings for us; she helps with the knitting of underwear for the children, she lugs things and looks after the animals, everything. But she irritates Pank, and Pank becomes even more irritated when she realizes that she gets criticism from two sides. Juus does it to help, but it isn't right, and it also makes me irritated and makes me a different person than I normally

---

33 At that time, women were expected to be secretive about menstruation.

am. No, Dicks, my paradise is to live with you and the two little ones in a small easy house, with a helper only during the day. And then our trusty Juusje can come and help us when there's sickness or an emergency. Ungrateful? No, I'm deeply grateful for everything that she does and will never forget it. But oh to be again among ourselves and free, free, free! Without Moeder Iete's well-meant remarks many times per week, without anyone else but only your dear presence. Imagine: Iete has promised to give a suit of yours to a guy who gave her a little bit of help a couple of times! I won't even consider it, but it irritates me dreadfully.

Thursday, 9 November. Today it snowed! What will come of *that*?

Friday, 10 November. Today is a somber, sad day, the sort of day in which all the misery, shortages, cold, hunger, and longing overwhelms you and in which you can no longer rise above it. All the primitive circumstances here in the house, the slogging all day long for food and drink while it either pours rain or you have a constant threat of falling bombs and artillery fire. No news from Dicks any more: his last was from 11 September so that's 2 months old. Marianke, who is bothersome and, according to the schoolmistress, has to be handled firmly. *Enfin*, a thousand and one things that just make you exhausted and depressed.

And then come all the worries from all the other people around you, falling on you. From my evacuees I hear that other evacuees live like dogs in a pool of mud at de Halm, 19 of them in a little wooden shed. One of my evacuee ladies is expecting a baby in 2 to 3 months and has literally nothing for it.[34] All their troubles among themselves and all their difficulties. Then when I was out shopping I met the funeral cortège of the Maarsbergen

---

34 Madzy doesn't indicate which of the two women this was, but it must have been Mrs. Molhuizen who, with her family, moved away a week later (see entries for 16 and 17 November, below). Had it been Mrs. West, who remained with us, Madzy would probably have referred to the birth of the baby when it occurred.

stationmaster and his wife. (Suus de Boer walked sadly in the procession.) It gives you a pang in your heart to see those children walking, crying, behind the coffins. Beside that, you were silent. Then this afternoon I thought I would go to Maarsbergen to see if I could get some rye,[35] and when I then visited Suus I became even more depressed, and then they began to shoot, and as soon as it was quiet again I fled home like a hare.

And now this evening, when I'm sitting by the lamp, an evacuee comes to me with all her worries and sadness. What can you do then? You just say that it will be over by Christmas, which is something that you yourself don't at all believe, you listen attentively and sink a bit further into the bottomless pit.

Saturday, 11 November. Armistice Day![36] When will the new one be celebrated? Today again there was a horrible lot of shooting, just when I was out on the black-market path,[37] and so I raced along like a hare and thought, "If I ever see Dicks again, my cry will be, 'I was *so* frightened, so *terribly* frightened!'" All of a sudden there is not much left of my courage. Odd, isn't it? Could it be because I have pain again in my left breast, and because I'm afraid of cancer and that that breast might have to be removed and that Dicks will find an ugly, mutilated wife back? And I would so dearly love to be entirely sound when I stand in front of you on that first evening, Dicksy.

For the rest, only sad news: bread ration lowered to 1,400 gr (Gerard 600 gr) per week. No butter these two weeks, half the meat (35 gr per week) and half the milk (1 ¾ L skim every 14 days). The famine has therefore arrived, and for how long still? That is something that we keep asking ourselves in these blackest of times.

---

35 Several of the farmers to whom Madzy went regularly were located near Maarsbergen.

36 She gave the words in English.

37 The Dutch phrase is *"op het swarte pad."*

Monday, 13 November. Dearest, we are sitting in a "damned little corner."[38] South of the rivers they have been liberated and now receive increased rations. Yes, they've had an awful time, but that's finished and they are free and can start rebuilding. But we? Our food is steadily less, we now get 1¾ L of skim milk *per month* per person, only Gerard 5¼ L of whole milk every 14 days. This is what our meals look like:

Breakfast: each of us 2 slices of bread (the children with butter, and Juus has her own butter, but I save mine for the children) and some porridge made with water. Juus eats rye bread and Pankie too, but Gerard and I can't digest it. At 11 o'clock a cup of Maggi[39] with warm water, or nothing. At 12:30 potatoes and some vegetables (whatever can still be picked in the garden, because from the greengrocer we get at most 2 days' worth twice a week). Because we have potatoes from the garden we have enough, with water gravy and whatever butter each of us might want to add. At 3:30 a cup of imitation tea without sugar, and at 6:00 in the half-dark each of us 2 slices of bread and warm porridge with some milk and water). All this is supplemented with apples, because we have plenty of them, but the cities don't.[40] This week we have a loaf of wheat bread with it, and some with fat. So that's extra. The butter that Moeder bought on the black market (32.50 guilders per pound) is for Juus and the children. If you ask, "Why for Juus?" then it's because she pays for it herself and because she says that she can't live without it. She also has her own sugar, because for the children, on coupons, we receive ½ pound every 2 weeks. Moeder also bought 10 pounds of honey for 100 guilders for us and every evening I eat a spoonful of that. Oh, that's so delicious! In the

---

38 She was quoting someone; the reference is to the fact that the Allies were pushing eastward south of the rivers but leaving the part of the country north of the rivers in German hands. See Chapter Six headnote.

39 A soup seasoning; diluted with hot water, it was a savoury drink but not very substantial.

40 There was an apple tree in our garden.

evening we also drink a cup of surrogate coffee; we don't even get any of *that* on coupons but I still have 6 packages. Gerard still gets 3 packages of children's flour every 2 weeks and he eats 4 slices of bread per day, so that is about 2 ½ slices per day over the ration. I'm not actually hungry, because the reduction in the rations happened gradually, but I'm definitely weak and the bicycling takes a lot of effort.

The children have a rash because we ate a fat rabbit.[41] I have to put ointment on the suppurating swellings and cover them with bandages, but the doctor didn't have much first-aid tape any more (fortunately I did) and not much calcium any more (I also have some of that still).

Tuesday, 14 November. Today was Dientje's birthday and we all sat together in the dusk. Chris poured real tea, with sugar! And there was delicious cake! No light, naturally, and it's very dark today, but it was still cozy. During such a visit you again hear what's going on. In Rotterdam 30,000 men have been conscripted to go to Germany. The food situation of the province of Utrecht[42] is the worst of all the provinces, and also the coal situation. In Groningen [a province in the northeast of the country], for example, they have coal for the whole winter, and we [our household] have one "mud."[43] And they say that very soon we won't get any food at all any more. All rationing coupons have suddenly been declared invalid.

All day, through the thick mist and rain, we heard in the distance the rumbling of artillery fire.

Thursday, 16 November. Today a card from Dicks! From 25 September! So it was out of date, my boy, but oh, for a moment it

---

41 This may be one of the rabbits mentioned earlier.
42 That included us.
43 A "mud" is a measurement of volume and also a container. In quantity, it is about 70 kg [155 lbs] of something like potatoes or coal (Dutch Wikipedia, "Mud," accessed April 14, 2017).

was as though you were a bit closer to us. And then I suddenly long for you so intensely that it hurts physically.

Tomorrow morning early the Molhuizen family is leaving us. That doesn't mean, however, much reduction in the number of evacuees; after that we will have 7—that is to say husband and wife West and 3 children (15, 6, and 2 years old) and an elderly grandfather and grandmother. These 5 families[44] who came as a group have absolutely dreadful quarrels among themselves. The West family regards our house as a paradise of rest and peace and coziness. May this time indeed be a blessing for them.

Friday, 17 November. This morning in the early cold the Molhuizen family departed on a flat farm wagon with a white flag. When I see a wagon with a white flag I get a lump in my throat. Mevr. Molhuizen, butcher's wife, sat in her fur coat plunk on the floor of the wagon and all her children around her and they took along piles of things which, it later turned out, belonged to other people here. My remaining refugees are badly off and I dig up this and that for them. This evening I gave your flannelette shirt to West, who had nothing else, and also your sweater, that old blue one, because he was so cold. I hope you don't mind it too much, Dicks, and I will try to knit another sweater for you before you get home. At this moment I can't let someone else freeze when I know how many clothes you still have in the trunk. Perhaps I'll give him a pair of trousers—he does some chores for me.

We're recovering from a scare: the doctor was afraid that Gerard had diphtheria. Fortunately it's only tonsillitis, but even with that we have to be careful. He has no fever at all; that makes a difference. But his breathing is difficult. He sits in my bed, therefore near us, so cozy. He is such an angelically sweet patient, never for a moment difficult, sits quietly playing with blocks or buttons. With little stuffed animals he lives in his own

---

44 This apparently included the Molhuizen and West families, and possibly others billeted in the neighbourhood.

fantasy world and beams with his little blue peepers. He is so soft and delicate that sometimes I'm afraid for him: life will be so hard for him. He is just like a gentle little doe. Marianneke is like a headstrong little buck; a good heart but with hard little buck's antlers. When she's with me she is the most manageable. Juus always wants to get involved with her upbringing and that makes her irritable. She's right, because two adults against one small child is not fair, and I'm sometimes angry at Juus about it. That's why it's so harmonious and cozy and festive when we're just with the three of us, and then it's as though you are more with us.

They say that a major assault has begun from Venlo to Basel, and that the Germans will sacrifice this part of Holland to the Allies in order to be able to shelter behind the IJsel River. But that would be too good to be true.

Chapter Ten

18 November to 30 December 1944

This chapter begins with what was for Madzy a catastrophic event: her sister Hansje's conversion to Roman Catholicism. Dutch society at the time was shaped by a system of "pillarization," a division into different "pillars" according to different religious beliefs. These divisions applied to all areas of life: "Thus [there were] parallel Catholic, Protestant, and nondenominational [labour] unions, [political] parties, educational institutions, newspapers, radio stations, recreational clubs, and numerous other groups."[1] Since the end of the Second World War this pillarization has greatly diminished,[2] but at that time it was very strong.

Madzy's reaction to her sister's conversion indicates the emotional dimensions of the issue. She felt that she had lost Hansje, almost as though Hansje had died. At an immensely difficult time, this was one more loss, one more shock. And Madzy was deeply hurt by the fact that Hansje decided to convert on the anniversary of their father's death, pushing a button that was already painful for Madzy, linked to another major loss.[3]

---

1   Warmbrunn, p. 158.
2   Judt, *Postwar*, pp. 65–6: "the post-war 'depillarization' of Dutch society, the breaking down of the centuries-long denominational divide between communities of Catholics and Protestants, began with personal links forged in wartime." He specifically cites the links created during the Resistance, when people of different religious affiliations worked together under difficult and dangerous conditions.
3   In future years, this division was bridged, and the two sisters were again on very friendly and even close terms.

Madzy's belief that Catholicism was *wrong*, a turning away from God, shows how deep the roots of the pillarization went. Though frequently analytical of established ways of doing and thinking, she clearly accepted this system unquestioningly.

Nonetheless, in spite of these feelings about Catholicism, Madzy was giving shelter and support to a family of refugees who were Roman Catholic. In fact, on the same day that she wrote about Hansje's conversion, Madzy took part in the Catholic celebration of the golden wedding anniversary of two of the refugees.

By now, as the notorious Hunger Winter set in (see headnote to Chapter Nine), Madzy wrote more and more about food: what we ate, what the rationing allocated, what she was able to obtain by begging and bartering, what she received as gifts. As elsewhere in the diary, when she referred to the food situation, it is often not clear whether she was referring to the country, the village, or our family, but it was bad almost everywhere.

*****

Saturday, 18 November. Today my soul has sunk to the deepest depths of unhappiness and misery. Hansje is going to convert to Catholicism, and moreover has chosen to do so on the anniversary of Vader's death.

I could write about this extensively, Dicks, but it is better that later on we discuss it quietly. However, it is an enormous test which God has given me, and it will take time to accept this. But every evening I will pray to God to give her back to us.

No one except you, Dicksy, will ever know how heavy it was today for me to go to Moeder and to say that we had better regard this as "a bagatelle."[4] I know that that cheered her up, and she doesn't have to know how awful I find it.

Moreover, no one else will see the humour in the fact that just today I had to attend the golden wedding anniversary of my elderly evacuees and therefore that, with the priest and about

---

4   Apparently Iete was also unhappy about Hansje's decision.

fourteen other Catholics, I have been drinking coffee and eating pastries. I gave them a plant which I had bought for 4 guilders.

No one will know how, next Sunday, Hansje will *desecrate* the anniversary of Vader's death for me.

Sunday, 19 November. Today Maarn again received the attention of the Tommies. I had wanted to go to church, but already during breakfast there began a rumbling in the distance, and flying. At 9:30 a couple of dive bombers with machine guns. I still thought about church, but it got steadily worse, and finally I stood in the passage with three children clamped against me (Pank, and Fia West, and with Ger on my arm).

In church this is how it went:[5] when it got so bad (the bombs fell close to the church) there was panic and crying children. Mevr. Jos asked, "Can't they play the organ?" But the organ lady had already disappeared. Then the verger came to say that the service was cancelled. And there should have been baptism. Eventually the baby was baptized in the consistory room because the family had come such a long distance, and Mevr. Jos and Mevr. Bentinck decided that they might as well stay for that.

I spent the night half crying, half coughing, and finally sleeping. Oh, if only next Sunday were past!

Today I first walked with the children, then we had lunch, then I had a little Bible lesson with Marian. She understands it very well.

Wednesday, 22 November. Today a busy day: in pouring rain and storm to Amersfoort for the money for the car.[6] Oh! what a trip it was and how tired I am. Mr. Koolemans Beijnen went with me. Arrived at 10 o'clock, soaked to the skin, at the Kolffs (KB went on to the van den Bents). There I got Dick's signature [on a document about the car?] and on to the city hall. When I had got the money (1,400 guilders) and went out again I found

5   Evidently she had heard this from someone who was there.
6   See entry for 4 June 1942.

that my bicycle had a flat tire, and had it repaired for 10 guilders by Ravensloot.[7] Then I went back to the Kolffs. My ski boots were soaking wet inside, your raincoat had leaked, *enfin*, a sad situation.[8] There I stayed for half an hour drying out a bit and catching my breath, and then bicycled home, heading into the storm which blew from the southwest. On the way I stopped in at de Greef to get 4 kg carrots (our vegetables for this week) and handed in coupons for peas and beans. I was home at quarter to 2. There I found Lies, looking for food. Hadn't seen her in 3 months. Gave her a couple of pounds of brown beans. We don't have any rye yet; maybe we will get 3 pounds per person.

This evening we ate mashed potatoes, and 2 small slices of bread, a little dish of oatmeal boiled in water, without sugar (a little bit of imitation honey) and apples. A cup of coffee surrogate with a bit of milk and no sugar. And compared to what other people have this is an extensive meal. At 9:00 to bed because by way of light we have only a little floating candle fueled with the rapeseed oil that we got instead of other oil on our coupons.

And now I really do see, Dicks, that we will be going into the new year like this. Bread without butter is now ordinary. Juus still eats it with butter and jam, but the butter she buys herself. But I've told her that it seems a shame that she eats 2 slices of bread with the jam she made herself, while there is imitation honey (which she doesn't like).[9] It cuts me to my heart to have to say such a thing. She works so hard. But when she falls asleep at 8:00 already, snoring, it can sometimes irritate me so.

---

7   This may be someone Madzy still knew from the time, only a few years earlier, when she and Wim had lived in Amersfoort. Pneumatic tires were a great rarity by now.

8   The ski boots, cleats removed, were by now her only outdoor footwear; shoes had been unobtainable for at least a couple of years.

9   This is one of those instances where we probably don't understand all the issues, but I've kept the passage because it hints at the human dynamics under such circumstances.

Besides, it's already such an effort, with all this stress, to keep your nerves under control.

Amersfoort looked bad because of the bomb that fell near de Witte,[10] many windows broken. And all the stores closed.

Goodnight, darling, do you think a bit about me? It all weighs so heavily on me, and I am still crying over Hansje.

Thursday, 23 November. Today it was already at 4:00 too dark to see anything clearly. Because it pours and pours rain. I have never seen so much rain at one time as yesterday and today. All our coats hang dripping, and my precious ski boots are soaked inside and out. It will take a week for them to dry because they mustn't stand near the stove (the leather would become stiff and hard). The problems are therefore huge: where can we dry things, and how?[11] I bathed the children in the half-dark and after that there was just enough light to slice the bread. Then until close to 6 we sat in the dusk while I invented the most fantastic stories about dwarves, and the children ate their slices of bread.

This morning I went to Stameren to borrow a pan for my evacuees. There it was also a mess; the staff had been fired by the Germans and there had been all kinds of arguments with Annetje, who was bursting with anger.

I came home with a pan, a little can of milk, a small rye bread, 2 bottles of buttermilk, and Pank on the back of the bicycle, in the pouring rain, with soaking wet feet, hair, gloves, etc. It was after all so ridiculous that Pank and I made up a song and sang it gleefully.

Monday, 27 November. I couldn't fight it any longer physically and was in bed with fever and a headache yesterday, the day of

---

10 Bill's note: "A well-known restaurant."
11 With the limited fuel, the house would be damp, and everything would take a long time to dry, and with the overcrowding there was little room to hang wet things.

Hansje's communion. You might think it affected, Dicks, but at this moment her action is for me such a huge unhappiness that I could *not* fight it. Yesterday while I had that fever I again lay silently crying, just as I did on many evenings before that.

Now I'm so far recovered that I can tackle life again with all its struggle and misery. Gerard is wearing out his clothes, has very few socks any more, and a new pair will have to be knitted quickly with odds and ends of wool. Marianne has a stomach flu. Come on, horse, you have to plod on. That's how it goes, Dicks, and I push on until I can rest in your arms, until I can say, "Here, lad, you take all the responsibilities. Help me, and together we will carry on." "Company in distress makes sorrow less." How strongly I feel that now, and how much I miss your support. But still (just now when I'm at a very low point), I know that the day of reunion is coming steadily closer.

Saturday my shopping trip was again disturbed by much flying and I arrived home pale and with a thumping heart. Even Pank remarked on it.

Yesterday (Sunday) at 9 o'clock they started again, because 30 Germans with horses and carts spent the night round Chris's house. I was terrified for her. The [Allied] fighters dove so low that you could see the fire spitting out of their tailpipes. You also hear, from time to time, a droning bang, and that is apparently a V-1 which is being launched from somewhere near here, but as long as the thing is working properly we won't have any trouble here.[12]

Tuesday, 28 November. A day like today is quite a day. This morning I quickly dressed in the half-dark, did up my hair more or less by feel, and washed (sort of)—but come on, horse! Otherwise Juus can't manage to have everything ready in time, and Pankske has to be well cared for. I still felt wobbly on my

---

12 It was when the V-1's engine stopped and the weapon fell that it was dangerous.

legs. Our breakfast we managed mainly by touch until finally at 8:30 the growing daylight began to help us. Then I tidied the bedroom and the living room, and then I had had it. Just when I was sitting down, Moeder arrived and then, yes, you're busy for an hour and a half giving her some support and cheering her up a bit. Really, Dicks, that also takes an effort. Then quickly prepared a meal, ate it, fed the children, washed the dishes. Then another diver came to the door asking for food; he got the leftover that had been meant for our supper.

At 2:00 I rolled exhausted into bed for a rest. When I'm lying down it's OK; my spirit can manage if my body can only rest. This afternoon Gerard was bothersome, not like him, and I'm worried that he is also getting sick. And then at 4:00 the awful darkness begins already. Until 6:00 we manage; we prepare supper by touch. The children sat with their feet towards the stove and we sang songs. Chris came, dripping wet (because it rains constantly) to have a chat in the dark. We ate supper, we did the dishes, the children to bed (actually unwashed but I was too tired and Juus too busy), and now I'll also turn in. My back is breaking and my feet are blocks of ice.

Thursday, 30 November. Moeder Iete is kind and good, but .... This morning when I came home from doing errands I found her sorting beans (we suddenly got 700 gr per person!) with the words: "We're just sorting them, and then Juus will set them to soak and then tomorrow you can eat soup; I will bring the strainer but you'll have to be careful with it!"[13] So Iete is now also going to dictate my menu! Will I have absolutely nothing to say any more? No, dear Moeder, we are *not* going to eat soup tomorrow.

---

13 Madzy wrote to Virginia Donaldson and Rosalie Worthington, in a letter of September 1945, that kitchen utensils were wearing out and were (even then) not replaceable.

Saturday, 2 December. This morning I suddenly regained some courage and went to Joost. It was as though his heart called me. Juffr. Toos said that he often opens the door to see if we might be coming.[14] On the bicycle path I saw that 2 big bombs had fallen about 75 metres (yards) behind me the last time. Joost was so happy, but all of a sudden I was afraid that they will also conscript him to go and dig. May God take him to Himself first.[15]

This afternoon again a real homey bath-day in a little tub. Gerard again has that nasty rash that causes him a lot of itching, but oh Dicks if you could see him sitting building with his little blocks, so sweet and full of concentration. My paradise now is to have the whole house empty except for the children and me (without Juus and without Moeder in the neighbourhood: by the way, she came every day last week, so that I can hardly bear it any more) and entirely clean and tidy, Willem in the garden, waiting for you. With that lovely vision I will go to sleep.

Tuesday, 5 December: St. Nicolaas[16] 1944: Whatever misery we are going through, however perilous the circumstances in which we live, the children had a wonderful Sinterklaas. There was lots of excitement, and setting shoes ready in advance was great fun, and today there was a real Sinterklaas party at Huis te Maarn![17] What a delight, what pleasure! Little Gerard was the big success; with his high voice he sang a song ("Sinterklaas kapoentje") for

---

14 Juffrouw Toos was the oldest of the three sisters looking after Joost.

15 Joost was about thirty-seven at this time; his Down syndrome and total lack of physical fitness should have made him ineligible for the labour draft, but Madzy's fears were not groundless.

16 St. Nicolaas, or Sinterklaas—the Eve of St. Nicholas (5 December)—is a big event in the Netherlands, with parties, presents, and fun and games. The children set their shoes, traditionally wooden shoes, by the stove or chimney down which St. Nicolaas would come. In the shoes would be a tuft of hay for the saint's horse.

17 No doubt Chris van Notten's visit on the previous Tuesday (see above) included planning for this event.

the whole company of 60 people.[18] It was a wonderful distraction for all the children, because their anxiety level is very high.[19]

I had decided, as a treat, to bake pancakes. They were thick, made from a mixture of flour, 1 egg, little milk, lots of water, and almost no butter. But they were still delicious and we had jam and even sugar on them.

Because, oh Dicks, the times are becoming so wretched. Even here we are hungry.[20] Sometimes I can buy an additional loaf of bread per week for 5 guilders, and then I do that, because Marian is constantly hungry and then I can't say, "Child, I have nothing." The upshot is that I try to fill *my* stomach with potatoes, but that means that I have to get up 3 times during the night because I can't digest them.

Today I also decided that we will sleep without bed-sheets. *You*'ve been doing that for 2½ years already, dearest, therefore why not we? Now that we do the laundry at home there is nowhere to dry them, and no soap.

And now, today, disaster struck: the "fork" of my bicycle broke in two places. Out of sheer necessity, for emergencies, I had your bicycle put in order but hardly dare to ride it for fear of confiscation.[21] So I'm doing everything on foot, so long as my ski boots hold out.

And now again a big camp of Germans is coming here; it appears that they are going to repair the railway track again and will defend it with strong antiaircraft artillery installations. That won't be a lot of fun for us! Already I almost don't dare to

18 Gerard was two and a half years old at the time.
19 A passage like this gives more insight into our daily lives. Madzy would find time during her busy days to teach Gerard the song, or at least to make sure that he could sing it well enough for the performance. She contributed to the festivities by reading aloud a poem that she had written for the occasion. The writing of humorous verses was part of the typical Sinterklaas fun. The poem was preserved in Dientje's diary, where I found it. See Appendix B.
20 Conditions in the cities were worse.
21 Men's bicycles were confiscated much more often than women's.

cross the railway tracks when there are airplanes overhead, so then I will hardly dare to go out the door. But because of the food shopping I have to do it.

Because of the lack of light we go to bed at 8:30, and then between blankets. For me that's a big thing because, Dicks, you know how I value having sheets. But if you can stand it, so can I.

There are many people who at this moment can't manage any more: no food, no freedom, and all the misery around us. The dike near Arnhem has been breached so that the Betuwe[22] is under water, the Canadians have pulled back. But when I did my food shopping today I thought all of a sudden, "Now I know why I can still bear everything so cheerfully: because Dicks is supporting me from the distance." And then suddenly you felt so close by!

The business with Hansje still makes me intensely unhappy, mainly because she treats everything that I consider holy in such a lighthearted way.

Sunday, 10 December. Evening. My dearest Dicks, now I'm going to have a quiet talk with you; in this way at least I have contact with you. Since St. Nicolaas I've been constantly on the go to look for food, because there is such a shortage and I have become *so* thin that I'm afraid that if I fall short I won't be able to be for my children what I have to be. From Vlastuin I got a bottle of milk (the dairy plant was bombed and we get nothing any more from the milk store) and 2 kg old [dried?] green peas. From van Beuningen I got a bottle of skim milk and 5 pounds of ground

---

22 The Betuwe was a fertile area not far south of us, famous for fruit production (Wikipedia, "Betuwe," accessed April 21, 2017). It was where Madzy went to get cherries (see entry for 2 July 1942).

wheat.[23] Someone was able to barter 3 sheets and 3 pillowcases for me against 35 pounds of wheat.[24]

Then I decided yesterday to go to Rika.[25] It had snowed hard during the night, but better to go out then than in fine weather, and I slogged through it on your bicycle. It was an indescribable journey, 1½ hours there and 2 hours back. I left the house at 9 o'clock and was back at 1:30. I came home with 7 pounds of rye, and kind Rika gave me a whole piece of balkenbrei[26] and a bag of green peas and all the makings for pea soup—sausage, bone with meat on it, two pig feet, and onions. Also 5 pounds of rye flour. I gave her my red woollen dress. That soup—oh, my boy, how we did enjoy it; naturally it was our whole meal, we ate only one slice of bread in it,[27] without butter, so it saved on bread and butter. That makes a big difference over the whole week. Rika also gave me milk, and now we can have an extra cup of coffee. How important it is, that food, also especially for the children to have enough.

But about yesterday: the trip was actually too heavy for me, especially because of the thick snow and mud, because I sometimes sank in over the pedals, and in fact I had to walk for quite a distance. And truly, Dicks, at the end I could hardly go any further because of the hunger. In the morning I did have a little

---

23 C. S. van Beuningen and his family were an important resource for Madzy in the next few months. On Anderstein, their estate near Maarsbergen, they had a dairy farm (Wikipedia, "Anderstein," accessed on September 8, 2017). Her specifying that what she got was "ground wheat" suggests that what she usually received was the unground grain.

24 This may have been some of the linen that was no longer being used on our beds.

25 See entry for 8 October 1943.

26 Balkenbrei was a sort of meat loaf made at the end of the pig-slaughtering process to use "the less desirable parts" of the carcass. These were cooked, mixed with other ingredients, and formed into a loaf, slices of which were then fried (Wikipedia, "Balkenbrei," accessed September 29, 2016).

27 "In it" no doubt means that we dunked the dry bread in the soup.

dish of porridge made with water and a thick slice of bread *with* butter, and at Rika's a cup of milk, and Rika had offered me a slice of bread: notice, Dicks, my former servant, who understood that I was hungry (after all, I had come to beg food of her), offered me bread. I didn't accept it. But when I was in the middle of a lonely stretch of the road I thought, "I can't go on any further because of the hunger, but if I stop here to have a rest then I'll never reach home."[28]

I got home, exhausted and with heart palpitations, but I again had this and that in the house. I rested for an hour and had something to eat, then went to fetch the milk and the loaf of bread that had been baked with our wheat.[29] Then the children in bath, then myself. The bathing happens only in a basin with a little kettle of warm water. *Enfin*, we get clean.

I have to have quite a bit of food in the house, Dicks, because everyone who comes to visit is hungry. Friday morning first Moeder, who got a little bowl of oatmeal porridge; she is so thin and walks so much. Then suddenly Tante Lot Roest van Limburg[30] and Tante Lotje Suermondt[31] on the bicycle. Tante Lotje looked ashy grey because in Doorn she had been overcome by cold and hunger. Both were cobbled together again with coffee

---

28 This passage is full of nuances. Madzy went to barter, rather than beg; she had the dress to give in exchange for food. The glass of milk appears to have been acceptable as hospitality for a visitor, but the slice of bread would appear to be considered as charity and therefore (to Madzy) not acceptable because of her pride. Part of this complex of meanings reflects social mores of an earlier time, and part reflects the new social relationships that were evolving because of the wartime conditions: Madzy, Rika's former employer, was now in a subordinate (needy) position.

29 Bill, in his notes to a later passage, wrote that the baker, lacking coal to heat his oven, was heating it with a wood fire, then raking that out and putting in the loaves to be baked—the same system that was used in earlier periods in history and in pioneer times in Canada.

30 A cousin of Wim's father.

31 A sister of Wim's father.

and our last milk. (We adults don't get any milk any more on the coupons, Marian 1 L skim milk per week, Gerard still 5¼ L milk per week.) In the afternoon came Juffrouw Gleichman,[32] cold and wet, because her room has no heat yet, and hungry: therefore again 2 cups of tea and 2 little slices of our home-steamed rye bread with a scraping of butter. (We adults get no butter any more, only Gerard ¼ pound every two weeks.)

And so we come to today. Because the weather was good I hardly dared to go to church. Last week I also ran back, and the two weeks before that there was constant shooting in Maarn, and bombing. This time the church service was again at de Hoogt.[33] I went on your bicycle, but at that moment the planes began to fly and one Tommy came over very low because just then a German vehicle was passing me. Then I was again so frightened that I jumped off and wanted to turn around but had to let my heart calm down, and just at that moment Dientje came by with the van Notten boys so I went on with them. Fortunately there was no flying during the service.

So the days go; in the daylight hours we rush through all the things left undone during the preceding dark hours. About 7 "light" hours against 17 hours of dusk and darkness. Fortunately only 11 days more and then we will have had the shortest, darkest day. The nights are long, but the children often wake me, sometimes 10 or 12 times per night, and then each time I have to get a match, light a candle[34] ... oh, Dicks, with children everything is *still* more primitive and difficult. If you think of the potties that

---

32 Miss Gleichman had been Madzy's music teacher when she was a child and Madzy, because she loved singing, had warm feelings toward her. Miss Gleichman was evacuated to Maarn, where she was one of the many people living in Huis te Maarn. During this winter, when there was no running water, Madzy (sometimes? often?) took pails of water to her.

33 In a later passage she mentioned that the church itself was occupied by refugees for a time.

34 Actual candles were very scarce, so probably she was referring to one of the little homemade oil-fueled lights.

have to be emptied, because the children are not allowed to use the toilet for fear of their getting a rash that the evacuees have. It's impossible to describe to you all the primitive details of our life nowadays, but I will bless the day on which we again have electricity. No, there's only one day that I look forward to, and that's the day on which we are again with the four of us alone together![35]

Tuesday, 12 December. Still 9 days and then we have the shortest day, and we can *say*—even if we don't yet actually *see*—that the days are getting longer. There is again a lot of billeting of Germans in Doorn; at Stameren a staff unit, and we in Maarn will probably get that too. Today we were for a little while alone with the three of us, which was wonderful. But oh! how tired my back is! From Suus a cry of despair; I should go to her tomorrow, and in the afternoon to the Everwijn Lange's to thank for *all* the presents.[36]

Wednesday, 13 December. Suus is really desperate. I always find it so awful when older people look for support from the younger ones. I feel that when you're older you should be proud to be

---

35 Other writers also described the living conditions as primitive. "It is impossible," reported Dr. Pfister of the International Red Cross, who visited the Netherlands in March in connection with "relief" negotiations, to his superiors in Geneva, "to describe what radical and dire consequences the lack of coal is having for the Netherlands, and how incredibly primitive life has become." Dr. Pfister reported that at the beginning of March, 20 to 30 percent of arable land was flooded, and since the pumps could not be used (because of the lack of coal), the sewerage systems in the cities no longer worked. The water levels in the lavatories rose, causing serious health hazards. Emergency hospitals— very primitive places—were set up in addition to the regular ones; all hospitals saw large numbers of patients with "deficiency" diseases" (van der Zee, p. 189). Beevor (p. 671) wrote that the malnutrition "exposed everyone to disease, especially typhoid and diphtheria."

36 Presents, at that time, almost certainly meant food.

allowed to support the younger people.[37] But Moeder Hans and Suus look for support from me (also Moeder Iete, but not nearly so much, and in a different way).

I have trouble with my breast again, now both breasts, and that always makes me rather tired.

Friday, 15 December. Today was another bad one for me. I went to Maarsbergen this afternoon to try to get meat and milk from van Beuningen. It was nice fresh weather, for the first time no rain, and in the distance there has already for the last 24 hours been heavy shooting, but there was not much flying. However, when I was half-way there three fighters began diving. And then I'm no longer a human being. I plunge into the woods and can't breathe any more because of the heart palpitations. They fired their guns close by. I would have turned around but just then Nico Kamp and Julia ter Kuilen and her brother came along and I went on with them and came home with meat and milk.[38] But even on the return trip I could hardly ride the bicycle because of the heart palpitations. Should I ask the doctor? I feel that I'm gradually becoming too weak, nervous, and underfed. Now I also have chilblains, lumbago, and rheumatism. I'm skin-and-bone and have a "potato tummy."

Saturday, 16 December. Evening. Do you remember how cozy it used to be on these evenings, Dicks? Do you still nourish yourself with these memories? In Leeuwarden we so cozily had a bath[39] and then ate raisin bread. Remember? How we could eat in those days![40] Today we've also had our baths, in the large basin, while it's light, therefore about 3:30. First Juus, then the

---

37 Madzy was thirty-four.
38 Bill's note: "Nico Kamp was a very distant relative of ours, living near Driebergen." August de Man's information is that Julia was also our distant relative.
39 Bill's note: "No bathroom." So this was a tub placed near the stove.
40 But neither of them was ever overweight.

children, and then I. We empty the basin on the lawn and then ...
who's next? And then in the dusk, around the stove, we eat a
piece of rye bread, the children with butter. But everything is so
sad. Everyone is craving light and spring. And we still have to get
through the whole winter. And yet, when January comes we've
struggled through a fair bit.

Dicks, do you know what I do at the moment to keep myself
going? While bicycling along the bleak paths to get milk and
food, while lying awake during the long nights, I imagine how,
later on, with the four of us we will go to America to build there
a new future for our children. At the moment I see the future as
being very dark for our country. If only you knew how much has
already been destroyed. Brabant and Zeeland totally ruined, the
Betuwe and other areas under water. All the cities laid waste, the
country plundered empty.[41] Before anything can again flourish
in this land you and I will have been under the green sod for a
long time. The question is, "Should we stay here to help with
the rebuilding?" or "Should we seek another country and make
room here and thereby make it easier for those who stay?" They
say that probably many people will *have* to emigrate because at
first this country won't be able to feed such a large population.
It's something to think about.

Today there was an announcement: there are new coupons!
All of us to the stores, where we waited for a long time in line.
What did I bring home? 1 little package of wheat flour for Gerard,
and for each of us ... 50 gr [¼ cup] of sugar.

Sunday, 17 December. Evening. The primitive conditions get
worse; Gerard on the pot while we're eating our meal, Marianneke
who eats messily and is disobedient, Moeder Iete who comes
with all her unpleasant criticisms—I can't handle it any more.

---

41 "From September 1944 on, German economic policies turned to acts
   of outright spoliation involving the wholesale removal of manpower,
   machinery, and rolling stock [from the Netherlands] to Germany"
   (Warmbrunn, p. 69).

The mess in this one room, that is completely wearing out and stays dirty even though I try to tidy up, the crowding, the noise, the darkness, oh, Dicks, I could scream or, out of sheer protest, crawl into bed. But even then I'm not free. Nowhere can I come to myself, and then I think of you who are prisoner in that camp and also can't walk out, just for a few minutes, to draw your breath in nature.

And then all the unhappiness everywhere. My evacuee came back from Arnhem today (after many futile trips, when we had already given up hope for him, which caused me great anxiety) to tell us that there is nothing in his house any more. The Germans have a horse and wagon standing in front of the houses and take *everything*: a violin without strings, tea services, children's clothes.[42] He has lost everything. And it's the same with thousands of other families. What scoundrels, Dicks. And yesterday I was at Vlastuin's, who said, "Mevrouw, before the Germans have left, they will have taken everything from us too." What a poverty-stricken country will be left for us.

And so the days pass in sad darkness, and still we have to see the Light of Christmas shining ahead of us. Yes, I see it all right, but it's often darkened by the darkness on earth.

If they start looting here, what will we do? I don't know.

And then I'm also afraid that my health will give up before you come home to take over the lead. Moeder stands ready like a shark to take over the leadership; I already have to defend myself with tooth and nail to prevent being pushed aside, but if I should get sick I'm lost.

---

42 The looting of Arnhem "was done with German thoroughness. There were teams specializing in textiles, others in china, there were squads on the look-out for sewing machines and others for vacuum-cleaners. Specially trained women ... were experts in the detection of hiding-places. Floors were ripped apart, wallpaper torn away, and gardens dug up in the hope of discovering the treasures that the evacuated Arnhem [residents] had left behind. Finally, the goods were stowed in trucks and driven to the different regions of Germany" (van der Zee, p. 222).

Monday, 18 December. Today I pedaled once more to Joost; he was so delighted with the surprise. I brought him this and that, and he helped me load the bicycle with all kinds of things that Moeder wanted from there, including a blanket. When I had the bicycle loaded I was again beset by fears for the return trip; these days I'm so tired and my heart is so uncooperative. But then I was given a delicious slice of bread with butter *and* sugar, and so the return trip went fine. Still I was tired—imagine! from that short trip. Sometimes I get such heart palpitations that everything goes fuzzy in front of my eyes and I can't go any farther. If this goes on I will ask Ad [van Kekem]'s advice.

Tuesday, 19 December. We're rather downhearted because a new offensive has begun from the German side against Belgium and Luxemburg, which is having some success.[43] What is *now* ahead of us? Is it the last convulsive movement or is it new [German] strength? What will we still have to endure? Also for days now there has been more artillery fire in the Betuwe, and we've also had more artillery installations set up near here. One shell exploded right over our house. The children therefore have strict orders: "As soon as they start shooting, go into the passage."

Today I made the rounds to gather some more food from a few reliable suppliers—I got 1 kg potatoes from each. Altogether I got about 10 kg and so I can bring happiness to some friends who have nothing.[44]

For the rest I'm irritable and tired, have a lot of trouble with rheumatism in my left shoulder and sciatica in my left leg. From time to time I eat a bit of sugar because otherwise my heart won't work at all any more. Everything irritates me: the clutter and the dirt in this one room with the dirty laundry and the things to be ironed[45]—with the mess from firewood, pans, pails of

---

43 This was the Battle of the Bulge.

44 A "round" of about ten stops was a long trip.

45 This would now have to be done with an old-fashioned iron heated on the stove.

water, toys, children who hang around on chairs and tables, etc. etc. etc., not to mention children having to go on the potty. And then nearly every day visitors coming to criticize, and Juus who always leaves the door standing open so that the evacuees can hear everything we say. *Enfin*, dear Dicks, life is not easy without you, as you see. With you there would at least be someone against whom I could snuggle, and all would be well again and I would again be able to manage everything.

Thursday, 21 December. Today a messy day. As always, I walked with Marian to the little school. I had a bulging tote bag because I wanted to send something to Hansje for Christmas, and I had to take that to de heer Posthuma, who regularly bicycles to Utrecht. I gave Hansje (you may never forgive me!) our bottle of champagne, but if we ever get to the point of drinking it, it will be a long way off—and then we won't need champagne. Oh, Dicks, forgive me, but I need to give something and she can use it so well and willingly, and we don't need it. For me at this time alcohol and all that luxury is not necessary, it's just unnecessary baggage.

Enfin, to return to my day today: from de heer Posthuma I heard that Hansje was planning to come *here* today! That again gave me a fright,[46] but I walked to Alberts [the baker]—took wheat to him for our loaf of bread for Christmas—and then to the dairy store (no milk), to Pater (no more wicks for the little lights) to the little school, and back home. That was a long walk of more than an hour and a half on heavy ski boots.

And then all of a sudden there was Hansje. In spite of everything it was enjoyable because I love her very much, but the atmosphere was strained because, at her request, we were not supposed to talk about "it." Treated her of course with all sorts of things, and from her received beautiful Christmas presents,

---

46 The fright would have been caused by her awareness of all the emotional issues connected with Hansje's conversion.

including a wonderful tote bag, that I desperately needed for all the lugging. She looked very well, but I could have wept the whole time. After a hot meal she left at 2 o'clock, visiting Joost on her way home. When I talk with her I'm constantly on edge, to avoid saying something wrong. It's dead tiring and intensely saddening.

After that Moeder came, and that was just as tiring. Then came Mevr. van Beuningen, who brought us at least 2 pounds of meat for the holidays! Including steak! I didn't know how to thank her.

And now, after all the other worries, I'm sitting here with an obstinate attack of heart palpitations that I can't get rid of, and full of sadness because only now do I realize how *completely* I've lost Hansje.

Sunday, 24 December, Christmas Eve, 9:30. The whole house is in wonderful peace and I'm sitting by the fire, which gives me just enough light to write this.[47] My Dicks, I don't have to tell you how very much I miss you on this evening. It is a gnawing sense of longing. But beyond that there is a sorrow in me, a despair about everything, that pervades my whole being. Besides that, however, I've already for days seen the light of Christ coming closer and in these days that gives me hope. So does the waxing moon, the hard frost, the bright sun—in a word, all the light in nature after that endless series of misty, rainy, dark days.

And so I sit close to my unsteady little light, that constantly abandons me, and think of you, my only love. I try to imagine what you are experiencing and wrestling with, and it is as though you are very close to me. I'm so grateful for everything that I have: your love, the two children, and everything around me.

This afternoon I held a Christmas service for all the people living in our house, with a couple of lights on our little tree, that

---

47 The little upright heater had an upper door that, when opened, would provide some light for anything (such as a book or a piece of knitting) held very close to it.

is serving for already the 4th year.[48] How will it fill its function next year? Will you be here then? Will we still be here? I asked myself that last year too, and the little note that I then put in the box of Christmas decorations I will enclose here as a noteworthy little document.[49]

Oh, my Dicksy-dicks, how much longer ...?

Monday, 25 December. Christmas is fortunately again behind us. It was a day full of good things. This morning by the Christmas tree I again read the Christmas story to the children. Then came four Germans who wanted to billet themselves here, but it was too small for them. Then we sang Christmas carols with piano accompaniment until 5 anti-aircraft guns came rattling by on the road. Then we went out. It's clear and freezing—bitterly cold—and we put on many layers of clothing to save our calories. Moeder had come to drink a cup of coffee and then walked with us until we were at the family Jos' house, which was our destination. At 1:00 we had dinner (meat! and canned peas and rice pudding made with half milk and half water!) and at 3:00 we went with the four of us to Stameren to visit Annetje and Floris, where we got *real* tea and *white* bread—pinched from the Germans—to serve instead of cake! By moonlight home through the snowy woods. Then I really missed you! And now with all our clothes on we go under the blankets.

Friday, 29 December. Yesterday I received three letters from you, Dicks; how delighted I was! If you only knew how dear every letter is to me.

Today I decided to light the stove here in our bedroom,[50] and oh! the luxury of a *dry* bedroom, once the fire, after a lot of

---

48 It was a live tree.
49 See end of Chapter Five.
50 "Stove" is Bill's translation, but in the entry for 17 January (below) Madzy called it a fireplace. I remember a small fireplace in a corner of what at that time was our bedroom, adjacent to what was then the living

trouble, burned well. I want to let it burn until the coal is finished and then we'll see what happens.

For weeks already I've had heart palpitations. It has been getting bad and I went to ask Ad about it. He looked grave; I'm too thin (there's nothing to be done about that) and I do too much. There's something wrong with my heart, it's not just anxiety. I now have a week of "house arrest" and a stiff dose of digitalis and valerian. God will help me. But how can I keep it a secret from Iete?[51]

Saturday, 30 December. I feel much better today; my heart is again as calm as ever, calmed by the medicines. My legs are also not so swollen any more. In two days my house arrest will be over and I can go out again. Tomorrow New Year's Eve and then comes the new year *with* my Dicks!

---

room. I imagine it was in fact a coal-burning grate or a little stove-type unit built into the fireplace. Bill noted that it was unsuitable for burning wood. In this desperate winter, Madzy was using up the last bit of coal she still had. In the entry for 14 November 1944, she referred to having one "mud," and Dientje, in her diary, recorded that on 3 December she and Chris had brought us a bit of coal as a Sinterklaas present, leaving it secretly near the door.

51 As we've seen, Madzy was afraid that if she became seriously ill Iete would use the opportunity to be even more helpful/interfering. It's not hard to see the other side of this: that Iete, worrying about her daughter's difficult situation, just wanted to help but was doing it in a tactless and overbearing way. The wartime conditions put an almost unbearable strain on all relationships.

Chapter Eleven

1 January to 6 February 1945

Part of the story behind Madzy's narrative is the life of the local Resistance, and if we know what we're looking for we can catch glimpses. Some of the war news that she wrote in the diary after her radio stopped functioning may have come from the network of divers and the Resistance. I have already commented on the possible significance of her frequent tidying of the barn and on the many inconsistencies between her reports of food that she obtained and what we actually ate.

Many of those engaged in the Resistance were, to all appearances, normally-functioning members of the community, but they had a behind-the-scenes life of opposing the occupying regime, and that included helping divers. It was dangerous, and many lost their lives.

Madzy knew at least something about this. Many years later she told us that she had lent English-language books to downed Allied airmen. These included her copies of the Jalna books, by the Canadian writer Mazo de la Roche, which by the end of the war were very battered—obviously much read. Her friend VaVa Hoogeweegen sheltered people active in the Resistance and also provided accommodation for a clandestine radio transmitter and its operators.[1] VaVa helped to hide at least one of the Allied

---

1   Caspers, p. 144. Dientje Blijdenstein, in a note added to her diary when it was safe to do so, wrote that in February 1944 VaVa Hoogeweegen

soldiers who had survived the Battle of Arnhem but had been unable to escape to safety with the rest of the evacuated troops.[2] The Idenburg family, mentioned in Chapter Nine in connection with their straying goat, were active in the Resistance, printing an underground newspaper and harbouring Allied soldiers.[3]

Madzy certainly knew far more than is recorded in the diary, but, as I indicated in the Preface, it would have been dangerous to write such things down. For instance, her reference on 28 November 1944, to "another diver" coming to the house begging for food indicates that this was a fairly common occurrence. Dientje also recorded that people frequently came to the door asking for food.

Some years after the war Madzy wrote a narrative in which there was probably some slight fictionalizing but that was mainly factual. She wrote:

> During World War II our village was teeming with underground activities. When, after the war, a map of Holland was published on which each active underground group [was] marked with a round black dot, the space around our village on the map was one large black blotch ....[4]
>
> One of the men responsible for so much ... ink was the retired minister of our church. ... "Dominee," as he was called in the village, was a short, portly man with snow-white hair .... When the war broke out, Dominee was seventy-eight, but this ripe old age did not prevent him from taking an active and very perilous part in

---

had already for months had two English officers with a secret radio transmitter in her house. It's likely that, after the silencing of the radios, some of Madzy's information about the larger war picture came from VaVa's guests.

2   Van der Zee, p. 130.
3   Van der Zee, p. 141.
4   This was largely because our area was wooded, unlike much of the Netherlands, and offered hiding places.

underground matters. For a long time the enemy did not suspect the charming old minister .... Only much later in the war years did they become suspicious, and [they paid] him several unannounced visits at all hours of the day and night, but they were never able to find proof to corroborate their suspicions.

His friends warned him often. ... To them Dominee would listen quietly, and then answer: "I am an old man, I have few years ahead of me. Allow me to do for God and Her Majesty what little I think I can do."

... I never knew the extent of Dominee's part in the underground work; one never spoke of these things, one either guessed or knew. I knew he had helped Jews, [and] hidden young men who had to keep [out of sight of] the enemy; his wife had nursed a Canadian who had parachuted down one night and broken a leg while landing. This Canadian had stayed in their house, and operated a secret [radio] sender for a while.[5]

Another brief glimpse into Resistance activity in the Maarn area comes from the account of the escape of General Sir John Hackett, commander of the 4th Parachute Brigade, which landed at Arnhem. During the fighting, Hackett received severe abdominal injuries, was taken prisoner by the Germans, and was put into a (by then German-controlled) hospital in Arnhem. Members of the Dutch Resistance smuggled him out of the hospital and found shelter for him with a family in Ede. When he was sufficiently recovered to ride a bicycle for many miles, the Resistance helped him to reach the Allied-controlled territory south of the rivers. His escape route took him through Maarn, where, for three days, he was given shelter by the Idenburg family.[6]

*****

Wednesday, 3 January. Nothing new, only I again had a bout of severe heart palpitations in spite of the medicine. My helpers are

---

5   "Our Dominee," written in English, never published.
6   General Sir John Hackett, *I Was a Stranger*, passim; van der Zee, p. 141ff.

abandoning me; no Willem,[7] [and for a few days] no household help. But starting tomorrow Jansje will come regularly to help me. The rooms are so horribly dirty, and cleaning them is too much for me.

Thursday, 4 January. The doctor was here today. Fortunately he was very satisfied with the state of my heart, but I still have to continue for another three weeks as a heart patient and then we'll see. It's possible that I will recover entirely, but I have to take it slowly. Until Saturday I'm not allowed to walk farther than to Christie, and on Monday I'm allowed to bicycle, but only as far as the viaduct[8] if there is no wind, and I'm not allowed to tackle heavy roads and hills. And on Wednesday he will come and have another look at me. I do so want to go to Doorn to the dentist with Marian, but there's no question of that. I have at least 3 cavities, and Marian 2. I also have trouble with my eyes (itchiness and redness) because of the poor light. For many of us it's high time that the war ends. For many it's already much too late.

Friday, 5 January. I see more and more clearly that we will have to go to America.[9] In the first place because of the children, to be able to provide them again with the good food that they need. Then because of their future. Then because of your future. Then because I have my money in the bank there.[10] I'm getting

---

7   Even though he had been drafted to work for the Germans, Willem seems to have been living at home in Maarn, not in a camp, and up to then had apparently still been doing a few chores for Madzy. However, what Madzy wrote here suggests that this had stopped.

8   The viaduct led under the much-bombed railway tracks.

9   Wim, in the camp, was thinking along the same lines. The fact that they had lived in the United States before the war made emigration easy to contemplate.

10   In a memoir written in his old age, Bill wrote: "In 1939, after Germany had invaded Poland, we had sent $6,000 to [a] bank in New York to be invested for safekeeping."

used to the idea. I'm teaching Pankie English words.[11] In my imagination, I am already selling my belongings to our evacuees, who have nothing. We have to start entirely anew without old baggage, and the things that we acquire will be *simple, few*, but *good*. Oh, Dicks, if we can only make a start!

Saturday, 6 January. The children found the story of the Three Kings so marvelous! I read it aloud by the light from the open door in the stove, after we had all had our baths and were drying our hair.

Today the railway line was bombed again, close by the van Kekems' house; Ds. Koolhaas was walking around sweeping up the glass from his broken windows. There's no new window-glass to be had.

Today for the first time in a long while I had no heart palpitations. I could sing and dance, it feels so wonderfully pleasant and healthy.

Sunday, 7 January. Juus's birthday, and in spite of all the wretchedness we spent it cheerfully. From me she received a rabbit, which all of us gobbled up with canned peas, potatoes in their skins, soup first, an apple as dessert—in other words, a feast of Lucullus. For the rest, she received a bit of butter and as a treat a slice of wheat bread *with* real butter (50 guilders per pound[12]) and some cheese. Furthermore a cup of *real* coffee and a cup of *real* tea. Well, could it be any better? I'm so grateful that we can still provide a treat for such a day as this. It's so important to Juus, and she really appreciated it. Today I felt again how much I love her, how she is entwined with our lives, as much a part of us as a leg or an arm.

---

11 At some point—perhaps now—Madzy read *Winnie the Pooh* to us in English, translating into Dutch but teaching us a bit of English as she went. She borrowed the book from VaVa Hoogeweegen, who was English.

12 This would be the black-market price. We remember that Wim's (active) salary was 125 guilders per month.

Thursday, 11 January. Today again a bottle of rapeseed oil on the coupons (180 gr per person); that means tummy nourishment, and light. Again there's shooting in the distance and the house trembles. Walked to the doctor and in that neighbourhood saw the damage from Saturday's bombs. What a sad sight, a house half destroyed, and all the broken windows and roofs round about.

We have deep snow and cold; what a misery for all the thousands of divers who have been newly added—because all the men aged from 17 to 41 in Noord and Zuid Holland and Utrecht have been called up.[13] You constantly see boys walking past, heading across the IJssel. There is a campaign to send children from here to Friesland and Groningen because here they are starving.[14]

Saturday, 13 January. There is heavy artillery fire in the distance; could something be happening again? It sounds like approaching thunder. All the men from 17 to 41 are in hiding; the world becomes emptier and more female.

Monday, 15 January. Today for the first time since 29 December I went out "on the black path." Annetje and I went to van Beuningen where they would be threshing rye. The road was icy like a mirror, and in less than no time we lay with our men's

---

13 These were the three most densely populated western provinces, which included us. It went without saying that many of these men would go underground rather than obey the conscription order. As for the "misery" that Madzy mentions, it was not only the actual cold that was a hardship for divers hiding in the woods or in barns and other unheated shelters but also the fact that any tracks they and their helpers left in the snow would betray them.

14 In the provinces of Friesland and Groningen, in the northeast of the country, there was still food—which, because of the railway strike, the German embargo on moving food, and the severe winter (which froze the canals and prevented barge traffic), could not be moved to the western provinces (van der Zee, p. 154).

bicycles on the road, so that we had to walk there and back. We will get a good amount. We still have to fetch it—it was not yet winnowed—but they will keep it for us until it's no longer so slippery.

I noticed that I could manage the trip again. That gives me courage. Fortunately it's thawing now.

Wednesday, 17 January. Yesterday I walked to Joost. In itself it's already an achievement, but this was doubled by the fact that the road was icy, so that you went backwards more than forwards, and I had to go there and back in the morning so as to be home in time for [mid-day] dinner. I left at 9 o'clock and was home at 1:15, almost 1½ hour there and 1½ hour for the trip home, not counting the distance I covered in Driebergen to visit Juffrouw Toos in the hospital and to ask for help from Julia ter Kuile in the event that Juffrouw Toos should die and we would have to find another home for Joost.

For 20 days we could burn a fire in the fireplace but now the coal is finished and the clammy cold penetrates our rooms again.

Friday, 19 January. Worries pile themselves up. Juffrouw Toos died this morning. What can now be done with poor, poor Joost, who depended so much on her? How glad I would be for the lad himself if he were to pass away, then he would be free of all the sorrow. Moeder wants him to live with a nurse. I had thought to bring him here for the war months. I am his official guardian and have a voice in the decision. Oh, Dicks, what should be done?

And then: because of all the meddling of Moeder and Juus I feel that I am sometimes unreasonable towards my children— yes, that I even lose contact with them, or rather that I don't have the contact that I would like to have. Darling, do you understand that sometimes my mood sinks and that I need all the support that God can give me?

Sunday, 21 January. Is it possible that you might come home earlier than I expect, my Dicks? It would be too beautiful to be true, but the Russians have taken Tilsit and Krakow and Warsaw, and are pushing into Germany on all sides. We have to continue to set our patience on "high."

Outside it snows and snows. It's a bitter winter, high snow, hard frost. This morning Bob and Jet Hudig arrived here on skis with little Ferand in the sled.[15] They brought a bottle of milk and a piece of meat! Jet, who expects a baby in May, was stiff from the skiing and left her skis here, so that this afternoon Marian and I went to Anderstein [to return the skis and fetch the promised rye]. I went on the skis, and Pank pulled our sled, with the suitcase tied on it.[16] But quite soon I tied the skis also on the sled and walked companionably with Pank. We got 6 pounds of rye and also 6 pounds for Annetje and came home through a heavy snowstorm via inner paths past Vlastuin. It was exceptionally beautiful in the be-snowed woods and even though we constantly heard heavy artillery fire in the distance, and now and then the bang of a V-1 or V-2, it was still beautiful, almost in a holy way.

I've now wrapped each of the children in a blanket in a little nest, with a fur coat around their feet. It's terribly cold in the bedroom.

Tomorrow Moeder and I have to go in our mourning finery to the funeral of Juffr. Toos. Fortunately I can take along some extra bread (we received some from Moeder) because my stomach is so soon empty and then I have trouble with my heart. If, in the future, we get good food again that will immediately be over.

---

15 Jet was the daughter of Mr. and Mrs. van Beuningen, already mentioned, who lived at Anderstein; Bob was her husband (information from Gijs van Roekel). As for the skis, with the heavy snow and the lack of other transportation, skis and a sled were a practical way to get around.

16 Madzy seems sometimes to have used a suitcase for transporting things. We remember her mentioning, in connection with Hansje's giving her a tote bag at Christmas, that she was short of such bags.

Monday, 22 January. Today Moeder and I "buried" Juffr. Toos. Yesterday there was another snowstorm; the snow was at least 15 cm deep and we had to walk along the uncleared bicycle path. But the sun shone and there was no wind, so that (apart from the purpose of the trip) it was delightful. I had a thermos with coffee and some sandwiches, Moeder had cognac!—which we did *not* drink—and we walked cheerfully in our mourning garb.

In a shut-down café we were allowed to rest for a moment, and then the little cortège came past: the hearse, 6 mourners, and 1 carriage. At the cemetery we [Madzy and Iete] were led into the chapel after the coffin, and then the people emerged from the carriage. No one we knew! I said, "Moeder, this is a different funeral!"—but no, when we inquired we learned that no family members had followed Juffr. Toos's coffin. So we laid little Toos in her grave. Dicksy, can anything be more tragic? And yet, what is such a funeral? I can now understand Christ's words: "Let the dead bury their dead, and follow me." In the chapel a man said the Lord's Prayer (which he didn't entirely know); at the grave Moeder spoke some well-meant words and even had a few tears to go with them, so that was all as it should be. We rode in the carriage to the house, where Juffrouw Anna and Juffrouw Dina and Meneer Gerard[17] sat chilly and hunched and unhappy. But Joost beamed when he saw us, especially Moeder, whom he hadn't seen since August. They all looked thin, and Moeder gave them some money again (400 guilders in a week[18]) and said that they should buy all the food that they could find.

Thursday, 25 January. Today I ploughed through the snow for 3 hours and got 1 pound of rye! *That* was a pathetic result. I walked to de Rumelaar, who had promised to have some rye for me in January (in December I had gone there in vain) and … he sent me

---

17 The sisters and brother of Juffrouw Toos.
18 The implication is that this was a special gift, bringing the week's total payment to more than the usual fee that Iete was paying for Joost's care.

away with empty hands.[19] Then I went to Kees Wolfswinkel[20] and there I got that one pound of rye (because I had already been twice in vain, and had come walking so far in this weather). Then I got a ride for a short distance on a cart and went to have a chat with Suus but wasn't offered anything to drink. Fortunately I had brought with me some warm coffee—that is to say, brown liquid with a drop of milk—and 2 slices of bread saved from breakfast. At 1:30 I got home starving.

There I found that Pank didn't want to go to school because, oh darling, yesterday our little tyke almost got a bomb on her head. A very large bomb fell right near Droffelaar's house, and Pank was just on the way home from the little class with Mijnheer Jos. They were walking close by the place.[21] I had *such* a scare and don't know if I will still let her go. Actually I should have enough trust in God, but I would so dearly love to receive you back together with the children. Tomorrow I'll see, and otherwise I'll work with her here at home.

But I'm on the road every day, now always on foot, tomorrow to Doorn to the dentist, and if I don't have my period I'd like to walk to Charlotte on Monday. Dick still has those lovely boots of yours without having given me anything for them, and now I will bring him your corduroy trousers and then I hope very much, when I tell him that we're suffering from hunger, that I might get some beans or something. I've already bartered matches for rye, and two of my sweaters to Marietje for food. I'm going to barter

---

19 De Rumelaar was the name of a farm near Maarsbergen. "He" would be the farmer, but Madzy never gave his name.

20 Owner of another farm near Maarsbergen.

21 Bill translates as "not far from VaVa Hoogeweegen." I remember the incident. Mr. de Josselin de Jong, who was too elderly to be affected by the labour draft and therefore free to be out and about, accompanied the van Notten boys and me to the school and fetched us home again. While we were walking on a path alongside a small field, a bomber flew over very low. Mr. de Josselin de Jong gathered us children under the skirts of his overcoat, but not before I saw the bomb land and explode, spraying up a huge fountain of earth and snow. We were unhurt but badly shaken.

my diamond ring for food, and your tobacco pipes (that is, 2 of them, but I will keep 1 for when you come home).

Yesterday I opened my last can of butter, 2 kg. That will last us to the beginning of March, and "whoever is alive then can do the worrying then."[22]

Sugar is something I miss very much because of my heart; I've never felt that so much as now, now that it is finished, and the honey is also almost finished. We never eat porridge any more, only rye flakes or oatmeal (as long as the supply lasts) as a sort of soup or with imitation gravy and a tiny bit of butter in it. Even the children receive little butter, less than what they need now that they are also not getting any cod liver oil or meat.

Sunday, 28 January. Sunday evening and my last little drop of coal oil is burning in the waxine light. I'm wrapped in a blanket, sitting beside the stove, because today I felt really sick. I'm expecting my period and at those times I sometimes have a nasty infection in my breast. Yesterday when I was washing myself I was shocked at how thin I was. All my ribs stuck out and my abdomen was flat between projecting hipbones, two empty little hanging bags by way of bosom—*enfin* not an example of female beauty, but rather a picture of starvation. But one breast was a bit swollen and painful and that was causing me to feel shivery and feverish.

During the night I dreamed fiercely and clearly about you, my darling, and that startled me awake with such a shock that I couldn't go back to sleep with longing for you, with loneliness and emptiness. I had a headache and pain in my right breast and arm. I got up and sat by the stove; it is so icy cold in the bedroom next door. But this afternoon I went to bed and when I woke up the fever was subsiding and the breast less swollen. Then all of a sudden there were airplanes flying again and then there was a whole string of bombs falling, at least 25 or 30, so loud and

---

22 A well-known Dutch saying, "wie dan leeft dan zorgt."

heavy that the house didn't know what to do with itself and the children crawled screaming under the blankets with me. When it was quiet again I decided that I had better get dressed, in case something worse happened, but it stayed quiet.

Yesterday the elderly heer van Beuningen came on skis with a knapsack and brought us a fat chicken! So you see, Dicks, that it's true: "Do not worry about what you will eat nor how you will be dressed, God will look after you all." Moreover I was able to trade your uniform coat for 2 pounds of butter and 4 ounces of fat. Since butter is currently 90 to 100 guilders per pound and fat 50 guilders per pound it was a good piece of bartering. Now we're supplied with butter for at least six weeks, counting also what we have in the tin.

Tuesday, 30 January. Today we heard all of a sudden that we have to make do with our bread ration for two weeks instead of one. That means that we have 500 gr per person per week, Gerard 400 gr. So Gerard will get one slice of bread per day and we 1½. Dicks, this is a disaster. Although we have probably 35 pounds of wheat and maybe 20 pounds of rye, if we eat constantly from that it's used up in no time. This evening we ate a bit of warmed-up green peas and Juus and I each 5 small cakes baked with wheat flour and oatmeal with skim-milk powder and water, Marian 4½ of these and 1 slice of bread, Gerard 4 with 1 slice of bread, Juus and I each a little slice of rye bread, and the four of us shared 2 apples. You don't find that skimpy? Well, I know that my stomach is rumbling with hunger.

They say that the Russians are approaching Stettin.[23] Oh, Dicks, what will happen then with you?

Wednesday, 31 January. Moeder Iete and I today: I am shopping, because I heard that de Greef has potatoes after weeks of [useless coupons]. After the work in the house I quickly went there. It is

---

23 Bill's note: "Stettin was in the region of my camp."

now really thawing. I put on my old grey coat, scarf over my hair, your snow boots.[24] At de Greef I have to wait; there are still 4 people ahead of me. Besides, Juffr. de Greef is telling a long story—but that's why we live in a village, no? You wait and listen and wait. Then comes Moeder: "Oh, had you heard already about the potatoes? Wait ..." (I continue waiting) "... then we'll go together." She looks at chattering Juffr. de Greef and abruptly says, "Eh, couldn't you just attend to us?" Juffr. de Greef gives her a sidelong look and says, "Yes, if you will be patient," and talks on.

Because of my irritation I can't quite appreciate the humour. *Enfin*, we wait and when our turn comes we get 4 kg potatoes. We walk back and I stop in at de Josselin de Jong's house. "Look," says Moeder when I come out, "I saved the hard-boiled egg from my breakfast. I just peeled it, so eat it right now." How can I stand up against that, Dicks? It's a shame to bolt something as good as that, and with no salt. Besides, I have to do it under the eyes of the Kempers and whoever else is walking on the street or living round about. Nevertheless it's kind of her to have saved it for me. So I swallow the dry, hard egg in two bites and am ashamed.

We plod home through the mud and slush, I feeling morose. When we get home, I get from Moeder: "Hey, why have you changed Marian's hair? Why hasn't she gone outside to play? What a lot you eat! Juus is getting too fat, and the children also. And you too thin." Etc. etc. Do you understand, Dicks, why I'm gradually going crazy?

Thursday, 1 February. They say that the Russians are 70 km from Berlin and that Hitler is planning, if the armed forces surrender, to start a guerilla war.

Saturday, 3 February. This afternoon the three of us walked to Anderstein, because little Ferand Hudig turned 1½ and everyone

---

24 She uses the English term, so possibly these were boots that Wim had brought back from the United States.

was treated to oliebollen and chocolate milk.[25] You can imagine how the children beamed. It was quite a trip, pulling Gerard in the little wagon, an hour there and an hour home. My stomach was rumbling again when we got home.

But oh, Dicks, it was so beautiful outdoors. Marian was also fascinated. After the hard frost and cold (we have regularly had 8 to 10 degrees of frost, sometimes 12 or 15[26]) it began to thaw on Tuesday night and even though the snow lay 30 to 40 cm [12-15 in] deep in places, everything disappeared in 2 days, and today it was a spring day, so beautiful, so beautiful. The sun set rose-pink behind the hills and the birds sang, but except for that it was silent, and then the children discovered the first evening star. Then we thought again of you. Do you know what Marian said to me recently, when we were walking together? "Mamma, when we walk together like this, I always have to think suddenly of Papa." And I answered: "Yes, when we walk like this, Papa is closer to us than ever."

Now it is Saturday evening, my dearest, and oh, how I'm looking forward to all the Saturday evenings that we are going to spend together in the future. Good-night, my darling.

(P.S. They say that you're going to be moved again. Where to? It can't be very much farther from here than you are now, because the Germans' territory is steadily growing smaller. Nevertheless I'm a bit anxious.)

Monday, 5 February. Today I walked to Charlotte, pushing your bicycle, and because of the bicycle confiscations I took the small roads. I had West's basket on the back and my knapsack hanging from the handlebars. I walked it (with short stretches of cycling in between) in two hours. Charlotte rejoiced to see me but did not have many potatoes or vegetables. Still, I came back with 5 kg potatoes and the basket filled with leeks, and 1 kg of rye and

---

25 Oliebollen are a kind of Dutch pastry, rather like doughnuts but with no hole.
26 Centigrade.

a little piece of bacon! That last we hadn't tasted in years. When I got home we ate brown beans with bacon. What a treat! The Kolffs looked well and were shocked to see how thin I was. Yes, that's how I am, but such a trip as today's I can still manage all right, and even though I'm now tired it was not too much for me. Admittedly, on the trip home the bicycle was very heavy, especially because the paths were very muddy and the heavy bicycle got stuck. I reached home at 5 o'clock.

Unfortunately I found, at home, that not much had been achieved. Marian's homework was messy and dirty, so that I immediately set her to doing make-up work as punishment. Everything was messy and I couldn't find anything. Juus has no conception of that. If you were expected home I would make sure that everything was nicely tidy. I've never received that thoughtfulness from her; it's always messy and uncozy. How I long to have our own little arrangements again, even if it is only in a couple of rooms, in which the real homelike, cared-for atmosphere reigns.[27]

Tuesday, 6 February. Moeder is trying to wheedle out of me the four silver candlesticks, about which formerly she didn't care in the least but but which now all of a sudden seem to have "historical value." Juus says, "Put them away and she'll forget about them." But I'm far more inclined to give them graciously back to her; I know that we will be just as happy without them.

Moeder has told me repeatedly that Marian looks like a slum child and that Gerard looks like a girlish, childish boy.[28] Can you understand how tired I am of this, Dicksy?

---

27 Homemaking was one of Madzy's great skills.
28 It couldn't be helped that Gerard had curly blond hair. As for "childish"— well, he was only two and a half years old.

Chapter Twelve

10 February to 12 April 1945

During this last winter of the war, communication between Wim and Madzy became very irregular, partly because the rail strike disrupted postal service and partly because of the general chaos. On 25 February 1945, Madzy referred to receiving "many letters" and having "much contact," but evidently these letters were out of date, because on 24 March she wrote that she'd had no news in two months. Whenever she was not receiving letters, she also had no letter-forms on which she could write to Wim. This lack of news, together with the difficult situation in the household, stretched Madzy's nerves severely.

The primitive living conditions caused almost intolerable stress for everyone. By now, overcrowding would have been common everywhere in the country. People who still had homes were taking in those who had lost theirs because of bombing, expulsion, evacuation, or evading conscription or imprisonment.[1] The lack of electricity, shortage of fuel for heat, scanty food supplies and resulting illnesses, poor sanitation because of the lack of soap and the shortage of water— all these contributed to the problems. Strained relations are part of the human story of that time. In London, where Queen Wilhelmina and the Dutch government-in-exile were keeping a very anxious eye on events and conditions in the Netherlands, the Dutch prime minister

---

1   By the end of the war, 400,000 people were homeless (van der Zee, p. 306) out of a population of about 9 million (http://www.populstat.info/ Europe/netherlc.htm).

commented to the queen on "the considerable mental instability of our people after all that has happened."[2]

The twin threads of increasing food shortages and of approaching liberation run through this section of the diary. Approaching liberation meant fierce fighting as the front approached and then engulfed Maarn.

*****

Saturday, 10 February. Evening. Yesterday I visited Joost—and happened to be present when Juffrouw Anna Toos died! Two sisters dead within 3 weeks! Joost was very cheerful throughout, but now he is left with only Juffr. Dina, who has never cared about him and does not want to keep looking after him. What can now be done with him?

Today a postcard from you from 10 December, precisely 2 months old. I'm very happy with it. Marian giggled for hours over the fact that Pappa thought that she had to go to bed at 5 o'clock. What, my dearest, are you thinking of? Children sleep for, at most, 12 hours at a stretch and are then jumping to be out of bed.[3]

Monday, 12 February. Today I went to Rika in Renswoude: 1¼ hour cycling there, 2½ hours walking back pushing a broken-down bicycle and with 25 pounds of rye through streaming rain, while there was constant booming of artillery and bombing in the distance. I'm now really tired, and along the way I had heart palpitations, but still my heart came to rest as soon as I had eaten something.

Moeder Iete was here when I got home at 2:30. She was rejoicing in the fact that perhaps the evacuees will be forced to move to Friesland [where there was still food]; she wants them to leave here, perhaps because she wants to come and live here

---

2 Quoted in van der Zee, p. 162.
3 Wim had no experience at all with six-year-old children; his only sibling was an older sister.

herself, perhaps because she resents the fact that I am doing something for other people. How strange that as daughter you sometimes dislike your mother. May God forgive me this guilt because I can do nothing else, but it seriously bothers me.

Marian said this evening in her prayers: "Lord, will you make sure that Pappa gets enough to eat and comes home to us soon, Amen."

Wednesday, 15 February. Today, first, we did extensive cleaning, and when all the furniture was standing out of doors there was Chris with a whole bottle of oil for us! And then Douwe Hoytema came to ask how you were.[4] I couldn't possibly invite him indoors so we sat outdoors. There, for at least ¾ hour, we had a chat while he drank a cup of coffee, and then he went off again. Then there came a postcard from you of 22 January in which you report that Piet van Notten is coming to your camp—or perhaps is already there!

Then the word came that my evacuees have to leave because of the food shortage in Maarn. Wailing and lamentations in the kitchen! West himself was not at home. However, when he came home everything was much more orderly because he (with my approval) will report himself as being sick. Dicks, for a moment today, in my thoughts, I saw us again alone in our little house, freshly cleaned, and free. In my thoughts I set up one room as "Pappa's room" and the kitchen as our dining room. I would again get my own bedroom with storage space and washbasin. Then I saw the sad evacuee-faces and thought how it would feel if we ourselves had to move constantly. Then I knew what I had to say: "You are welcome here from the bottom of my heart, and if you dare to stay here with the food shortages, you can stay until you can go back to Arnhem." You would have done the same, wouldn't you, Dicks darling?

---

4   This was an old friend of Wim's.

Friday, 16 February. Today I walked to Lambalgen,[5] 19 km [14 mi] total, there and back, to look for apples, but no success. I left at 9 o'clock and was home again at 1 o'clock with 3 apples (a present) and 2 eggs (which I bought). So I lost more calories than I brought home. But Meneer West bartered your little bit of left-over genever [Dutch gin], less than half a litre, for 20 pounds of rye.

Today West pretended to be sick, but Dr. Rinkes was not fooled and said that they nevertheless had to move. This evening Mevr. West went to Ad [van Kekem] to ask once more if they might stay, and he said that they had to think of me, that I was living in primitive circumstances because of their desire to stay and that I would sooner sacrifice myself—and was breaking down because of it—than that I would ask them to leave. What a beautiful thing to say!—but when I heard it I knew immediately, "Moeder is behind that." She hasn't been here in 5 days, and I was already thinking that she was up to something. She's been trying for a long time to get the evacuees to go. But I am glad to keep them—1st, because then Moeder can't come to live here and, 2nd, because with divers wandering around, and hungry passers-by, razzias, Germans, the Landwacht, etc. I don't want to be alone with Juus, especially at night.

They have taken Mevr. Bentinck and her daughter-in-law prisoner because weapons were found in her shed.[6] Freule[7] Verschuur, when she went to ask about Mevr. Bentinck, was also taken. Since yesterday they're in prison. It's frightful; something like that could happen to any of us.

---

5   Bill's note: "Where an estate manager lived where I worked for half a year mostly surveying. It is just south of Scherpenzeel."

6   Mr. Bentinck is not mentioned in this entry because he died in 1943. Madzy didn't record his death in the diary, but I obtained the information from a member of the Bentinck family, Ursula den Tex.

7   "Freule" is a form of address used for unmarried female members of noble families, (Dutch Wikipedia, "Freule," accessed January 6, 2017).

Sunday, 25 February. Evening. Haven't written for a long time, it's busy, and we have little light. Everything continues, many letters from Wim, so that we have much contact. On 24 January he was happy and full of future-plans. Yet about the future we can still say so little; I don't visualize anything beyond the day of Dicks' return.

Last night three V-1s flew over one after another; one of them suddenly stopped and crashed with a big bang. Later in the night a fourth came over, so low that the house trembled and I held my breath to hear whether it stopped, but it went well. Marian dead-scared under my blankets. She doesn't want to go to her little class out of fear, and I myself am also frightened.

There was further news about Mevr. Bentinck: the house has been plundered empty and will be blown up.[8] They say that Mevr. Bentinck is free now but promptly went underground. Here close to us, near de Halm, there was also a container of munitions, probably dropped by Tommy.[9] I didn't dare let it lie there and have reported it to the Luchtbeschermingsdienst; isn't that cowardly of me?[10]

Tomorrow I will probably go to Charlotte in the hope of getting some more food. I will walk because *all* the [bicycle] tires are used up except the surrogate tire.[11]

---

8 Lägers and Veenland-Heineman (p. 106), writing in 2003, made no reference to the house having been blown up, so presumably it did not happen. But the looting does appear to have taken place.

9 Briedé (p. 171) refers to the Allies' dropping weapons for the use of the Resistance.

10 The Luchtbeschermingsdienst was a Dutch volunteer organization set up in 1939 to warn people against dangers and air raids; local units also instantly came to the aid of victims of air raids (Wikipedia, "Luchtbeschermingsdienst," accessed December 12, 2018). Mr. Koolemans Beijnen was the leader of the local group (van der Donck, p. 11). As for Madzy's reporting the munitions, ethical issues of this kind added to the stress.

11 There were (non-rubber, presumably non-inflated) tires in use, which made a bicycle extremely heavy to pedal, and there were also wooden

Saturday, 3 March. Today real March showers.

For a moment we lived in hope that Sweden would join the Allies or would intern our officers but both hopes vanished.[12] I did hear from Dick Kolff that the [POW] camp had been moved to Lüneburg but I won't believe it until I hear about it from Dicks. And we still don't know where Piet van Notten is.

Far more things happen than I can ever write down. There was a raid on a purported nest of terrorists here in Maarn. Many divers were picked up. At de Hoogt many razzias.

Dearest, forgive me if I say that I can hardly stand up against Juus and Moeder. I have to fight tooth and nail to defend my rights as housewife and mother, and that makes me so tired. When Juus wants something there's no point in my trying to dissuade her: she has her way. She doesn't eat potatoes in the peel, even though everyone else eats them like that; she sputters against it every time.

Then I simply have to fight for us to get our share of the food. She eats the most potatoes, she still eats butter, she had sugar until the day before yesterday. She drinks milk from the litre ration that I get every two days for the children. And she never says, on her own initiative, "There now, why don't you take a bit of extra food, you need it." If I didn't have her, everything would come out better and I would have to do less lugging.

And then when I come home the place is messy, and the table is untidily laid or not laid at all, so that I, tired as I am, immediately have to look after the children and the house. The mood in the house is also spoiled by her. I can never write a letter without "Who are you writing to?" "Open!" she shouts if she wants a door opened. "Give me that!" etc.

"tires." Some people had tires made of garden hose. As a last resort, people rode on the bare rim.

12 Sweden was neutral. The words about internment come from Bill's translation—he may have known what Madzy was referring to. Being moved to Sweden would have been preferable to being interned in Germany.

Ach, it's not all like that, there are some good things.

Moeder also makes me so sad with her endless meddling. I'd better stop this.

Wednesday, 7 March. Yesterday I was so unhappy; I had dreamed of you, dearest, and went about all day crying in my heart. Not openly, because I never do that. Only with you can I deliciously cry. I walked to Joost today and came home sad. My dear boy misses out on a lot, now that Juffr. Toos and Anna have died. Moeder came up with the idea that Juus could go there sometimes and help, and Juus would rather like that. Suddenly I see her again in another light, and I'm ashamed of what I wrote above. Because she said: "But I'm not going to desert you." She also said, "Moeder will certainly not pension me off so soon; she'll let me look after Joost because then she keeps me in the family."[13] It would be a solution, but first Dina [the surviving Toos sister] has to approve.

Now I'm going to have a good sleep. Cologne has fallen; the Allies are standing in a solid block along the Rhine. Now they have to cross; that will be a very big step towards our liberation. Who knows—perhaps in a couple of weeks we'll be free. But then still you, oh my dearest. I feel such anxiety about the coming events.

Wednesday, 21 March. I'm writing by moonlight because there is so much flying.[14] Tomorrow Joost is coming [to live here]. Today we put everything in order.[15]

---

13 Juus was still an employee of Iete's.

14 i.e., She didn't want to use a light because of the danger of attracting bombing.

15 He would stay with us until just after the war ended. Madzy didn't record the discussions that led to this arrangement.

Moving him from Driebergen to Maarn was a big problem; long after the war Madzy told me how she had managed it. Joost, who was not physically fit, would have been completely unable to walk or bicycle such a distance, and there were no cars available, but Madzy found

For days there has been lots of flying and heavy bombing. This morning at 6 o'clock two bombs fell between Schut and Christie[16] (5 windows broken, 1 hen killed). One bomb was left hanging in a tree and exploded there, and that gave the worst bang.

Saturday, 24 March. Evening. Today Joost has been here 2 days, and he says he is entirely settled and at home. I'm going to urge that later on Moeder take him along [to The Hague], with Juus, and put him in a separate part of her house.

Meanwhile we wait for the liberation, because it is coming closer all the time. Also your homecoming, dearest. One day I was very down, and I'll tell you honestly that I had awful visions of myself as a widow with two orphans, but fortunately I got over it and even though I haven't had any news from you in two months, I know that God is with us. All of a sudden I can manage everything again, am much calmer with the children and have real contact with them.

For a week it has been unbelievably warm weather; today I was bare-legged and in summer clothes (such as I still own, which is not much), and the children were outdoors the whole day, which did them a great deal of good.

Willem is all of a sudden going to leave me, I don't know precisely why.[17] It grieves me a lot.

I'm so thin that my summer dresses hang loose around me. Still, I feel fine and have little trouble with my heart.

---

someone with a horse and an ancient carriage, and in that vehicle he and his belongings were moved from Driebergen to our house. He and Juus shared one of the upstairs rooms.

16 In other words, it fell about one kilometre from our house.

17 Evidently he had still been doing some chores for Madzy.

Monday, 26 March. Have I already told you about the reign of terror in Maarn and the sad days during which 4 Maarn people were shot dead?[18] And now there are again more Germans here.

This afternoon I bicycled to Charlotte and came home out of breath because for the last stretch I was followed constantly by 6 low-flying, circling fighters, who were looking for something and finally made an enormous attack on the railroad near the station, just when I had to cross. Finally one came over very low, just when I had to pass two wagons with horses (also a beloved target of the machine guns), and someone in the woods started to shoot at the fighter. Fortunately I was home soon, and Joost was happy. I brought spinach and potatoes. Tomorrow I will put on my "bold" shoes and again try to get some rye at de Rumelaar, and eggs for Easter. That will again be a really unpleasant begging-expedition. Maybe Vlastuin will have some milk for me. I don't like begging.

Last night there was such dreadful fighting not far from us that the house sometimes swayed back and forth.

Thursday, 29 March. All organized opposition by the Germans has stopped, the English will determine the moment when they lay down their arms.[19] Liberation is close.

It's impossible to describe how it appears to our hearts, our poor battered hearts that have been turned to stone. The pulse

---

18 This "reign of terror" was in reprisal for an incident that took place just north of Arnhem. There, on 6 March, a Resistance group attacked a vehicle in which, as it turned out, the passenger was Hanns Albin Rauter, one of the most powerful Nazi officials in the Netherlands, known as the "evil genius" of the Nazis in the Netherlands (van der Zee, p. 182). Rauter was seriously injured (but survived), and his second-in-command ordered reprisal killings. At least 250 and probably more like 400 Dutch citizens were killed, including, from Maarn, two Resistance workers and two men who may have been only divers (Caspers, p. 237ff).

19 I have not been able to discover what Madzy was referring to here. There must have been a rumour to this effect, but it was misleading because, as the next entries make clear, the fighting continued.

beats in our throats, our stomachs feel woozy (and not only from hunger), we wait ....

Today was for the first time a day of incredible silence. One V-1 came over in the distance, and one airplane. The tension hangs in the air. No bombs, no shooting, no rumbling, no fighters diving, no squadrons of aircraft flying over, nothing, nothing, only silence ....

But in the house there was excitement. Our dear Pankie advanced to the second grade and brought a marvelous report card home: reading, writing, arithmetic, language, all received an 8 [out of 10], and for diligence and drawing a 7! Yes, she's not always diligent, because it comes easily to her. Now she is amply ready for the second grade, and if there really is a truce then she will go to the "big" school, which will by then be cleared of the Landwacht and the NSB supervisor.[20]

And where are you, my Dicks? Why have you not been able to share the joy of this step up to the next grade?—Pank's shining eyes at the sight of my gift (3 little pads of paper) and the "cake" (a pathetic "broeder"[21]), the bottle of tomato juice, and the rusks that Gerard had been allocated as "additional allowance"? Are you still alive, my Dicksy, and, if so, where?

Good Friday, 30 March. Evening. This afternoon, while the barber was shaving Joost, bombs suddenly fell nearby, enormous bangs. The battle for the Netherlands has begun[22] and we wait breathlessly for what is going to happen. Will we still have to endure a lot of awful things? I can't stand much more; I really feel that I'm coming to the end of my endurance.

---

20 This use of the school building is confirmed by Caspers, p. 240.

21 A "broeder" was a sort of bread boiled in a bag and then sliced (Dutch Wikipedia, "Broeder," accessed January 9, 2017).

22 The phrasing suggests that she was quoting a news report.

Moeder heard from Tante Kuuk[23] who had heard from someone in Groningen that you are on Sylt Island.[24] If that were true! That would really not be too bad, I think, although maybe you might have food problems. Let's hope that no bombs fall there. There are planes flying over low again; might they start something here?

Tuesday, 3 April. Too many things are happening to write about them all. Besides, I'm overcome by a paralyzing exhaustion; it's as though I can't handle the last straws. It could be because since January I haven't had my periods, and that's a sign of the times (many women have that problem[25]) but it's a fact that it makes you feel very tired. Meanwhile the front is approaching from all sides. And what is still facing us?

However, there are some amusing things happening. The Germans are streaming past and sometimes leave something behind that can't be taken along. Annetje came yesterday with half a pail of pea soup (with meat!), a loaf of kuch[26] from 14 March (but usable for us, especially in soup), and ... 3 soles [fish]. One went to the kitchen [the Wests], the other two were wolfed down by us (not by me—I can't stand fish) because we haven't seen any fish since 1942. Then what happened today? Comes Bob Hudig bringing "something that we hadn't seen for a long time," as he put it ... 5 soles! Two fat ones to the kitchen, 3 again fried and gobbled up by my four hungry mouths. Moreover we received, for Easter, a total of 37 eggs! The kitchen also received an ample number of these (also portions of the pea soup and the bread, and also milk). The more the war progresses the

---

23 Kuuk was the wife of Sam van den Berg. See entry for 11 July 1942.
24 Sylt Island is off the German coast.
25 Van der Zee also recorded this (p. 157).
26 "Kuch" (or "munitiebrood") was a sourdough bread specially baked for the military, made of rye and other grains and noted for its long shelf life (Wikipedia, "Munitiebrood," accessed November 23, 2016). What Madzy wrote indicates that the loaf was date-stamped.

more windfalls we will get, I think. When Joost came we opened Moeder's last tin of butter. She also still had a bottle of real salad oil. So we're not starving, although I've had more than enough of rye. My digestion isn't good; I soon feel full and half-nauseated and can't eat heavy things.

Friday, 6 April. The battle is coming closer; the Canadians are in Arnhem. Today was a quiet day, really an oppressive stillness before the storm, but just now, at 9:30 this evening, the far-off rumbling of gunfire began again, that sound that we already find so familiar that we almost listen for it. It's bad weather, rainy and cold, but the sun comes out between the showers, the wind has shifted to the north and the barometer is rising quickly.

Monday, 9 April. Since yesterday we again hear constant shooting from the direction of Arnhem. It's an accompaniment to our daily lives, and the regular trilling of the windowpanes is music to our ears, because this is shooting and flying *for us*: the approach of liberation. We know very well: don't put your faith in Tommies and shooting. But however deeply we trust in God, with the coming of these sunny days our ears and eyes remain "in the air." And they keep on shooting. Then again some airplanes close by, then heavy artillery in the distance, so the air is hardly ever still.

This morning, under cover of the morning mist, I went by the small roads to Charlotte, even though a farmer tried to frighten me with stories about "bicycles being requisitioned by Germans retreating from the front." Fortunately I pushed on in spite of fierce, penetrating cold (I was faint from the cold) and came home with 8 kg turnip tops and some potatoes and 5 bantam eggs.

This evening I had all of a sudden an intense longing to have another baby and then to experience the first days with you, Dicks. Silly, isn't it? Good night, darling.

Thursday, 12 April. After a few days of rather frightening silence, this evening suddenly, not far off, from the direction of Arnhem, began a constant drumming of gunfire. At 9 o'clock Willem risked his young life to come and tell us that the Allies have crossed the IJssel[27]—a front of 1½ km [1 mi] wide and 3 km [2 mi] deep—and that a new offensive has started near Arnhem. What will happen now? Courage and trust.

---

27 A river that branches off from the Rhine near Arnhem and flows north.

Chapter Thirteen

13 April to 27 April 1945

The front continued to be close to or on top of Maarn; some of the place-names that Madzy mentions in connection with the fighting are familiar to us because she has gone there to visit friends or in search of food. It is clear how lucky we were to escape with our lives and with an intact house.

At the end of April, the Allies began relief flights to drop food on the starving country. Queen Wilhelmina and Prime Minister Gerbrandy had for some time been urging the Allied leaders to give attention to the famine in the Netherlands. It took time for the relief flights to be organized but at last, on 27 April, the food drops began.[1] The distribution of the food was to be handled by Dutch Resistance fighters and former members of the Dutch army.[2]

Madzy continues to give glimpses of daily life in wartime. Though hampered by the curfew, people are moving around; information—and rumour—are circulating. There are trips to the shops and brief visits, and there are encounters in connection with Madzy's hurried scrounging expeditions. Madzy's mother comes with stolen food, friends drop by to offer accommodation in a bomb shelter. These are glimpses of what daily life becomes when it is skewed by abnormal circumstances and when word-of-mouth is virtually the only form of communication. In this respect—and a few others—conditions had become almost mediæval.

*****

---

1   Olson, van der Zee, and other sources.
2   Olson, p. 410.

Friday, 13 April. When I lie still in my bed listening to the world, there are 11 quietly breathing people around me in this little house, but outdoors rumbles an interminable shooting; there is no pause. Moreover I think I hear cars on the road to Doorn, at least there is a zooming sound. What is waiting for us in the coming days?

This morning early I went to Woudenberg and to Rika. The military installations through which I had to pass were being feverishly strengthened.[3] For the first time I had to show my identity papers, and on one road the gate through the fortification was already closed but I could still take a roundabout little road to get home. The attack on Arnhem seems to go well, the bridgehead over the IJssel is 10 km [6 mi] deep and 6 km [4 mi] wide, the tanks are streaming into the Veluwe.[4] The Ruhr has collapsed, Vienna is free.

I am busy making plans to empty the house before you come, also to move Juus and Joost out, so that you will find only me and the children.

Saturday, 14 April. A quiet day, though it began with mortar fire close by. Tremendous explosions, probably Soesterberg [the airbase] going up in the air. Few airplanes, but now this evening some more, and also a sort of mist that probably means that there is a smoke screen not far from here. This morning little groups of young men went up the lane [to Huis te Maarn]: underground people, or SS dressed in civvies? This evening the news came through that Arnhem has been liberated and also that from there the fighting has moved towards Apeldoorn, where they are fighting in the streets. What is still awaiting us? We have wooden poles that we can put against the house,[5] and we'll close the shutters. Beyond that it's just trusting in God.

---

3   The Grebbe Line and perhaps other defence installations.

4   A forested ridge of hills just north of Arnhem, therefore not far northeast of us (Wikipedia, "Veluwe," accessed December 5, 2018).

5   Presumably to prevent it from collapsing.

The English are very close to Berlin, and the Russians are also fighting there.

And you, Dicks? Are you really on Sylt? Are you safe? Do you have food? We are still getting only 400 gr of bread per week, Gerard 800. Beyond that G. gets something which we haven't had since September, 250 gr of syrup. And again some milk, and buttermilk for Pank. The only problem is whether it isn't too dangerous for me to go and get it. I think that with the food I have in the house (potatoes, vegetables, rye, wheat) I will make it for another 2 weeks, and then everything will be clean used up.

Sunday, 15 April. Today is an eerily still, misty, soft day. The weather is abnormally warm. Many fruit trees are already in bloom, our apple tree is on its tiptoes, and the oaks are already looking greenish even before the beeches shed their little brown shells. The spinach and peas are growing like crazy; in a word, it is unusually early.

Not one airplane has come over and we haven't heard any shot or explosion except far, far away. And still people say that Apeldoorn has fallen to the Allies, that the Germans are retreating from Putten, where fighting is taking place, that there are 2,000 Germans in Woudenberg and also the same number in Maarn, that VaVa will get 15 billeted on her tonight, that Amersfoort is encircled and that no one is allowed on the road with a bicycle. In short: tension. People are saying that the 3 northernmost provinces—Friesland, Groningen, and Drente—have been taken [by the Allies] without a fight and the Tommies are storming across the Afsluitdijk.[6] How much of it is true? There are only a few lucky people with batteries for their radios who can spread the news.

Today I put all your letters in order and will reread them from the beginning, a couple every evening when I'm in bed.

---

6   This is the dike and causeway connecting the northeast and the northwest parts of the Netherlands (Wikipedia, "Afsluitdijk," accessed September 20, 2017).

Monday, 16 April. This morning I raced to the Kolffs in one rush, back within 2 hours. Very dangerous especially as regards the requisitioning of bicycles, but I came safely home with 10 kg turnip tops, radishes, and at least 5 kg potatoes.[7] I did see Germans, some of them drunk, but they didn't harm me. This evening (a beautiful evening with a new moon) there was news that an [Allied] army has reached Otterloo and is approaching Ede. The Germans are trying to establish themselves in safety in the cities.[8] They are destroying everything, factories, roads, etc.[9]

I'm very tired. This waiting for news and liberation makes one tired and very hungry. My breakfast was some rye porridge (made with water) and two dry slices of bread. When I was with Charlotte I saw that they had just finished a plate of porridge with milk; bread and rye bread lay in a dish in the middle of the table, for the taking, (not just a little slice on each person's plate) and on the table stood butter, cheese, peanut butter, syrup, jam, and another kind of spread. With that they had real tea with milk. What luxury! We have no jam and no butter. I fry the children's slices of bread in oil, but I can't digest that. How long

---

7 It's not clear why she had to make this trip, which she admitted was dangerous, when two days earlier she wrote that she had enough to see us through for two weeks. Presumably there were again demands on her food supply that she didn't mention, or perhaps the increasing danger made it desirable to get more food while she could.

8 They still held the west of the country, where the big cities are located.

9 In addition to the dikes already breached, in late March or early April the Germans were given orders (by Hitler, says van der Zee, p. 185) "to ready the demolition of all electrical plants, gasworks, bridges, railways, and, most deadly of all, [the] dikes. If [more] dikes were blown, the nation would be inundated by water within three weeks, resulting in a calamity of unimaginable proportions." One dike in the north of the country *was* blown at this time, flooding more than 30,000 acres (12,000 hectares) and many farms. "More than twenty residents were shot as they tried to escape the floods" (Olson, p. 408–409).

will this still last? Sometimes I'm so hungry that Juus cleans a carrot for me. Dry bread or a cold potato is a delicacy.

Tuesday, 17 April. Evening. The armies are approaching: Barneveld is already being named, and Scherpenzeel. Oh, if only a miracle could happen now whereby everything was finished! The attack on Berlin has begun.

We hear a lot of shooting close by, and there are warnings not to go on the roads. There is much traffic of motorbikes and cars, even on our little road. Oh, will an English or American tank or car ever drive along it? Will we here in the woods (Ai! That was a big bomb! The children are terrified.) know precisely when we are free?

Last night I took a sleeping pill again; because of the hunger I again couldn't sleep.

I can always go to Vlastuin if we don't have anything anymore. I still have about 6 pounds of rye, I think, and the same of wheat.

Beautiful weather; we sat in summer clothes in the garden. (Another of those big bombs! I'm lying shaking in my bed; all the windows are open.)

Wednesday, 18 April. Evening. They say that today the Germans will leave this area.[10] During the night I was frequently shocked awake by enormous explosions. The Germans again laid a telephone line in front of our house to Huis te Maarn.

I really believe that I hear a train passing. Yesterday enormous tanks came along the old highway in Doorn; you could hear them here. We are really in the middle of the front. Every sound makes us anxious (it's clear moonlight). Just now we heard 8 planes which dove over the [German] line with bombs and machine guns.

---

10 This didn't happen. There are references in later entries to their continued presence.

Thursday, 19 April. Early morning. During the night there was such an uproar that eventually I got dressed and leaned out of the window for a while and then went back to bed still dressed. But nothing happened—fortunately, because at night I always find it more difficult than by day. It's a beautiful day today. The German cannons bark from time to time but here it seems peaceful enough in the intervals. All night there were tanks and horse-drawn vehicles rolling by on the old highway in Doorn.

Afternoon. I'm lying on bed (2:30 p.m.) enjoying a calm moment, because 4 nights of having had only half-sleep leaves me a bit tired. Many bicycles are being requisitioned (mine is sleeping in the woods, yours is dismantled in the little hutch in the barn). There were many Germans in the village, passing through during the night. Wageningen, Ede, Barneveld, and Voorthuizen are free, and the Allies are less than 30 km from Amsterdam! How will they manage in inundated Holland?

Evening. Now cannons have been moved in all around us, and they are doing their work with enormous bangs and a frightful droning. No wonder that the children are anxious and that Gerard, during a dreadful nightmare, woke up soaking wet with sweat and didn't go back to sleep. His little bed now stands against my feet, but if it gets worse he'll just have to sleep with me. It's not necessary that at the very end he still gets an anxiety complex.

I crept through the woods after dinner, and before 8 o'clock came back lugging 5 pounds of rye, a bottle of milk, and a bottle of buttermilk. Now we can at least eat some porridge tomorrow; the bread is nearly finished. And then still your birthday, Dicks![11] With the very last flour I made a broeder, a "cake," and a little loaf of rye bread and with that will entertain all 12—with Willem 13—people in the house! How long until there is food coming

---

11   The next day was Wim's birthday.

again? Marian is constantly hungry and actually all of us too, but Juus and Joost and Gerard not so badly as Marian and I.

Just now it's quiet, better profit from it by getting some sleep.

Friday, 20 April. Well, Dicks, even though we don't know whether you're still alive, we sang the "Lang zal hij leven!" for you.

It was a crazy day, first a very quiet night during which we slept well for the first time after 4 unrestful nights. At 6:30 I got out of bed (I was already half-dressed) and immediately walked to Maarsbergen. An hour later back with 6 pounds of rye and 3 pounds of wheat—no milk. At home great rejoicing (because of the birthday) and flowers from the children. Breakfasted on rye porridge with buttermilk. Then did the housework but not too much because we could easily have a shell falling from those cannons round about and then it would be a shame to have taken the trouble. Then Moeder came unexpectedly, in spite of the danger, with a pound of butter! What a feast! Then Annetje and Floris with a tube of German toothpaste and some flowers. Then Bob Hudig with his son. Then Tante Lotje Suurmondt with some flowers. Then it was lunchtime.

All of a sudden there was a German who demanded billeting! After a quick meal we emptied the two front rooms, Juus with Joost to the little upstairs room, the old West couple into the room with the rest of the West family.[12] Furniture in the barn.

---

12 The German officer demanded our two front downstairs rooms, which were our family's living quarters, so those rooms had to be cleared. All seven members of the West family would squash themselves into one of the upstairs rooms, and the plan seems to have been that our family would use the other two bedrooms; presumably all of us (we and the Wests) would use the kitchen.

One of my most vivid memories of the war is connected with this episode. The German who came to requisition the rooms left his knapsack on the floor of one of them when he went away. Out of the knapsack rolled a round, red-waxed Dutch cheese. We had not seen such a cheese in years—indeed, to judge by Madzy's account, almost no cheese at all, in a country that was presumably continuing to make it.

Everything was just ready, when ... another German! It wasn't going ahead.[13] They had—please note—planned to set up a cannon here right next to the house and 5 on de Halm. Well, we've just escaped a grim end.[14]

Enfin, you never know what is still going to happen. They say that Elst has fallen and half of Amersfoort, that there is fighting there. Also near Baarn. Here, Germans are setting up artillery on the other side of the railway. Why don't those idiots give themselves up? Sometime or another there will be an end.

Tomorrow I have to go out early again to get milk, and I now have something like 10 pounds of rye and 6 pounds of wheat in the house. From the German we got a loaf of bread, fortunately, because we had none left.[15]

In bed: I'm wearing my corset and bra and summer dress. In the distance there is constant shooting and flying and the tramp of horses, and if they again go to work with artillery I'd rather be ready. Therefore we picnic on a little bridge table[16] so that if necessary I can put mattresses on the floor of that room. Meneer West fortunately sleeps like a hare [wakes at every sound].

Saturday, 21 April. Tonight I lie in bed pleasantly in my nightgown again. It's quiet and it appears that we still have to have some patience, so that I afforded myself this luxury. The whole day

---

All of us gathered around the cheese, and someone suggested that we grab it. Madzy knew that if we did we could all have been executed on the spot, and she forbade everyone from touching it. It was to be left precisely where it was, on the floor beside the knapsack. If necessary, she would stand guard over it. So there the cheese lay until the (or *a*) German returned.

13 In the 1976 narrative Madzy said this plan didn't materialize because the Germans had to retreat farther.

14 The cannon would, of course, have attracted Allied attacks.

15 She may be saying that the German who came to the house gave us bread.

16 Presumably the furniture had not been brought back from the barn.

silence except cannon fire in the far distance. The radio gives no news about Holland. We sit in the middle of the front; soldiers come regularly along the road, and now and then a car or truck, and I was just in my bath when a Tommy came over low firing its guns so that I sprang out of the bath again and, half wet, started to dress myself, but that was all that happened today. At 6:30 this morning I was already out to look for milk, without success, but at 8:00 this evening I came home with milk and buttermilk. Moeder brought a stolen kuch and pork, and so we can manage for another few days.

Sunday, 22 April. Morning. I had not yet blown out the light when an appalling fight began. The artillery in Maarn roared. Shells shrieked over our heads and the little house shook. Children scared to death and both with me in bed. It went on like that until 4:00—we didn't shut an eye. After that we dozed a bit.

Afternoon in bed. I tucked the children in nicely and am also going to catch up on some sleep myself. It was, it appears from further information, the English firing. We are in the middle of the firing line, and a number of houses were damaged. Chris slept with the boys in the cellar.

Today was a day of good gifts: 1½ litre of milk from Zuster Greeve,[17] meat, fat, and bread from the Germans,[18] all kinds of delicacies from Els. (I find it so difficult to accept anything, Dicks, but I have to do it for the children and for Joost and Juus.)

Evening. Now the roar of shooting is coming from the direction of Soesterberg-Amersfoort, as though the Allies have moved around Amersfoort and intend to surround us. I went to

---

17 Bill read Madzy's squiggle as "Zr"—i.e., Zuster, "Sister" (meaning "nurse"). Later Madzy mentioned this person again. Elsewhere Madzy referred to a district nurse; perhaps this is the same person.

18 It's not clear whether this food was given to us by the Germans or whether someone like Annetje Nahuys stole it.

Maarsbergen; starting tomorrow we're forbidden to leave our own communities. I was given all kinds of things so that now we really can survive for probably two weeks as regards food. (The Wests received at least half a big basket of stolen potatoes.) There are Germans walking around here, of a bad sort.[19] We're allowed to be on the street only from 8-9 and 5-6. I gave Pankie ⅓ of a sleeping pill, the little mite was so frightened and nervous. They say that tonight 200 Germans will have to be billeted here, some in our house; if that's so, Joost will have to sleep in my bed, Juus with Pank, and I on the 2 mattresses on the floor. Everything is ready so that we can shift in one move to the kitchen. What an existence, eh, Dicks? But we have to sacrifice something to gain our liberation. The shooting last night fortunately took no lives but did cause damage; in Maarn many shells fell, in Woudenberg nine. Many people in the village slept in their cellars, or stayed up. After all we should also probably have gone downstairs, which in future we will do, but it turned out all right.[20]

Monday, 23 April. Evening. Because the cleaning help didn't come, we had to do the laundry ourselves; not such a bad thing, because if you don't have anything to do the day at home is so long. Not when you're here, Dicks, and we with the four of us can enjoy being at home, but definitely if you have to huddle with 12 of you in a state of tension. Last night there was a lot of shooting and I lay in bed awake, while the children slept quietly. Half the village, though, slept in their cellars again.

Everyone uses the two hours that we're allowed to be out. We raced through the shopping and just managed to get it done in the hour. Tomorrow morning I will just fly to Vlastuin for milk. Now that I'm not using the bicycle any more it's really a dash.

---

19 These were presumably ruffian-like, undisciplined soldiers, who were always more dangerous than the well-trained, disciplined ones.
20 "Downstairs" may refer to our small earth-floored cellar, which we rarely used as a shelter.

During the day it was cold, raw weather and except for a couple of explosions in the neighbourhood we noticed nothing of the approaching front; it's almost spookily still. The children can now sleep peacefully. All the same, I think that, now that the weather is clearing and the storm has died down, I won't undress but just take off my skirt and shoes and sleep like that. On purpose I slept this afternoon so that I could stay awake tonight in case of need. I also saved a bit of real coffee, for such a night of waking and watching. Berlin is practically taken; odd that it falls sooner than Maarn. The latter seems to be almost untakeable![21]

Tuesday, 24 April. Last night quiet—that is, constant heavy shooting near Woudenberg along the Grebbe Line and 2 enormous explosions, but we're so used to that that for us it's a lullaby. I slept from 12 to 5 and really felt rested. During the day it was also quiet; at 8:30 I was at Vlastuin's for milk, got 1 L ordinary, 1 L buttermilk.

Last night a big troop of Germans came past with carts; all of a sudden they began to sing in two-part harmony at the tops of their voices and that sounded so fantastic in the moonlit woods that I was overcome by a strong feeling of unreality. They kept singing until they were far away and their voices rang out for a long time.

Meanwhile nature has progressed a good way. The apple tree has nearly finished blooming, the spinach and turnip tops we'll be able to eat on Sunday, cress we've eaten already. The lilacs are in bloom. All of this is phenomenal for 24 April.

This afternoon the Tommies began a new stunt: 2 planes began to circle low over the Line and sent messages to their artillery in which direction to shoot. Then you heard two shots, bom-bom, in the distance, and then a moment later the whistling

---

21 Our area, with its dense woods and strong artillery installations, might well have been hard to take.

of 2 shells and then 2 heavy explosions (boooom—boooom). That went on for almost an hour, unfortunately just at the time when we were allowed on the street, so that only a few people ventured out.

Huis te Maarn is without water (35 people, among them many evacuated hospital patients) and they fetch it from here [from the hand pump in our garden] in a tank-wagon. It's dangerous now to go out with such a wagon, and during the night the idiot driver left the wagon standing near our house. Fortunately no Tommy spotted it, otherwise we could all have been dead.

Annetje and Floris were in prison yesterday from 9 to 5 and when they got home all their belongings had been stolen, including the little "flight" suitcase.

Later. It's high time that it's over, also for our Pank. Just now there was severe shooting and flying, but not particularly close by, and then she was again so frightened that she lay with her hands over her ears screaming. Then a shell came whistling over and she was absolutely beside herself. Now it's quiet. People say that the Allies are near Scherpenzeel.

The doctors, nurses, and midwives are also not allowed to be on the street except between 8-9 and 5-6. Don't you find that crazy?

Wednesday, 25 April. Afternoon. Last night a terrible uproar and much shrieking of shells. Many people are sleeping in cellars.

This morning dead silence but this afternoon artillery fire in the distance. Dr. Rinkes thinks that we will remain in this situation until the fall of Berlin. If this lasts long, we will have absolutely no food any more. This morning got 2 L of milk on Gerard's coupon; it was sour, but we used it to make porridge. We eat everything: for breakfast we have porridge made with musty wheat and water, etc. The Tommies are going to drop food parcels on the cities, but how will that help if the Germans get most of it?[22]

Thursday, 26 April. Dearest, the days are endless. You won't believe this, but the English have stopped all action.[23] Only now and then do we hear the sound of a distant cannon, and for the rest there is in this sun-drenched, summer-warm world no war, only hunger, pinching hunger. People say that the English took the IJssel line only for the purpose of covering their flank but don't plan to push through further here. And that we have to wait until Berlin falls. Well, that can happen soon because it is ⅔ taken and entirely surrounded by the Russians. They are saying that at any moment there could be an armistice. But it could also last for weeks still.

At the moment I still have a little keg and 1 tin of rye, and 1½ tin of wheat. Then some bits of fat, and a bit of sugar, a bag of salt, and yesterday from Chris we got a jar of jam. Unfamiliar luxury! But the situation is such that we are grateful for a lump of (terribly old) bread thrown away by the Germans, and my evacuees are going to beg for food from the Germans. This morning I walked to Vlastuin again. Everyone else was being turned away, but I could get a bottle of milk and a bottle of buttermilk. And then they added, for the children, two slices of rye bread with butter. And Dicks, I was so happy with it. At home we divided that rye bread fairly, everyone a tiny bit. At this moment I could cry over it. But I wonder whether you have anything to eat still, and how you are. Where *are* you? It makes me so tired, all that worrying.

Yesterday three people offered me safe shelter in their cellars. They say that under no circumstances should I stay in this little house during a real artillery bombardment such as we had recently. I did put a mattress in the cellar and now am

---

22 The relief flights in fact began two days later (Olson, p. 409).

23 There were talks taking place between the Allied and the German leaders, but it is impossible to know what information was circulating on the grapevine.

sleeping on the springs of my own bed, in case it's necessary to go downstairs at night. I don't feel good about leaving the house and the evacuees [and going to someone else's bomb shelter], but I feel that it's my responsibility to you to do *everything* I can to keep the three of us safe.

The big road intersection in Woudenberg, together with all the corner houses, has been blown sky-high. In the direction of Amersfoort there is a big fire. For the rest it's frighteningly silent and you hear your heart beating.

Evening, very tired and drowsy: Our evacuees are near their deepest point. They have almost no food anymore and talk about setting out on foot to meet the English and in that way to be liberated—that is, when the curfew is lifted. What a lot of nervous tension and misery is caused by being in the middle of the front! Meanwhile it looks as though the Germans are running low on gasoline; many cars, motorbikes, and even trucks passed by pulled by well-fed, gleaming horses. I haven't seen such beautiful horses in a long time.

Every time I want to have a nice, quiet wash the bothersome cannons begin to bark so that I jump into my clothes again. I'm now going to sleep on my little spirals; it's mouse-still and I'm hoping for a peaceful night.

Friday, 27 April. The waiting and the silence oppress me so much that we're at the point of wishing for the dangers of a hail of shells instead. Nothing on the road, nothing in the air. Until now we had beautiful weather, though cold at night (I'm afraid that the apple tree has frozen, and the first strawberries are black) but sunny by day. But today it's endless rain, and our nerves are prickly in the extreme. During the night there was only occasional firing and otherwise silence, silence. And now also: little to eat, starvation everywhere, and ... no liberation.

Afternoon: I've withdrawn into the bedroom; for a time I just have to be alone in order to find myself again and to get a bit of sleep. I'm tired through and through from all the unrestful nights and anxieties and worries. Mr West is reinforcing the cellar. Oh Dicks, now that the end is approaching it's almost as though I can't deal with it. May God support me .... I love you so much.

And I've just seen that the Germans are again laying a telephone line.

Chapter Fourteen

28 April to 2 July 1945

The last weeks' entries describe the problems, confusion, uncertainty, and dangers involved in the transition from war to peace, both on the smaller scale—family, village—and the larger, national one.

Madzy's personal situation is dominated by the intense anguish about Wim's delayed return from the camp. It is the expression of someone who is at the limit of her endurance.[1] Once the war ended, the POWs began to filter back, but Wim was not among the first groups. Although some of those who returned were actually from the same camp, their reports about the delay in Wim's return were falsely encouraging or simply wrong.

However, the camp had indeed been liberated—on the night of 28 April, the same date as this next entry. It was liberated by the Russians, but the prisoners had to wait for weeks before transport could be organized to take them home. Bill wrote two versions of the story of the liberation and his return journey (see Appendix A).

The process of liberating the Netherlands—replacing German rule with a viable Dutch government—was a complicated and sensitive one. The remaining German troops had to be rounded up by the Allies.[2] There were enough German troops in the country so that there was danger of more killings of Dutch civilians and prisoners, and massacres of the kind that had happened at the Vucht concentration

---

1   I have edited some of this out.
2   On 2 May, during the negotiations, Prince Bernhard charged the Germans with continuing inundations (from breached dikes) and executions (van der Zee, p. 271). On 6 May there were still Germans looting and shooting (van der Zee, p. 287).

camp just before the arrival of the Canadian troops.[3] In fact, on 7 May, two days after the official end of the war, there was a massacre of celebrating civilians in Amsterdam that resulted in nineteen dead and 117 wounded.[4]

Moreover, it was necessary to prevent the Dutch from engaging in reprisals.

In books about the ending of the war there are abundant stories about (and pictures of) the arrival of the liberating troops, with parades of armoured vehicles, grinning soldiers, and rejoicing crowds. This jubilation did happen, but it did not reflect the state of the country as a whole. General Alexander Galloway, head of the British military relief effort, reported to his government that it "was deceptive because men and women who are slowly dying of starvation in their beds cannot walk gaily about the streets waving flags. ... It is an empty country, inhabited by a hungry, and in the towns, a semi-starved population."[5]

In fact, Madzy wrote very little about public jubilation in Maarn. For one thing, as she wrote, the area was still "chock full of Dutch SS."[6] Given their ferocity, it's understandable that the Allied authorities wanted to avoid a last-ditch battle or a massacre.

*****

Saturday, 28 April. It is almost incomprehensible, but they speak of peace, or at least truce. The Germans ask *us*: "Is the war over?"[7] And this evening Willem came panting to say that the last battle in Berlin is being fought and that a new government is being formed in Munich. About Holland nothing is being said, but both yesterday and today there has been no shot fired here, no airplane flying, no explosion heard.

---

3   See entry for 6 September 1944.

4   Van der Zee, pp. 293–294.

5   Quoted by Olson, p. 413.

6   The Dutch SS were a Dutch police force under German control, an integral part of the German SS (Schutzstaffel) (Warmbrunn, pp. 22, 89).

7   Madzy gave the words in German, evidently quoting bewildered German soldiers.

The sword of Damocles has hung over our heads by a silken thread, shells have gone over our roof, bombs have fallen all round us: will we really survive all this and suffer only hunger? Because again I'm really hungry this last while, and feel myself getting steadily weaker, while my heart again behaves strangely. But will we really escape so wonderfully well?

All around me is silence; just now I made my bed as it was formerly, and Pank is sleeping in her own bed. I am again wearing a nightgown and I could have my bath without being interrupted. It is as if a great quiet is descending on us, no longer the silence, the stifling silence before the fierce storm. We are again making plans, we dare to look at the future again. At any hour the last shot may fall. But there are still lots of Germans and Dutch SS here, and 70,000 troops on the Grebbe Line. I will take a sleeping pill because otherwise I will never get to sleep.

And where are you, Dicksy, and what are you thinking and feeling?—if you are still alive.

We still have 10 pounds of rye and 3 pounds of wheat in the house. We were told that we would get no bread, but now there is again 4 ounces per person. But when the English come this situation will soon be over.[8] Tomorrow we will eat the first spinach from the garden; we share everything with the evacuees, who also have nothing anymore and go begging from the Germans. This week we still have something to eat, and as for what happens after that—"who is alive then can do the worrying then." If only you are still more or less OK, Dicks. Actually we expect the end to come tomorrow. Oh, Dicks, how will it feel? I think that we will weep more than rejoice ....

Sunday, 29 April. And now it is just waiting, endless and impatient waiting for the latest news, for unconditional surrender. And oh! the last waiting, after 5 years of endless patient waiting, weighs

---

8   Madzy used "the English" to refer to the liberating troops in general. Presumably the local people had no information—at least not in advance—about which nationalities were involved.

so heavily on us. A day like today is just a matter of counting the hours and longing for someone who brings news. The curfew is still in effect so no church, and we can only go out between 5 and 6—because what could you do on the street on a Sunday morning from 8 to 9? Besides it was miserable weather: *wet snow*, please note, and icy cold, and raw rain showers. I held a quiet and extensive Sunday school and knitted the last wool that I had from unraveled little socks. Everything is the last: the last wheat and rye, the last gravy cubes, and rice and soup-thickener, and the last little bit of butter and fat and jam and sugar (all presents given during these past few days by people who now dare to give away what they had been hoarding).

Every now and then, near us in the woods, a German fires his last ammunition at a hare or a rabbit.

At 13 minutes before noon the English began dropping food parcels on the starving cities. In that respect we are also well off, although I have a pain in my stomach, perhaps from hunger but more likely from the rye. We ate the last eggs out of the preservative; they were slightly spoiled but nonetheless we ate them. Tomorrow in honour of the birthday of Princess Juliana we will eat a pudding that we got from Els, with a bit of orange sauce. The evacuees are thinking that they will leave before next Sunday. I will also find a place for Joost to go to: I want to receive you with only the children.

Monday, 30 April. It snowed seriously today, such a weird sight: snow on the young green, and it was very cold. 60,000 tons of food have been dropped on the cities. We celebrated the Princess' birthday as well as possible and sang the national anthem behind closed doors while outside a couple of Germans bicycled by, and Joost loved it all. But oh, what do we do if we have to be patient for much longer?

Tuesday, 1 May. A new month: what will it bring us? A day like today murders the soul: constantly huddled in the house with the 12 of us, except for those single hours in which like hares we can run along the road, and then again waiting, waiting, asking for news, and again tensely waiting. Today Neubrandenburg has fallen but you're not there any longer, are you? And you aren't free yet, or are you?

Liberation is only 7 km [5 mi] away from us, but oh, how far! This week we will be eligible for food from the Swedish Red Cross. We will get ½ pound lentils and Gerard ½ pound rice.

Wednesday, 2 May. The news today is that Hitler is dead, von Dönitz has taken his position, is prepared to capitulate to the English and Americans but not the Russians, so the fighting continues. There is no fighting here in Holland any more; England guarantees food, and the Germans will allow it to be delivered to the harbour at Rotterdam, where the ships are already arriving, and to 3 airfields. One highway has been declared free. We expect that one of these days we will get something via the distribution network, but the cities will get it first. I still have ½ basket of potatoes and received an ample 10 pounds of rye, which I share with the evacuees.

Just now we saw a food airplane coming over slowly and stood excitedly looking at it!

Evening: Today we had tremendous excitement, actually a foretaste of the huge liberation sensation which we hope to experience. We heard the droning of an airplane; the children were scared again, but I said, "That's the Tommies with the food parcels," upon which everyone ran out into the garden. We saw in the distance a large airplane flying low, and then it was gone. An hour later, there was again droning and then four airplanes came over the Knorrebuurt; they sheared over the trees, enormous white birds with red crosses! The rejoicing from the Knorrebuurt was deafening. But who can describe how overwhelmed we were when, just after that, five of those huge birds flew right over our little house? We screamed, waved, jumped, cried—what all didn't we do? The emotion was indescribable; it is as though a little window opens and one can again see a house of peace. My heart beat like a mad thing, the children clamped themselves against me—in short, it was an almost frighteningly oppressive sensation, a foretaste of the feelings which will storm through us when once we are free again.[9]

Thursday, 3 May. This morning many more Red Cross airplanes flew over. One group of 6 came skimming extremely low over the vegetable garden;[10] we ran out and waved and screamed as though our lives depended on it! And again the tears sat high.

But there was one even more emotional moment: I went to have a rest—I had a headache and took an aspirin—and suddenly Juus comes rat-tatting at the door. Chris was there and brought such good news, she couldn't delay telling me. Italy had fallen, Denmark was liberated, in Austria a million men had given themselves up, and there was peace! "But where, then, are the English?" I asked. "They are almost at the door, but why don't they come?" Do we have to believe it? Chris disregarded the curfew; all that was over, she said. But VaVa—when I dropped by at 5 o'clock—said that everything was true except that we here are not yet liberated. At 7:30 I went again, and at 9:15 again, but that is deadly dangerous, I won't do it again, because around here it's chock full with Dutch SS and even over the radio we are warned not to do it, that it's against the rules, because it's precisely *now* that we could still get into awful trouble because the SS is ferocious. According to Dr. Rinkes the SS is handing over its weapons to the Wehrmacht. But after all the emotions

---

9   I was one of the children clamped to Madzy, and I am still moved as I work on this passage.

10   Madzy used the word "rakelings," which means almost brushing against something, a vivid way of indicating how low they flew. I remember that it looked very much as though they would graze the tops of the trees surrounding our house, so low you could say they passed over the garden rather than over the house. It was a stupendous sight.

of today I no longer believe in "The End" until I see, with my own eyes, the English coming along the road.

Friday, 4 May. There's not much news. The Queen and the Princess are already in Brabant.[11] And almost the whole German front has collapsed, as has also been announced over the German radio. But here everything goes slowly, perhaps deliberately so. I think that people want to move inconspicuously towards capitulation in order to prevent bloodshed. Also the Dutch SS is fierce, as are some Germans (not all). Yesterday Dutch SS shot down a Red Cross airplane, the devils. The Wehrmacht immediately executed the guilty men, and all the SS have to turn in their weapons now. The food parcels have now also been arriving here, and next week we will enjoy something from them. At any moment we expect the arrival of the English; according to some people they are already here but they are moving in gradually so as to make it as unnoticeable as possible. Too bad; I would have liked the see the *moment suprème* clearly.

Evening, in bed. At 9:30 Dr. Rinkes stood on the doorstep: tomorrow at 8:00 the German armies in Holland, Norway, and Denmark have to surrender unconditionally. So that will be the *moment suprème*. What will we notice of it? I hold my breath. Will there still be fighting here along the front? Just now there was still gunfire. I decided to stay home, although I really need to go to the town hall to get Joost's coupons. Will you believe, Dicks, that I have a stomach-ache because of it? But that can also be because all of a sudden we again had something to eat: a little piece of liver that we fried in some ... butter! It came from the Swedish Red Cross on Joost's ration (brought by Nico [Kamp] and Julia from Driebergen), with some white bread. I can't eat much—it immediately disagrees with me; I've had trouble with my stomach for a long time. That will soon get better now. To my

---

11 One of the southern provinces of the Netherlands, in the area that had been liberated in the autumn of 1944.

pleasure, my heart stays steady in spite of all the nerve-shocking moments, a sign that at that time it was after all not a question of nerves but probably a matter of being overworked, together with the poor food. We are hoping very much for the Red Cross parcels that we can begin receiving at the beginning of next week. One of these days we'll run out of potatoes, but now we have lentils and rice. We are getting used to living on charity—all this is gifts. What will tomorrow bring us?

5 May 1945

We are free!

Yes, that's how it is, but we didn't spend the whole day in rejoicing. Not a bit of it; today was, like the former ones, a day of waiting without anything unusual happening. Since 8:00 this morning we're free, but except for a couple of airplanes we haven't seen an Englishman or an American. No one knows what is actually happening.

Last night for the first time I slept peacefully, but at 6:15 I was wakened by someone knocking at the door; it was Willem, who told me the news of the liberation. I immediately got dressed and walked to Vlastuin for a bottle of milk. Hurried back, dressed the children and had breakfast and at 8 went to the town hall for Joost's coupons. There I saw a deputation of people in their Sunday best. It was Dien, Chris, and the boys, M^r. and Mevr. de Josselin de Jong, and Freule Verschuur to welcome the mayor.[12] This was very risky because there was no Tommy to be seen and no flag.

This afternoon I quickly bicycled to Driebergen for Joost's coupons (English food parcel) and that was very dangerous because the curfew has not yet been officially cancelled. In Doorn

---

12 They were greeting Mr. Everwijn Lange (see entry for 23 May 1942), the pre-war mayor who had been replaced by a pro-Nazi one and was now being reinstated. According to J. P. Briedé (p. 177), the reinstatement actually happened the following day.

yesterday Mevr. Heybroek-van Eeghen was shot dead because she was on the street during the curfew.

It appears that all of Holland is waving flags and cheering, but we alone still have the SS and they are pestering us; in Driebergen and Zeist the decorations and festivities have been suppressed by the SS. But beyond Zeist and throughout the whole country there is celebration. How sad for us! Now we are just waiting for the arrival of the Allies, and then I will open my bottle of wine.[13]

Fortunately I came home safe, and now we hear that the SS are being disarmed by the Germans. There is still nothing like a liberation mood. We are told not to show ourselves on the street wearing orange.[14] Tomorrow I will go to church and then will learn whether the curfew is lifted. I baked a festive cake with the last of the baby-flour and custard. At 5 o'clock I went to fetch buttermilk from Vlastuin and got 4 large slices of rye bread with cheese, which we loved. After dinner VaVa and I tried to listen to the Queen's speech; this didn't succeed, but Prime Minister Gerbrandy did come through.[15] "We are free." Then it sort of penetrated to me, but I still don't feel really free so long as Germans with guns cycle past the house.

People are congratulating each other. From now on I will often take the children with me, now that at last we can again leave home without endangering their lives. For me, the children's safety is almost the most precious thing; the *most* precious is the approach of your return, my dearest darling. I don't know how I will be able to thank God for that. Later let us always be grateful *if* you actually come home safe and healthy. Where *are* you, my darling?

Sunday, 6 May. Even though we didn't know whether the curfew had been lifted (as it turned out, that took place only

---

13 If she was thinking of the bottle of champagne, there *was* no wine. She was forgetting that she had given it to Hansje.
14 Orange is one of the country's colours.
15 Evidently VaVa still had a battery-powered radio.

this afternoon), Pankske and I went to church. Because many people were still obeying the curfew, it wasn't full, and it was an improvised service, but because of that all the more spontaneous. At one point the reader couldn't continue because his glasses misted over with emotion, and halfway through the service the organist had to be revived by the district nurse. The minister, Ds. Koolhaas, sometimes couldn't go on because of the tears, but it was tremendous, and after a thundering sermon with many appropriate psalms and hymns we ended with the national anthem. No one's eyes were dry, and people often couldn't sing because of the tears. Even for me it was almost too much. For little Pankske it was an unforgettable experience.[16] "For the first time we really sang the 'Wilhelmus,' Mam!"[17]

For the rest it was a day of waiting. Now it appears that it is only this afternoon that the surrender will be signed between General Oberst Blaskowitz and Prince Bernard, although even this was not confirmed at 8:15.[18] But tomorrow the Allied armies are expected. So we still sit under the power of the Germans. This evening, two bicycles were requisitioned right in front of my door and we couldn't do anything about it. We still have to restrain ourselves, but it is now a matter of hours. The mayor is ready to resume his position. In the blink of an eye we will be truly free.

This evening I wrote a poem for Chris, in honour of Piet's birthday. I finished this emotional day with a severe migraine attack and will now go to sleep.

Outside there is a lot of banging from all the shells and bombs that have to be exploded. They took away 8 bombs from under the viaduct. God has certainly spared *us*, dearest. You too?

---

16 In fact, I have never forgotten it.
17 We had, of course, been singing it *sotto voce* behind closed doors and windows. It was important to keep singing it, partly for morale and partly so that the children would know it.
18 See van der Zee p. 282ff.

Monday, 7 May. Evening, past 11:00. What a day! Everything is in festive array; everywhere orange, Allied troops passing through Doorn, the mayor reinstalled, the underground on their legs again, flags everywhere. Raised the flag at Christie's house and drank punch. Marian went with me everywhere in her party dress with orange sash, Gerard also with sash. *Enfin*, splendid. One beautiful moment was when several hundred Germans passed here on the way to give themselves up as prisoners. This evening I spoke with a young Englishman. And the war in Europe is, today, definitely over.[19]

What occupies my mind most is how I will get you home. And how do I get rid of the evacuees? It's said that they can't return to Arnhem for two months. All the same, I've told them that they have to leave here as soon as possible: they have enough relatives to take them in. Tomorrow Mʳ West will go off to see where they can go. Joost will have to stay for a little while. Moeder hasn't been here for more than two weeks, even though the curfew was lifted yesterday. But she knows perfectly well that she has to make some decision about Joost and therefore probably prefers to stay away! Poor Joost, who is so happy here, and now has to leave again. But now you and the children come first. I expect you every hour of the day, but still I remain calm. Tomorrow the national day of celebration.

This morning when I was waiting near the town hall there came all of a sudden the first American automobile, and who stepped out of it? Jan de Beaufort in uniform.[20] I received from him via de Hoogt (Lies came to bring it) a little tin of corned beef and a tin of all sorts of delicious surprises. We ate everything in one go because we were *so* hungry.

---

19 Clearly Madzy had not heard about the massacre in Amsterdam, which had happened that day (see headnote).

20 One of the sons of Betsy and Ferd de Beaufort, and therefore a cousin of Wim's. He was probably serving with the Dutch contingent in the Allied forces.

Tuesday, 8 May. Every day *full* of experiences. This morning at 6:30 to Vlastuin for milk, buttermilk, and rye. Again received rye bread with cheese. Did the housework, began to air your clothes out of the "flight" suitcase. This afternoon Juus with Marian to Doorn.

All of a sudden a splendid American car stopped in front of the garden: Edward Hoogeweegen in uniform![21] He is on Prince Bernard's staff and lives at 't Loo![22] But he caused me great disappointment by telling me that nothing was known about all of you, also not where you were. But as soon as you were found you would be coming home.

Then my evacuee came back from Ede full of stories about the good food there, and he reported that after 15 May they have to evacuate back to Arnhem, everything compulsory and done according to definite regulations. But I want them gone before that, if possible, and now he will make an effort for that. I do so hope that they're gone by the time you return; it would be an impossible situation for you, and I don't have a bed for you.

Wednesday, 9 May. Bicycled to Charlotte. Close to her house the roads were barricaded by felled trees, etc. There I had a flat tire[23] but (pushing the bicycle) I still went on. Dick's mother's house had been bombed,[24] and Dick and Charlotte's house also uninhabitable, and the greenhouses. Spoke with Charlotte. Received some spinach but nothing to eat or drink. (Had breakfasted on rye porridge made with water, and one slice of bread, and my stomach rumbled.) At nearly 11:30 I had to

---

21 See entry for 18 May 1942.

22 One of the royal palaces.

23 Pneumatic tires had been unavailable for a long time. On 25 February 1945, Madzy had referred to having only one surrogate tire left. Perhaps Wim's bicycle, which she used less often, still had a pneumatic tire.

24 Bill noted that this happened on one of the last days of the war and that the house was totally demolished. Charlotte's nephew Carel Beynen told me this bombing was an accident (e-mail to me on 1 June 2017).

start walking back but couldn't go via the small roads anymore so went along the moor. I was half-fainting from the hunger, so that when I saw, on the moor, a [Canadian military] canteen with tents round it, I begged for food. At first I got nothing, but afterwards I did, delicious cookies and custard with apricots! And real tea with sugar! And I got 4 tins of fish and sausage to take home! Unbelievably strengthened by all this I danced home.[25]

There we had many visitors and confusion. Lies told us that Hans van Ketwich had come home from the camp. He said that you could also come at any moment, so that I am very keyed-up and lie listening to every sound.

Thursday, 10 May. It is still a matter of tense waiting. People are working hard on Holland;[26] we here experienced nothing

---

25 This incident came to have immense importance for Madzy. Years later she wrote a short narrative about it, and she also dealt with it in *Land for Our Sons*, her book about our early years in Canada. The three narratives differ slightly in detail; in what follows, I have incorporated material from both of the other versions.

The Canadian soldiers were, as she approached, just finishing their meal and scraping the leftovers off the plates onto the ground. "My eyes followed the falling food; I looked at [one of the men] and before I knew it I had said [in English], 'Is there some more left? Can I have it?'" The soldier explained that they had orders not to give food to civilians because "there are so many hungry people, you know." Madzy, turning away, apparently fainted because when she came to she was sitting on the ground with her back against the wheel of the truck and was given a mug of hot tea with sugar and milk. While they all waited for her tea to cool, the soldiers told about "their cousins and brothers who had died in the fighting." They gave her food to eat, and when she returned to her bicycle, she found food in the basket. The soldiers jumped into their truck and left. As Madzy continued her trip home, she wrote, she vowed that, to repay our debt to the Canadians, we would emigrate to Canada.

26 There was of course an enormous amount of reconstruction to be done, but for months after the liberation many workers were unable to do much work because of the long period of malnutrition (Kaufman & Horn, p. 133). It was the same with those who had survived the labour camps

special today. The Germans are gone from Maarn. The women who collaborated have had their heads shaved.

And I wait and wait ....

Friday, 11 May. The blackout has been lifted over all of Europe. Tomorrow we will get the first small food parcel from the English Red Cross: a pound of biscuit,[27] half a bar of chocolate, 1 tin of meat. Then I will after all have something for Gerard's birthday [on 13 May]. I still have 2 meals of potatoes, 14 pounds of rye, ½ pound of brown beans, and some vegetables, and a little bit of oil. That's all. Bread finished. We received only 400 gr. If this coming week the bread ration isn't increased we'll have finished the rye by Saturday, because we use 2 pounds per day for rye bread, rye porridge, rye soup, and rye cookies for 5 hungry people. The last days I'm again really hungry and my pound of biscuit will certainly be finished by Sunday. My mouth is already watering at the thought.

They say that you are in France to be deloused and given supplementary food.

Sunday, 13 May. Today our little Gerard is three; it was a delightful party, but we missed you. This evening visited at Stameren with the English. Wonderful. Home at nearly 11:00 and told the evacuees that they really will have to go. They want to stay, but I heard that you can come home soon and now I'm pushing through.

Monday, 14 May. Today I try to wrestle myself loose from the evacuees. I told them that they have to leave by Wednesday morning at the latest to make room for you.

---

in Germany and were now straggling back, mostly on foot; they had been living under appalling conditions.

27 This is probably "Holland rusk," which in Dutch is "biscuit." In the following passages I'm guessing that every time Madzy mentioned "biscuit," she was referring to rusks.

I tried today to press 4 suits of yours with old-fashioned irons.

Wednesday, 16 May. Evening. They're gone, the evacuees! And my house is my own again.[28] It took an enormous lot of trouble to get rid of them; this morning at 6:30 I still went to fetch potatoes for them because they had again gobbled up everything, and we worked like horses the whole day to create some order out of the dirty mess,[29] but now the house is completely ready to receive you—and we too, my darling.

And naturally I'm again getting anxious: will you ever come home? Could something dreadful have happened to you? Today the gossip in the village was that you and de Boer[30] would come home today; where do they pick up such a rumour?—and still I believe it and constantly look out to the road and listen to every car or motorbike, whether it stops here. Oh, Dicks, my impatience is now so great, so intense, and I sometimes don't know how I can contain it. Now that we have everything so entirely ready to receive you, all my thoughts go out to you and I live in and with you. It's as though the three years lying behind us shrink and the time when you were still with us comes again more clearly before me, comes closer to me, so that I see you more clearly in my mind's eye and I again remember all kinds of movements and words of yours.

May God bring you back to us tomorrow.[31]

---

28 Juus and Joost were still there: Joost is referred to in the entry for 1 June, below. I have no information about when he left and where he went. Juus stayed until shortly after Wim's return.

29 This would still have been done with inadequate cleaning supplies and no running water.

30 Captain de Boer, Suus's husband.

31 This is the end of the second hard-back notebook; the rest of the diary is written on loose sheets from a scribbler. (The scribbler may have been intact when Madzy was writing in it, but it was loose sheets that we found in the back of the second notebook.)

Saturday, 19 May. Evening, 11:30. When I was setting the table today, Juus suddenly gave several penetrating shrieks. My first thought was: "Dicks!", but it was Nel.[32] Very nice for Juus to hear everything and again to have one of her family to talk with.

A tiring day. At 6:30 on the road to get milk. Immediately after breakfast did our washing and went out for food; together with standing in line, I was busy with that until 11:30. Then quickly did the rooms, ate lunch and washed dishes and cooked porridge and read with Marian. Then out again for milk. At home drank tea, put the paperwork in order, bathed the children, bathed myself, quickly ate supper and from 7 to 8:30 went out for vegetables. Now fortunately two days in which there will be no food-worries, only Monday to the dairy-store and maybe to van Beuningen for milk. So we will manage fine. Out of the English parcels we regularly get something: Saturday ½ pound nutritional biscuits and meat and chocolate, Tuesday 3 ounces of rusks, Thursday again rusks and chocolate, and 1 ounce of sugar, today again rusks, 340 gr meat and 125 gr lard, all of the finest quality.

I keep watching for Dicks and need all my trust in God in order to feel that he is still alive and will soon come safely home. Where *is* he and why do we hear nothing?

Sunday, 20 May. Today the first sign of life from the camp! Thank God! Moeder came to meet me, just as I was going into the church, with *'t Parool*.[33] In it was the whole story about how the camp at Neubrandenburg (so after all not Sylt!) had been liberated by the Russians and everyone was well. Oh, how happy I was; during the church service I could hardly contain my tears. Now I expect to receive a letter from you soon, Dicks, and I expect you

---

32 Nel Slag was Juus's niece.

33 *Het Parool* was one of the major underground newspapers, begun in the early months of the occupation. By September 1944 it was a weekly. Several people who worked for the newspaper were executed by the Germans or died in concentration camps (Warmbrunn, p. 228).

yourself in a week or two or three. Oh, my darling, I'm so deeply grateful ....

This afternoon visited the Everwijn Langes, and also went to de Hoogt, where I spoke with Hans van Ketwich and Jan de Beaufort. This evening again to Stameren with the Tommies, but it is becoming disappointing to find how little conversation the English have. However, these are simple lads, even though the young girls regard them as heroes. Now I feel how old I've become in these last years ....

Wednesday, 23 May. The days pass and no Dicks.

There is not much news here. We regularly receive rusks, sometimes sugar, chocolate, tinned meat. But the supply of other articles has stopped: no bread any more, no meat. So it's still very limited. We have enough, but my rye is almost finished and also the wheat. But it should soon get a bit better. Maybe we will soon get butter.

I don't feel very well. What it is, precisely, I can't say: very tired, and nauseated and some pain in my stomach. I don't want to get sick now that I constantly expect Dicks. Maybe it's the reaction, maybe the different food, maybe the cold, because it is nasty cold weather.

Monday, 28 May. Yesterday the Prince[34] drove by, after having had dinner with VaVa. A big occasion for our little gravel road.

Still nothing from Dicks, except a card from the Swiss Red Cross, not bringing much news.

Chris has collapsed; apparently that is happening to many women. I still feel tired but am already putting on a good deal of weight and will have to restrain myself, otherwise I will split my one corset!

---

34 Prince Bernard, as commander of the Resistance forces, was at the centre of the negotiations that ended the war (van der Zee, p. 234 and elsewhere; Olson, p. 379).

Wednesday, 30 May. When the shutters were closed this evening and I was completely ready for bed, just on my knees to thank and beg to God, there was a knock on the door. I thought: "There he is!"—because since the liberation I see in every opening door, in every shadow passing a window, in every approaching step or car or motorbike my Dicks. But it was one of Chris's evacuees who came to tell me that Piet van Notten came home at 9 o'clock and that my Dicks will be home in 2 or 3 days. Oh!!![35]

Thursday, 31 May. Evening. Today has been one awful tension, so that my heart constantly hurt and Juus got some valerian from Ad. I will not leave home any more until he, my dearest, is here. This evening I nearly collapsed, but just then Piet van Notten came. That gave me a push again, and just now, as distraction, I washed my hair, on Piet's assuring me that Dicks can't be here before 6:00 tomorrow evening. Oh, God, how heavy this last bit is for me, not only emotionally but also physically, because the pain in my heart is so gnawing and irritating. I'll lie down and read a bit to get through the night. (The last one alone?)

Friday, 1 June. 8:45. It is evening, after a thunderstorm; outside the birds whistle their evening song; the air is woven through with the scents of summer, the rooms smell of the flowers that I've already received. I don't know how many people have come by already to tell me that you are coming, or they ask why you aren't here yet. Annetje spoke to a lieutenant who said that you should have been part of an earlier group and will certainly be here very soon.

---

35 At this point in the photocopy of the diary that he was using for translating, Bill wrote: "Translated up to here. I cannot go on." He told me that he found it too agonizing to live himself into Madzy's state of mind and mood during those days of waiting. But he continued reading, and he resumed translating with the entry for Monday, 2 July. Immediately after the last diary entry he wrote the narrative of his return (see Appendix A).

I'm alone; the children are in bed, Joost is in bed, and Juus keeps herself upstairs out of considerateness. I sit by the open window and listen to every approaching sound. Just now there was suddenly a car: but it was Edward. Also a jeep raced by but (I thought that my heart broke) it raced on.

And I wait ....

But I'm waiting patiently with, constantly on my lips, "Thy will be done, God." I no longer wait as I did formerly, when I impatiently walked to meet you and when you came I was, out of pure tension, unkind to you.[36] I wait in the firm conviction that when God wills it He will give me back to you. It would be a perfect evening for you to come home, but it is already so wonderful that you *are* coming back.

And yet ....

Just now a man came by to say that a car with officers is driving around, and that Capt. de Boer is home.

But where are *you*, my dearest, where *are* you?

Oh, God, I love you so much ....

Oh, if only you came now ....

10:00 p.m. Piet van Notten said that I could expect you from today 6:00. I will do everything I can to remain calm, otherwise this heart of mine will break down. I intensely wanted you home this evening: today I hung all your clothes ready, and now (like yesterday) your bed is open and your pyjamas are ready, while your place for breakfast is laid.

Saturday, 2 June. Evening, 7:30. My dearest, this day is hell. From minute to minute I've waited, and nothing has come except people to congratulate me! Oh, Dicks, I can't hold out any longer. All kinds of awful things go through my head about what could have happened to you. Now I know how much I love you and how

---

36 She may be thinking of the long evenings of waiting for him in the United States or perhaps of similar occasions when they were back in the Netherlands.

difficult it is without you. My heart really hurts from longing for you ....

When Pank and I were sitting outside in front of the house, a jeep approached, and suddenly stopped nearby. I *knew* that it was you! But the jeep turned around and drove quickly to the Hoogeweegens.

My God, how long do You still want me to hold on?

Sunday, 3 June. Afternoon. It was as though I couldn't continue. My heart was again behaving so strangely, I thought that it would break. Then I sent Nel [Slag] (who came yesterday) to Dr. LeHeux [in Doorn] to ask if Jan was already home. When Nel came back she told us: "There was suddenly a column of transport vehicles that arrived in the camp, and the officers had 20 minutes to pack. Brender[37] had then just gone for a walk outside the camp and when he returned he was too late. Now it may be two weeks before there is another chance to come home."[38]

I thought that I broke. Since 1:00 on Thursday I haven't left the house and watched every minute of the day and night. But now I took the children along and we walked through the woods to Piet. He wasn't home and, despairing, I walked home again. When I was home I couldn't contain it any longer and lay down on bed crying ....

When I had tidied myself up a bit and had drunk a cup of strong coffee and (with sunglasses) made myself a bit more presentable, the Kamps came by. After that Piet came with the whole family, and also VaVa and Andrusha[39] and Oom Ferd.[40]

---

37 Wim was often referred to in this way.

38 Beside this, in the photocopy from which he was doing the translation, Bill wrote in heavy, emphatic letters, "Not true." But it was partly true—see his narrative in Appendix A.

39 I haven't positively identified Andrusha, but I believe he was VaVa's young son.

40 J. F. de Beaufort, husband of Betsy. He was director of the Nederlandsche Bank (information from Bill) and spent much of his time in Amsterdam.

"Well, damn it, what nonsense," Piet said. "Listen, you can expect Wim home at any moment. Within two weeks the camp had to be empty, and when I left it was already the tenth day. No, the problem is with the transport. Those columns get split and then if you're in a column that stays behind it lasts another day. Don't worry, and keep watching for him."

Yes, but Piet,[41] you're home for four days already, and Wendelaar, van Tuyll, Piet de Boer, LeHeux and his brother-in-law, etc., all those prisoners of war from this whole area are home for a long time already.

Nevertheless I will be patient again and look for you, every moment of the day and night, my very dearest ....

Evening: This afternoon Dick [Kolff], Charlotte, and Bertie [their daughter] came to bring you fresh strawberries! We'll keep them for a bit. They came because almost all the people we know in Amersfoort are also home. Therefore I will again really watch for your coming, my dearest. The whole village laments and sympathizes with me.

*****

Monday, 2 July: Tomorrow at a quarter to 7 you will have been home for four weeks. These weeks have been an unbroken succession of wonderful moments, during which time I constantly had these words on my lips: "God, thank You for his safe return."

And how did it happen?

Sunday evening[42] passed in comfortless waiting, and also the following morning. But when, at 1 o'clock [Monday, 4 June], I was just sitting down with a cup of coffee, suddenly Dick Kolff's gamekeeper stood at the window with a note from ... Wim![43]

---

41 She used no quotation marks here; probably it was what she was thinking, not saying.

42 She picked up the story from the end of the entry made on Sunday, 3 June.

43 Bill, in his narrative (see Appendix A), doesn't mention writing this note. This message is not to be confused with the later one mentioned below,

From himself! He wrote that he was then (when he wrote the note, on Sunday afternoon) at the border and hoped to be home on Wednesday or Thursday after registering at the camp at Austerlitz.[44] My first reaction was, "Oh, *still* such a long time!" but then I was so happy and so thankful. In the afternoon I got on my bicycle and hurried off to Austerlitz to find out what was going on. Had a very friendly reception but was told that the officers would not arrive until Wednesday. I left a letter and a chocolate bar with them [for you].[45]

The next day [Tuesday], much rested after a peaceful night without constantly waiting and listening, I phoned the camp. They told me that the officers had become tired of waiting and might arrive immediately. The waiting began again.

At quarter past one Willem van Tuyll and Cornelie[46] suddenly came to visit and were still here at nearly 3:30 when suddenly a strange man stood at the window, with a note from ... Dicks! He had passed the Viersprong[47] and would try to get through the registration quickly and then walk home.

Now I've forgotten to tell that Vader and Jet also on that morning (Tuesday, 5 June) had come by car,[48] assuming that Wim would long ago have come home. They went, desolate, to have lunch at de Hoogt.[49] When I got *that* note, therefore, I sent Willem van Tuyll to de Hoogt (to tell Vader and Jet) and I myself jumped on the bicycle, and they and I arrived at the same moment

---

which was delivered by a stranger.

44 A small town four kilometres (three miles) from Maarn, with a big estate. The estate was being used as an administrative centre to process the returned POWs.

45 Bill's note: "Never received in the chaos."

46 Willem van Tuyll had been in the camp with Wim; his wife, Cornelie, was the daughter of Willem de Beaufort of 't Stort.

47 This was the local name for the intersection of two main roads.

48 Bill's note: This vehicle was the last remaining small truck of the gas works in The Hague. It ran on octane gas.

49 Betsy de Beaufort was Gerard's sister.

at the entrance to the camp at Austerlitz.[50] We weren't allowed into the camp. However there came a tall officer who had already registered and was looking for transportation to The Hague. I sent him on my bicycle to look for Wim. He came back alone to tell us that everyone was looking for Wim, and then went back. Very shortly after that (Jet and I were peering up the lane), the officer came cycling up with someone else, and only when they were close by did I recognize my own darling.

NOTE: When Bill reached this point in his translation/annotation, he added the account of his liberation. See Appendix A.

---

50 In his translation of this passage, Bill added that Madzy also sent Willem de Bruin, her helper, to the camp, riding his own bicycle and wheeling Wim's.

Conclusion

Madzy ended the diary there, but in the 1976 taped narrative she continued the story, speaking in English and addressing her children. "It was a strange feeling to see him back. [His hair] had begun to get slightly grey when he left, not very much; when he came back he was completely grey .... He was trim, clean, well-dressed; his uniform was in good shape. He had kept himself in good shape altogether. He looked healthy, well-nourished and happy, a little bit puzzled and confused of course, you can imagine, but everything was fine."[1]

Wim had to go back to the main building to finish checking out, and Madzy went with him. "Finally we could go home. And here we were, bicycling home along the very well-known little lanes through the woods, towards our little house. Well, it was quite a trip for Dad; he hadn't bicycled in three years, and after some time he began to feel it in his feet and his legs, I think, but he managed it."

In Maarn, we children and Juus were waiting. Gerard was at first eager, but when he saw a man in uniform, he ran indoors and hid under a bed. Madzy had to explain that his father was a *Dutch* soldier, not a German one.

*

As we know, Madzy had intended to give the diary to Wim when he returned, but she never did; he read it only after her death. It's easy to guess why she made that decision. One of her

---

1   For Wim's account of the reunion, see Appendix A.

main tasks in those first days and weeks would have been to reintegrate the family and set us on the course toward healing and rebuilding.[2] That would have included assessing the damage of the imprisonment on Wim; three months later she would write to Virginia Donaldson that his "nerves are still not as they used to be." Very probably she felt that he should not be exposed to the grimness of some of what she had written in the diary, that the best way to heal would be to look forward rather than back.[3] Before post-traumatic stress disorder became more widely understood, this was what one did.[4]

Wim, for his part, having had only Madzy's very limited and censored letters to go by, was reconnecting with someone who had been through events and conditions that he could hardly even imagine and who was even now glossing over the damage.[5] No doubt she was now telling him something about her wartime experiences, but she could be selective and, with him safely at home, she would certainly colour everything less blackly than she did when writing the diary. Undoubtedly she was mostly cheerful, relieved that we had all survived and were still in our own house, though the continuing shortages of everything and

---

2　Madzy told Gerard later that it took her a great deal of effort to persuade us children to look to Wim as the head of the family rather than to her, and this was only one aspect of the reintegration required. She also wrote about this in one of her semi-fictionalized (uncompleted) works.

3　Several times in her writings she referred to the biblical story of Lot's wife, who was turned into a pillar of salt because she looked back.

4　In a novel fragment titled *Never Too Late*, dating from ten or twelve years after this time and containing strongly autobiographical elements, she wrote: "There are moments of life through which I live without much reaction. I go through them with a numbness of mind which borders on callousness. [In the year or two following the war] I was still so overwhelmed by memories of war and terror, hunger, longing, and fear, that I [did not realize] whether I was happy or not. I just lived or vegetated, whatever you would call it" (quoted in *Frontiers and Sanctuaries*, p. 166).

5　We remember her intention to write only cheerful news to him.

the difficulties about Wim's health and employment (see below) were ongoing worries.[6]

Nevertheless, in his old age Bill told me that he wished he had read the diary soon after his return. Until he did read it after Madzy's death, he had no idea how bad those three years had been for us.

*

Madzy was thirty-five when she wrote the last words of the diary, and she was to live for another thirty-nine years. In *Frontiers and Sanctuaries*, I reconstructed the rest of her life as well as I could from my memories, her other writings, and outside sources. Here I will sketch it more briefly.

On that day in July 1945, the door to Madzy's inner life shut almost entirely. It was never to open again as wide or for as long, though glimpses appear in letters and in semi-autobiographical fiction and journalism. Much of what she wrote after this was directed to other readers and showed her public face. Although the public and private sometimes interrelated, there is ample evidence they often did not. The passage I quoted in the Preface (see page 8) indicates the gap between them.

However, she never stopped writing for very long, and she clearly had a deep urge to write autobiography, not only the narrative of her outer life but also the inner story. These writings included first drafts of works originally perhaps intended for ultimate publication but that she never managed to revise and

---

6   Madzy's niece Madzy Adama van Scheltema, the daughter of her brother Paul, stayed with us for a few months in the following year. Aged about fourteen at the time, she was one of the family who had been imprisoned in the Japanese camp in the Dutch East Indies; after their return to the Netherlands in March 1946 (see *Frontiers and Sanctuaries*, p.169), she stayed with us so that my mother could help her catch up on the schooling she had missed during the years in the camp. While I was working on *Frontiers and Sanctuaries*, this cousin wrote to me that both of our mothers were, in the years following the war, functioning physically and psychically at a very low level, both women exhausted by the gruelling war years.

that, in their rough state, were not ready for the public eye, though she preserved them to be read after her death. She wrote letters, diary fragments, history, and journalism.[7] She used her war experiences in several memoirs, short stories, and novel fragments. In all of this there is autobiography, direct and indirect. She never dealt successfully with the difficult issues of writing a connected, large-scale autobiography, but her preserving the attempts and fragments through all of our many moves indicates that she felt they were important.[8] Toward the end of her life she asked Bill—as Wim was known after our emigration to Canada—to destroy several volumes of the small five-year diaries in which she had kept brief records from the time of our arrival in Canada, but she gave no such instruction regarding her other work: she wanted it to be kept and read. The material fills about one and a half cardboard boxes of the kind used to store office papers.

*

The country to which Wim returned in 1945 was a shambles. Well over 200,000 hectares of land (over 500,000 acres; about 800 square miles) had been flooded, most of it deliberately, much of it by seawater. Sixty percent of the rail, road, and canal transportation system had been destroyed. Over 200,000 civilians had died.[9] In Amsterdam alone, a few weeks after the liberation, 30,000 people were reported as dying of starvation.[10] One family in eight was homeless.[11] "More than 400,000 people, driven from their homes, had to be brought back and often rehoused. More than 260,000 men straggled back from Germany, mostly on foot, and they had to be taken care

---

7   See Appendix C, and *Frontiers and Sanctuaries*, p. 387.
8   The one book-length memoir that she wrote was *Land for Our Sons* (see below, p. 316) and it covered only a relatively short period of her life.
9   Judt, *Postwar: A History of Europe since 1945*, pp. 17–18.
10   Van der Zee, p. 300.
11   Mak, *De eeuw van mijn vader*—"My Father's Century," pp. 336–337.

of."[12] Queen Wilhelmina wrote in her memoir: "We could not have suspected how widespread the destruction would be ... and how tired and physically weakened, and in what psychological condition our people would return to freedom."[13]

These conditions could not be remedied overnight. Though the food situation gradually improved, rationing and shortages continued for several years.[14] Judt wrote that, of the countries in western Europe that had been occupied, the Netherlands was the slowest to recover because of the serious damage to "farms, dykes, roads, canals, and people."[15] He noted that in "the first eighteen months following the Allied victory the mood of [Europe as a whole] swung from relief at the mere prospect of peace and a fresh start, to stony resignation and growing disillusion in the face of the magnitude of the tasks still ahead."[16]

Families had their own rebuilding to do. Although Madzy wrote that Wim looked healthy and well-nourished, he was in fact not well: he had contracted colitis, an inflammation of the colon, for which he had to follow a strict diet. As Madzy wrote to Virginia Donaldson in September 1945, there was also psychological damage.

As regards employment, Wim was still an army officer, and after three months' leave he was sent to a location in the southern Netherlands to be trained for work in tanks. He hated it, as by then he hated all things military. Because of the colitis he received a medical discharge, but then he had to find another job. He worked in an apple orchard to gain farming experience, and

---

12 Van der Zee, p. 306. The population of the Netherlands in 1939 was just under 9 million (https://m.ww2db.com.country/Netherlands).

13 Quoted by van der Zee, p. 306. Also see Kaufman & Horn, p. 133.

14 Months after the end of the war the rations were still inadequate. On 17 November 1945, Madzy wrote to Virginia Donaldson and Rosalie Worthington that there was still a scarcity of meat, fat, butter, and sugar. As late as the spring of 1947, "millions of people in [European] cities [were] slowly starving" (Olson, p. 455).

15 Judt, p. 89.

16 Judt, p. 86.

then in an office headed by Willem de Beaufort that managed the estates of the de Beaufort family. Although by now he had his certification as an estate manager, he found the work uncongenial. In disputes between "the office" and the tenant farmers, Wim usually found himself on the side of the farmers.

So he and Madzy decided to realize their dream of emigrating, which they had touched on in their correspondence during the war. They had to rebuild their lives in any case, so perhaps it should be done not in that battered and overcrowded country but elsewhere. Madzy was anxious to be free of her mother and in-laws.[17] They feared the Russian threat and another war.[18] When, in November 1946, a second son, Joost, was born, they had two boys who would in due course reach fighting age.

*

A cousin of Wim's, Peter van Stolk, had been living in Canada since before the war—in Terrace, a small logging town in northern British Columbia. Peter and his Canadian wife, Enid, came to the Netherlands in the summer of 1946 to visit his family, and Madzy and Wim had lunch with them. They discussed emigration. Peter agreed to sponsor us, so the following year we uprooted and set off. It was a huge venture for Wim to take a wife and three young children, and a few small crates and trunks of belongings, such a distance and to such a strange place.[19]

---

17 In 1963, in a letter written from Canada to Bill when he was in the Netherlands on a visit, Madzy alluded to being free of family pressures. "That is why I love it here; here I am free, though lonely."

18 Wim, in the weeks following the liberation of the Neubrandenburg camp, heard and saw what Russian domination would mean (see Appendix A). Moreover, as noted earlier, he was subject to re-testing for the colitis, and if/when he recovered, he could be required to rejoin the army.

19 It's hard for us in this time to imagine how little Wim and Madzy knew about their destination. Other than (as it turned out) misleading and romanticized information from Peter and Enid, they knew virtually nothing because there were no sources of information. We emigrated before the main wave; it is likely that later emigrants were better informed, if only through correspondence with those who had already

On an old freighter that carried a few passengers, we travelled from Rotterdam through the Panama Canal to Vancouver, and from there we went by coastal steamer north to Prince Rupert, then by train to Terrace.[20] It was a trip of about six weeks. We arrived in Terrace in mid-September of 1947. Bill (as he then became) immediately bought an eight-hectare (twenty-acre) property with a three-room cabin on it, and he and Madzy began making a new life.

It was hard work. The place they bought was not a working farm, and only a small part of the land was usable. More land had to be cleared of trees and brush, and the house had to be enlarged. Even with the addition of three bedrooms, it was still so small and simple that Madzy's mother, after a visit in 1952, reported to people in the Netherlands that her daughter was living in a "hut."

It was, in fact, a pioneer farm. At first we had a horse; a tractor and a small pickup truck came several years later. Madzy's housekeeping was primitive, similar in some respects to what it had been in those last war years, though in Terrace we had a washing machine. We still had no vacuum cleaner, nor a refrigerator, and cooking was for several years done on a wood stove. We had enough to eat, though it too was simple and dictated almost entirely by what the farm produced.

In spite of the labour-intensive housekeeping, Madzy found energy and made time to join in the work of farming and building. We remember her writing in the war diary that she enjoyed the gardening and asking Wim if, in the future, he would allow her to be his assistant, though surely at that time she had not pictured

gone to Canada. When we were in Terrace, Bill corresponded with several would-be immigrants, providing helpful and accurate information.

20 On the ship to Canada in the summer of 1947, Madzy was startled by the quantity and quality of the food served in the ship's dining room, which was much better than what was available in the Netherlands then, more than two years after the end of the war (*Frontiers and Sanctuaries*, p. 176).

herself driving a tractor or holding the other end of a board that Bill was nailing into place.

*

However, that active life changed drastically. In 1951 Madzy contracted rheumatoid arthritis. It began suddenly, and in a severe form, as the result of a bad flu. For the rest of her life the condition fluctuated, sometimes partly suppressed by medications, sometimes surging up to cripple her and cause agonizing pain, eventually impairing her physical mobility, vision, and hearing. From the age of sixty-two (in 1972) she was in a wheelchair, and for the last two years of her life (1982–1984) she was bedridden.

In the 1950s not much was known about the disease, apparently, and treatments were approximate and experimental, some of them making her condition much worse. Partly in the hope of finding better medical help, we left the farm in 1956 and moved to Vancouver.

By then, Madzy and Bill were ready for a change. She wrote, "The time was past when I needed a place of retreat, a spot in which to bury myself."[21] Moreover, they wanted to be something other than "small farmers." Both of them received credits for their Dutch education, and in two years of study at the University of British Columbia they obtained bachelor's degrees, Bill in Agriculture and Madzy in Arts.[22]

Because Bill was unable to find work in BC, they took the family to Antigonish, Nova Scotia, then to Burlington, Ontario, and finally, in 1965, to Carlisle, Ontario, then a crossroads hamlet in the countryside about sixteen kilometres (ten miles) north of Burlington. There, after nine nomadic years, they came to rest

---

21 *Land for Our Sons*, p. 188.
22 Madzy would continue learning for as long as she could. A few years later she took a course in Russian at McMaster University in Hamilton, Ontario, in which she received high marks, and later a correspondence course in Greek to revive what she had learned in school. Her reading was extensive and varied (see below, p. 319).

again. They bought a hilly, wooded property of two and a half hectares (six and a quarter acres) on which Bill had a simple wooden bungalow built (another "hut"!) and where he had an extensive vegetable garden and some goats and chickens. We called the place Brandstead, the homestead of the Brandis family.

*

With the onset of the arthritis, Madzy had to redesign her life. There were spells when medication allowed her to be somewhat more mobile, but in general she was increasingly handicapped and in pain.

So she turned once more to writing, and again, for brief moments, we are allowed insight into her mind and feelings. In 1954, still in Terrace, she wrote: "I plan to write a book. I have got to do something with myself now that I have to stop doing other things I like better. I don't want to write. I even don't know how to write."[23] However, she set out to learn, signing up for a correspondence course in Creative Writing and subscribing to a magazine for writers.

In one sense she was correct in saying that she didn't know how to write: she was a great reader but was never very interested in literary form and style. In her own writing she focused on being informative and, if possible, entertaining. Moreover, up to then (except in some letters) she had written only in Dutch, so doing "creative writing" in English would be a challenge.

In another sense, of course, she *did* know how to write. She had written the newspaper columns from the United States, the war diary, and narratives like the one about her and Wim's wedding and honeymoon. Writing came naturally to her, and for the rest of her life she continued doing it, for publication, for family and friends, and just for herself.[24] From now on she wrote in both Dutch and English.

---

23 Quoted in *Frontiers and Sanctuaries*, p. 216.

24 In the course of her life she wrote thousands of letters. The only ones that have survived are some that Bill kept and that family and friends gave me after her death. During my first years away from home she and

In the passage quoted above, she says that she planned to write a book, and she did so. During the last year or two in Terrace, she wrote a book-length account, *Land for Our Sons*, of our immigration and experiences on the farm. She wrote it partly for her half-brother Paul.[25] He found it so interesting that, with Madzy's consent, he arranged for its publication in England. When published in 1958, it came to the attention of a government department in the Netherlands that was helping people to emigrate. They asked her for permission to have it translated into Dutch. Madzy offered to translate it herself so that she could adapt and expand it for Dutch readers. The Dutch version, *Land voor onze zonen*, was published in 1960 and was widely read in the Netherlands.

In Antigonish, Madzy worked for about eight months in a one-room library attached to the Extension Department of St. Francis Xavier University, where Bill was working. During this time she wrote newspaper columns and short stories for local publications.[26]

At about the time of our move to Burlington in 1959, she realized that her experience of immigration could be relevant to others. That led her to contact the editor of a Dutch-language newspaper published in Canada titled *De Nederlandse Courant in Canada*, and between 1962 and 1964 she wrote thirty-two columns directed mainly to immigrant women, who, at that period, spent most of their time on farms while their husbands and children—being out and about—were integrating much more quickly into Canadian life. This created serious rifts in families and led to the women being far more homesick for the Netherlands than the men were. In the columns, Madzy adopted

---

I wrote to each other at least once or twice a week; I was saving those letters, but they were destroyed in a fire.

25 Her writing it in English suggests she was also considering other possible readers. At least she would have thought of it as being, in future, of interest to us children.

26 *Frontiers and Sanctuaries*, pp. 255ff.

a mediating, bridging role, empathizing with the women, discussing such issues as how to maintain contact with their children, and explaining aspects of Canadian life. She bore in mind the fact that she and many of her readers shared the experience of having lived in the Netherlands during the war and of having small children whose physical and mental welfare had been (and to some extent continued to be) a serious worry. She also wrote some short stories that were published in a magazine titled *The Atlantic Advocate* and some historical works that remain unpublished.[27]

In about 1977, she went back to writing memoirs and other narratives meant only for the family. Because by then her arthritic hands made it impossible to use a typewriter or to write more than a few words by hand, she found a typist, Barb Wintar, to help her. Madzy would dictate her narratives onto tape, and Barb would transcribe them; then Madzy would correct and annotate them, and Barb would produce a final draft. They worked together for about five years.

Part of the motivation for writing these memoirs was to provide us children with information about our background. Already in Terrace she had come to realize that emigration, though it had advantages, had created a significant gap between her children and their ancestral and cultural background. At that time, addressing us (though we never saw those works then), she wrote:

> Once upon a time we tore up our roots and sailed for new lands. We took you away from the comfortable houses of your grandparents, and with the eyes of all immigrants we stared and kept staring at the future, partly out of fascination, partly out of fear. So we briskly plunged ahead and forgot our past. And

---

27 In Burlington she also began painting, which was easier for her deformed and painful hands, though she continued writing for as long as she possibly could.

we omitted to tell you anything about it. That was a mistake, for now you lack the sense of a background. Well, my dears, here I go. I shall try to build up your past and mine. I shall try to arouse in you the same snug feeling of belonging to a world that is gone but will never die.[28]

In Terrace, she produced only brief and unfocused fragments. What she wrote during the Brandstead years, however, though still fragmentary, was much more successful. In each of several different narratives she concentrated on individual people or specific aspects of family history, relating not only what she had experienced herself but also what had been passed down by parents and others.[29]

She clearly enjoyed recording those memoirs. She and Bill were both homesick, sometimes severely so. They loved many aspects of Canada—the wide spaces, the natural beauty, the freedom to invent a new life. But it was not until they were living in Canada that they were able to measure—or perhaps even thought or dared to measure—what emigration had cost in terms of the loss of the community of family and friends and the cultural and intellectual life of the Netherlands.

*

The war cast a long shadow over Madzy's life. From the time when she resumed writing, she wrote about it, and those writings, which I've drawn on in the footnotes and listed in Appendix C, add dimensions to the story told in the war diary. They include her own reflections about the impact of the war on her and her family.

---

28 Quoted in *Frontiers and Sanctuaries*, p. 216. The passage was written in March 1954.

29 That substantial body of work, about 30,000 words, is the source for much of what I wrote in the Introduction and for some of the information about the work of Willy Schüffner.

The conditions of life during the war obviously affected her health. After years of worry and hunger, and extreme emotional and physical stress, her health never really recovered.

Furthermore, she was never able to overcome the fears, and the fearfulness, that the war experiences had imprinted on her. Her lifelong dichotomy between the need for freedom and the need for safety continued,[30] but after the major upheaval and adventure of emigration, the balance shifted to the need for safety. It was my realization of that that led me to give the title *Frontiers and Sanctuaries* to the biography. She needed frontiers, but also—and even more, in the later years of illness—she needed a sanctuary.

Much of that safety was rooted in Bill. During our years in Canada, he went to the Netherlands several times by himself (as well as once with the whole family and twice with Madzy), and each time they were apart Madzy suffered from agonizing homesickness and fear that something would happen *this time* to prevent his return. Each absence reawakened the wartime anxieties.

After the war, her sense of adventure could be indulged in only so long as she had the safe family capsule to retreat into. In her last handicapped years, the only adventure available to her was the intellectual kind, researching and writing about topics ranging from mediæval history and Dutch windmills to the archæological work of the Leaky family, a short history of the Netherlands, and an account of an ancestor of hers who was a ship's captain and corsair.[31]

---

30 It was shown in the war diary, for instance, by Madzy's need to be free of Iete's influence but to be sheltered by Wim.

31 She was always interested in mediæval history and studied it at UBC. In the last years of her life she read Icelandic sagas and a book titled *Medieval Culture and Society*. She loved a book called *The Medieval Machine: The Industrial Revolution of the Middle Ages. The Brendan Voyage*, about a modern-day crossing of the North Atlantic in a leather boat, had been read to pieces by the time I inherited it from her. She

It was against these limitations—a tangle of physical and emotional handicaps—that her creative energy kept pushing. She needed to do something worthwhile in what was left of her life, and she did what she could with her skills and experiences and with her failing physical capacity. This had already been one of her motivations for writing the diary during the war: her creativity pushed against the limitations and handicaps of the wartime conditions to make a space where the inner spirit could survive.

She died quietly at home in 1984.

*

In the Preface I indicated the importance of Madzy's diary as a document. There are other diaries about life in the Netherlands during the Second World War, and each of them makes its unique contribution to our understanding of that time and those conditions. Moreover, the specific details provide insight into what has been an ongoing element in human history. Madzy's record of survival through crisis illuminates the experience of other people struggling through all of the world's crises and disasters.

---

read about the historical background behind St. Nicholas. While reading Icelandic sagas, she ruminated (see *Frontiers and Sanctuaries*, p. 363) about the extent to which family memories are reliable history. This is only the barest indication of where her mental "adventuring" took her.

Appendix A

The life that Wim Brender à Brandis led in the prisoner-of-war camp is an important part of the story, but it is much less well documented than Madzy's life in Maarn. Because we have only three of the letters that he wrote during that time, we have no real idea what Madzy, letter by letter, was hearing. The only hints are the passages in the diary where she responds to or comments on what he wrote.

It is unfortunate that no more of his letters survive, and none of Madzy's. But to judge by the correspondence between Henk de Pater, another POW in Wim's camp, and his wife, Coby,[1] and by two of the letters from Wim that we do have, the threat of heavy censorship kept people from writing anything very important except constant anxious encouragement to keep going and reassurance that each of them was managing. Wim's resorting to confusing codes indicates how difficult it would have been to give real information.

From various sources, however, we have some idea of what she knew, and here I have assembled this material in roughly chronological order, beginning with Bill's own account, written in English in his old age, of the day he was taken captive.[2] Here, and in the other documents, I have done very minor editing to improve clarity and flow but kept as much as possible of Bill's own "voice."

---

1 Published online: http://oorlogspost.yolasite.com. See headnote to Chapter Four.

2 We don't know at what point Madzy learned all this—perhaps not until Wim returned home more than three years later.

[Following the occupation of the Netherlands in May 1940[3]] the Germans kept a check on the career officers. This consisted of requiring them to report monthly to the nearest occupation commander—in my case, this was in Amersfoort—who asked for my address and especially what I did. Working in agriculture was just fine as it supported indirectly the war effort.[4]

Then I received a notice to report at an army unit in Ede[5] on May 15, 1942. Gerard had been born on May 13, not in the hospital but at home. We had a private nurse who was a friend of a friend, and our nice doctor van Kekem delivered the baby. Madzy was still in bed with the baby on that nice spring day, and I said that I would be back with the train of 6 p.m. I took a scribbler with notes to study on the train as I was cramming for an agricultural exam, but not a raincoat.

On the railway platform in Maarn I met the family de Beaufort who were seeing off their son-in-law, also a career cavalry officer, who carried a small suitcase.[6] He told me that the night before he had been informed along the grapevine that we all would be sent to a prisoner-of-war camp. It turned out that all the [career] officers in the country had been ordered to report to only four German garrisons. Hence in Ede there were some 500 of our officers, all in civilian clothes and not prepared.[7]

---

3   See Introduction.
4   That meant, of course, the German war effort.
5   He always went to Amersfoort (ten kilometres, six miles) by bicycle, but Ede was twenty kilometres (fifteen miles) from Maarn, and that meant a train trip.
6   This fellow officer was Willem van Tuyll, whose wife, Cornelie, was the daughter of the de Beauforts of 't Stort. Evidently Wim van Tuyll was being seen off by the whole family. The two Wims went to the same camp: in the cigarette-paper letter Wim Brender à Brandis wrote to Madzy that he was reading a book borrowed from Wim van Tuyll.
7   Wim was wearing a business suit; he had no change of clothes or other personal effects until the suitcase reached him several weeks later.

The Germans separated a small number, of whom they had a record and who were later fusilated.[8] We received a printed card to be filled out with our addresses, without any other words allowed, stating that our uniforms had to be delivered somewhere for sending to the camp.[9] I wore a belt with my suit pants but would need suspenders for my army breeches. Being afraid that they would not be packed, I included the word "bretels" ["suspenders"] in the address.[10]

The news travelled fast; by late afternoon on that day Madzy and my parents had heard that we were on a heavily guarded train on the way to the POW camp,[11] which proved to be Nuremberg in southern Germany.[12]

*

As we know, during the first three and a half weeks after Wim's departure, Madzy heard nothing except rumours. On 9 June she received the card giving only the address to which she could send letters and parcels. Then, in mid-June, information from the camp began to reach the Netherlands. The first word from Wim was a terrible disappointment, but then, a few days later, the army doctors returned, and they spread information as quickly and widely as they could. Madzy seems to have spoken to two of them personally and, through Mrs. LeHeux in Doorn, and Mrs. de Beaufort and her daughter, heard what others reported. In two cases she wrote down what she

---

8   Executed by shooting.

9   The imprisoned officers had to wear their uniforms all the time; being in uniform would make it more difficult for them to escape.

10 He guessed that Madzy would get the point, and she did.

11 In fact, the diary shows that it took longer than this for the details to reach Madzy and that it was weeks before she knew precisely where Wim had been taken.

12 In his old age Bill told me a bit about the moves from one camp to another. Each trip took five to seven days in small cattle or box cars, the men packed so closely that they could not all lie down at the same time. There were two small windows in each car, and the men took turns standing at them looking out. Wim, seeing the cottages and small farms of the countryside, formed the dream of taking the family to America and being as nearly self-sufficient as possible.

had heard, typing it in multiple copies so that she could send the information to members of the immediate family (and, fortunately, keep one copy for our family archives).

The first report was written on 15 June 1942. The speaker is Madzy, addressing family members.[13]

This morning I heard from Mevrouw LeHeux, the wife of the doctor in Doorn, all kinds of news about our prisoners of war in Nuremberg; she had had a visit from Dr. Boer from Groningen, who returned the day before yesterday from Nuremberg as a released army doctor. Maybe you haven't heard such detailed information, so I am just writing this—we can never have too much news about our loved ones in that distant location.

In general they are fine. They are living in good barracks, are sleeping in bunks (three levels, one above the other), have blankets and a pillow with pillow-slip and will still receive sheets. The food is adequate: in the morning grey bread with a little bit of butter and jam. They get a bit more bread than we do—2,000 gr per week. At noon thin soup, in which they dip their bread. At 6:00 each gets a half L of stamppot.[14] At 11:00 in the morning they can buy a cup of soup in the canteen—they get 3 marks [German currency] per day allowance to buy something, but the canteen isn't in regular operation yet.

This buying of soup is a distraction in the morning because they don't have much to do. But they can walk round in the enclosed area, which is of a size for 100,000 men,[15] surrounded by barbed wire, with in [each of] the four corners a tower with searchlights at night and machine guns. In front there is a main street called Wilhelmina Street.

---

13 Madzy wrote these reports in Dutch; the translation is mine.

14 Stamppot is a traditional Dutch dish made of potatoes mashed with one of several other vegetables and served with sausage.

15 When I was doing the research, I was astounded at the huge numbers of prisoners the Germans were accumulating, in various kinds of camps, all of whom had to be accommodated, fed (even if inadequately), and guarded.

Their trip took place in stages: Cologne, Aschaffenburg, etc. They arrived on about Tuesday.[16] While the train was moving the windows had to be closed. When they arrived in Nuremberg there was a small train to the camp, which is 3 km [2 mi] outside the city.

They are supposed to go on to Linz as soon as the bedbugs now in that camp have been fumigated. The letters that they receive have to be read in half an hour and then returned.[17] The suitcases that we sent arrived two weeks later, and they all had to be searched, which also took time, but the guards, who are mostly older men, are kindly. The contents of the suitcases— that is to say, food and letters—were left [in the suitcases]. The civilian clothing will be sent back to us in a bag, but no written messages can be included, at risk of severe punishment.

They spend their days walking around, sunbathing, and talking.

Next door is a camp of Serbians, who receive quite a lot from home, especially cigarettes, so that each of them can smoke about three per day. They (the Dutch and the Serbians) communicate in French.

They all wash together[18] at big washbasins, in which everything has to be washed; until now there is only cold water, but they are soon supposed to receive warm water too. The mood is perfect. Soon they will probably also be able to write.[19]

*

---

16 They had been taken prisoner on the Friday.
17 This may be why we have none of Madzy's letters to Wim, but the letters that Coby de Pater wrote to her husband (see headnote to Chapter Three) have survived.
18 Bill explained that this meant that all ranks among the Dutch officers washed together.
19 If indeed the number 4 on the cigarette-paper note indicated that it was the fourth letter Wim wrote, the prisoners were already allowed to write letters home. This is another of the many obscure or conflicting details about this whole situation.

On 20 June 1942 Madzy wrote another report, giving information she received first-hand from an unnamed doctor. The inconsistencies between the two reports could result from the fact that the first one was filtered through Mrs. LeHeux. Again Madzy is the narrator.

Doctor _____[20] came on Sunday evening, 14 June, to bring greetings from IJman[21] and has told me all kinds of things. The [reporting to the German camp in the Netherlands, on 15 May] was awful.[22] As soon as they were inside they saw that something was wrong: machine-guns had been set up and there were soldiers with bayonets, etc. Their papers were checked and the NSB men separated from the others.[23] All the same, about 20 of them went along to the camp, where their lives are not worth living.[24] Before their departure each of [the prisoners] received half a kuch,[25] some sausage, and corned beef. Altogether there were 8 train cars. In Cologne they stood still for a long time

---

20 The name is thoroughly blacked out. That suggests that Madzy, after writing the account, was asked by the doctor (or advised by someone else) not to give his name. There are other signs of self-censorship on Madzy's part: the use of personal names that appear nowhere else in her war writing (no doubt pseudonyms), and the fact that she does not mention this very important visit in her diary. But most likely the information does refer to Wim's camp, or there would have been no point in the doctor visiting her or in her recording the information and passing it on to the family.

21 This is almost certainly a pseudonym for Wim; it's not clear why she used pseudonyms here but not in the other report or why they were necessary at all. Possibly there had been a rumour circulating about the danger of using real names.

22 This doctor (see below) reported to a location in a different Dutch city, but no doubt the circumstances in Ede were very similar.

23 The members of the NSB would be allowed to go free because they supported the German occupation.

24 In other words, as Nazi sympathizers their lives were made uncomfortable by the other Dutch officers.

25 See entry for 3 April 1945.

during the night because the group from Ede joined them.[26] At 11:00 a.m. they arrived in Wiesbaden and were given soup. From there they went via Aschaffenburg[27] to Nuremberg where they arrived at 1:00 during the night. It was then too late to go to the camp so they stayed in the train that night. From the train they saw the searchlights moving over the camp and therefore figured out where they were going.

There are 9 different camps. Each camp is 8 km [5 mi] square (therefore I think 8 square km)[28] and is divided into 2 blocks. Each block has 12 barracks; in IJman's barrack 105 men, including all the doctors. They sleep in bunks (3 high), with 2 blankets, on a paper straw-sack filled with wood shavings. Between every two barracks is a place for washing, very primitive, water out of a pipe. The toilets are also primitive, all next to each other so that the men can have pleasant chats and offer each other toilet paper.

When they arrived in the camp, nothing was in order. Probably the camp officials had been expecting, the day before, a little group of communists or something like that[29] but not 2,060 officers. So the first night they slept in tents where Russians had just been sleeping. Nice and fresh! It's a big SA[30] camp and there is room for 250,000 men. Next to them are Serbs who are very friendly and agreeable. They have already been there for a while and therefore are receiving parcels from home. They immediately throw cigarettes, bacon, cookies, etc. over the barbed-wire fence, and the relationship between the Dutch and

26 That was the group that included Wim.
27 Here Madzy wrote "Schaffenburg" but the spelling she used in the earlier report seems to be the correct one.
28 Madzy's parenthetical comment.
29 The implications of this remark are not clear. No doubt Madzy is simply quoting her informant.
30 SA: Sturmabteilung. This was the original paramilitary arm of the Nazi Party. In 1934 it was "effectively superseded by the SS, although it was not formally dissolved until after … 1945" (Wikipedia, "Sturmabteilung," accessed May 20, 2017).

the Serbians is excellent. Five barracks together is a "company." Twice per day there is a roll-call; then they sometimes stand for 2 hours because everyone is counted. Two have already attempted to escape but failed. Tonnet[31] jumped out of the train during the trip; no one knows how that turned out but some people say that he is dead.

Their schedule is to get up at 6:00, fetch their kuch and eat some of it, and attend the roll-call at 8:00. After that they all have to get out of the barracks, which are then cleaned. There are no servants so the officers have to do it themselves, and also the cooking. There are kitchens, and some officers volunteered to do the cooking.[32] So they do everything themselves, peeling potatoes, cleaning vegetables, everything—and also, for instance, playing barber with a scissors, cutting each other's hair. While the barracks are being cleaned, the others hang around, play chess, etc. At noon they eat stamppot in which sometimes, if you look really carefully, you'll find a little piece of meat. Once a week stokvis [dried fish]. After dinner, two hours for resting, probably needed because of the fatigue,[33] and then again hanging around. At 6:00 thin soup and the rest of the kuch. At 10:30 they have to be in the barracks and at 11:00 the lights go out.

Several of the officers wanted to teach some kind of course— astronomy, languages, or something like that—but up to now it is forbidden.[34]

Each of them has a small bowl with a spoon and that has to serve for everything—eating, washing clothes, shaving, etc. The

---

31 This may also be a pseudonym.

32 Evidently some food was supplied by the camp administration, but the prisoners supplemented this with what they received in parcels from home and from the Red Cross.

33 It's not clear why they should be so fatigued, and Madzy seems not to have asked.

34 Teaching of this kind would later be permitted and would flourish. See below.

suitcases from their families arrived a week ago Friday[35] and the distribution took until Monday. Out of the suitcases from Bussum[36] all the food and smoking supplies had been taken. The medications were taken out in the camp and given to the Dutch doctors. The letters enclosed in the suitcases had to be read quickly and then returned. Also all books were taken so that they could be censored, and they are now slowly coming back, including books that here in Holland are prohibited. Odd, isn't it, that there they are permitted! Also now there are more letters getting through so I'm going to write more.

There were no medicines in the camp but now a big case has arrived from the Red Cross with everything. Two people have already had a gastrointestinal perforation and have been operated on by a Serbian surgeon. The patients are doing well.

The whole thing is therefore a very primitive affair. Four of our doctors stayed behind and will be exchanged on 15 August for four others who have already been designated. But now it's being said that that is not necessary. Whether these 4 have to stay, or what the reason is, he also didn't know.

In all of Germany you don't see any men and it looks absolutely deserted.[37] Cologne[38] is unbelievably broken and battered. The return trip took the doctors from Thursday 5:00 until Saturday 11:00, so that's not too bad.

The mood in the camp is excellent. For instance, they held a chess competition with the Serbians. Every move was signaled

---

35 It's not clear which Friday this was.
36 This was probably another of the collection depots.
37 The shortage of men in Germany helps to explain the Germans' need to draft workers from the occupied countries.
38 It's my guess that this is the city in question: Madzy gives only "K," the initial of Köln, the German form of the name, and the narrative mentions that the train passed through Cologne. It was very severely bombed by the RAF on the night of 20 May 1942, just a couple of weeks before the returning army doctors passed through it, and it was natural that they should comment on the damage (chronology in the Time-Life book *WWII*).

across the fence, and Holland won. They and the Serbians are constantly throwing notes to each other.

Before long a number of the Dutch officers will come back because they have some health condition and can't stand the life in the camp. On this occasion also two patients came with the group.

In the canteen there's virtually nothing to buy except cigarette paper, so I can send tobacco.[39] Every morning they ask who has a birthday that day, and he gets a double ration of food. Tins are all opened [by the guards] so we must not send very much in that form because of the risk of spoilage. The days are boiling hot and the nights very cold. It's good to know that there are no guards walking through all the time and that they [the prisoners] are more or less left to themselves, but I hadn't thought that it would be so primitive. Did you? Fortunately they are not hungry, but the food is very meager.

*

In the diary entry of 6 September 1942, Madzy referred to Dr. Tellegen, another of the returned army doctors. She apparently did not write down what she heard from him, but there is a website[40] giving an account that he wrote at the time. By then the POWs, except for the doctors and a few others who had been sent home, had been moved to Stanislau. Here I am including only some information about the travel conditions (quoted from the website) that is not given in the other reports that Madzy received.

The officers were divided into two groups; for one group the trip from Nuremberg to Stanislau took nearly 5 days and for the other nearly 6. The higher officers travelled in passenger cars and the rest in baggage-cars. In the baggage-cars, jam-cans served as toilet facilities. Food consisted of bread and liver-paste, with (three times during the trip) porridge. Many of the

---

39 Wim smoked a pipe and would undoubtedly have had one with him. Madzy's reasoning here is not clear.

40 http://eindhovenfotos.nl/TELLEGEN.htm, accessed April 7, 2017.

officers had diarrhoea, probably because of the [poor] quality of the drinking water. The trip was tiring and the men were in low spirits, partly no doubt because of the conditions and partly because they didn't know where they were going, but the mood picked up when they arrived and were again in the fresh air and walking to the camp.[41]

*

On 17 June Madzy received the note from Wim, written on cigarette paper, that another of the doctors had smuggled out of the camp.[42] I learned of its existence only shortly before Bill died. He must have found it among Madzy's papers after her death; she had put it in a small envelope of the kind used in the Netherlands for visiting cards. Both Bill and Madzy wrote notes on the outside of the envelope. Madzy wrote:

When all the Dutch officers were taken prisoner of war on May 15, 1942, some army doctors were included by mistake (they were non-combatants). Some weeks later they were released and sent back to Holland. One doctor managed to hide the enclosed 'letter,' written by Dad, in his fountain pen and smuggled it out of Germany, and brought it [actually sent it in a letter] to me. Mam.

On the other side of the little envelope, Bill wrote:

Enclosed is the note from Wim to Madzy, dated June 10, 1942, smuggled out of POW camp in [a] fountain pen by [a] medical army doctor released from the camp in 1942. This is a precious souvenir. I could read part of it. Dad.

I was able to read most of it using a magnifying glass and a good light. A few words are hard to make out, and bits are obliterated by ink blots from the fountain pen. Moreover, Wim was cramming as much as possible onto a tiny bit of paper, 3 x 6 cm (1½ x 2½ inches). The

---

41 *Ibid.*
42 See entry of 17 June 1942 and illustration on page 91

message is 386 words in length, so he expressed himself concisely. He seems to have written it with a very finely sharpened pencil.

The date given at the top right corner is 10/6. There is a number "4" at the top left corner. Wim numbered his letters, so this is presumably the fourth.

This is what I was able to make out and then translate:

Dear Mappie, Thank you very much for the wonderful suitcase and letters. I also find much support in the Bible, am reading Luke myself and Job with a group [of other prisoners].[43] I also pray _____ for you all. I'm making out well, am cheerful and optimistic. It's possible to manage here, especially if I have books. Will you _____ order *Kennis van de Grond*[44] and [a few words that he himself crossed out] *Houtteelt*[45] to be sent via the Red Cross. _____ leather canteen [bottle] which I enjoy [having?] and old table knife (sharp) and pocket knife. Food in the suitcase arrived in good condition and _____ [but] bread was spoiled—better first dry it a bit _____ next [time?] in butterbox.[46] Please send vitamins, calcium,[47] and [illegible brand name] among the candy otherwise it doesn't get through [the censorship of parcels]. Please send a change-of-address notice to *Boerderij Heide* _____ en *Boschbouw* magazines[48] [next few words illegible]. I ____ fine and will get through this time very well with our love as ____ just as you write yourself _____ that you have the strength [to get?] through this time and live for the children. I'm curious to know where you will be living. Try

---

43 Madzy had included a small Bible in the suitcase.
44 "Acquaintance with earth [or soil]."
45 A book or magazine about forestry.
46 Not clear what this is.
47 Dr. Tellegen also wrote about the need for "kalkpepermunt" (calcium peppermint) as a supplement that the POWs needed to get vitamin D.
48 These are clearly magazines about farming, moorland (common in the Maarn area), and forestry, and would be relevant for the work that Wim hoped to return to soon. Evidently at this stage the prisoners were allowed to receive magazines.

to write _____. Such letters do get through. I will be eager to hear everything. I'm [getting used to?] the life. The food is good but less [of it] than at home. Enough sugar but little to fill the stomach and [little] protein. Please also send nails for shoe-soles, from Vershuur.[49] Oom Sam[50] is doing well. I'm studying an agriculture book [from] van Tuyll[51] and the dictation that I had with me.[52] Seriously, darling, never doubt about my coming home, and in any case before Christmas. The thoughts about you give me much support and we both trust to God. Give a big kiss to Marianke and Gerard and know that you yourself are most warmly embraced by your Dicksy who loves you so much and in his thoughts is constantly with you. I hope _____ to write. We are expecting [a change?] of camp.

*

Except for this, the only communications from Wim that survive are two letters from November and December 1943 (see the end of Chapter Six). However, we have an account that he wrote in English in his old age. I edited and tidied slightly.

When I was in the POW camp I could write twice a month on a ruled form, hence limited space, as all letters were read by a censor.[53] On the margins of my letters I often drew pictures of farm animals or buildings for Marianne and Gerard. Those forms had a reply section attached on which Madzy could reply. No regular letters were allowed, but still we had contact, except in the last nine months when no mail came through.

---

49 The cobbler in Maarn.
50 Sam van den Berg. See entry for 11 July 1942.
51 Willem van Tuyll, the fellow-officer Wim encountered on the railway platform in Maarn on 15 May.
52 This would be the scribbler with notes that he took with him on 15 May to Ede.
53 As we know from the diary, families were, in the beginning, allowed to write long letters. I've noted already that I've been unable to find definite information about when the system of letter-forms began and how many of these form-letters were permitted.

Gradually more and more underground resistance developed in the Netherlands and many men and women took part. As an officer I would not have been able to stay out of it. Many were caught and either shot or sent to a concentration camp. Madzy then realized that I was much safer behind the barbed wire than living at home and probably in hiding. All men between 18 and 65 were forced to work in Germany, mostly in factories.[54]

The main thing on everyone's mind was to survive until the end of the war. In the camp we were quite safe and in general stayed healthy. We had our own military doctors and a dentist but few medicines. A few of us died from poor surgery in local hospitals, but otherwise we all survived. My eyesight when reading was not good, and with several others and a German guard we went to an eye-specialist in the town and got glasses. It was an outing to be outside the camp.

Life in the camp required adaptation; the first months were by far the most difficult, the lack of any privacy, poor sanitation, etc. We were never badly treated by the Germans, but it was essential to keep busy. Gradually books arrived from home, also food parcels but they took a long time to reach us and food spoiled. Many of us received black rye bread which was steamed at home, not baked,[55] and it was always mouldy inside and out with a yellow mould. We crumbled it and washed the grains. Later, Red Cross parcels arrived but we received far fewer than prisoners from other countries. They were not gifts but ordered and paid for by the Dutch government-in-exile in London, who were very stingy.[56] It was good not to be amongst the smokers, who traded their milk powder, Prem,[57] Nescafé, margarine, canned fish, etc., to get cigarettes, allowing the rest of us to stock

---

54 This is Bill's simplified version of the various labour drafts; because he was out of the country, he may never have known precisely which groups were drafted when.
55 See entry for 28 October 1944.
56 Probably the Dutch government-in-exile was also very short of funds.
57 Canned meat loaf.

up on food.[58] The camp food was poor, potato or cabbage soup, mostly water. One loaf of hard bread weekly containing sawdust and camphor against sexual urges.

After four months in Nuremberg we were moved to Stanislau, in the Ukraine, a week-long trip in crowded freight cars not knowing where we were being taken. A stop inside the fence of the concentration camp in Auschwitz gave a scare, but we moved on.

The food was better there as the poor farmers were forced to deliver. We got musical instruments, requisitioned from the civilian population, for a 40-instrument orchestra, which gave concerts as we had good musicians and a conductor. Study groups were formed on countless subjects. I led an agriculture group, for which having books was helpful. Fourteen languages were taught, including those from Asia. We had a theatre group giving regular performances. There was a Protestant chaplain and a Catholic chaplain, who held services, catechism classes, and Bible studies. I was confirmed and when asked if I had been baptized I did not know, hence I was baptized anyway.

In general there were two groups. Those who studied every day and all day, even for exam credits in Holland, or were occupied in various jobs (for instance in the kitchen or sick bay, or working for escape activities) were cheerful, clean and shaven; they darned socks and repaired clothing.[59] For them the time passed much faster than for those who played bridge all day, were grumpy, complained about the lack of cigarettes, and were dirty and shabby.

---

58 As noted earlier, Wim smoked a pipe for much of his life. If cigarettes were included in the Red Cross parcels, he would be able to trade them for food. No doubt Madzy included pipe tobacco in her parcels to him —although according to his note (see entry for 26 June 1942) not many of the parcels reached him.

59 After Wim returned home I remember seeing, on his uniform, the immaculate darning, and I remember his saying he had done it himself. He was good with his hands.

Russian prisoners, who came into our compound to do the dirty work, would take shoes or clothing back to be repaired by their friends who worked in German workshops, to be paid with cigarettes.

I was fortunate with my interest in all that pertained to farming, having already hopeful plans for emigrating and living with Madzy and the children on a little farm. We could request study books, not by title but by subject, from the Red Cross, which were sent from the U.S.A. via Geneva,[60] reaching us months later. This gave me books on farming in America, which I wanted.

In the last two years we were well up-to-date on the war news. There were several home-made radios. Some [radio] parts came from German guards, traded for cigarettes. We had a secret group listening to the BBC. Nobody knew who or where as there were always a few who would tell the Germans for personal favours. Each afternoon the group—one reliable man from each barrack—came together at a different place where the news was dictated, then during the evening meal, with our guard outside the door, the news was read aloud, then the paper destroyed.

In January 1944, after the battle of Stalingrad, when the Germans retreated fast through Russia, we were moved to Neubrandenburg, between Berlin and the Baltic Sea. This was again an eight-day train trip. Accommodation there in old wooden barracks was far worse than in the big stone building in Stanislau and so was the food, and there was no fuel. The Germans had no resources anymore, and farm production was much reduced for lack of manpower, equipment, fertilizer, etc. In the Ukraine they just took it from the population, which was not allowed in their own country.

*

Bill wrote two accounts of his liberation and return to the Netherlands, both in English, one in an unpublished short

---

60 Conditions in the POW camps were governed by the Geneva Convention. See entry for 18 May 1942.

memoir titled "Our Lives Together" and one at the end of his translation/annotation of the diary. The latter, which is more detailed, is the one given here, with a few bits from the shorter narrative inserted. He is the narrator. I edited and tidied slightly.

Neubrandenburg, where the POW camp was located, is in eastern Germany, lying about halfway between Berlin and Stettin.

On April 27, 1945, we knew that the Russian army was very near and could hear tanks firing. Our German guards and their officers were in a panic, and they wanted all the POWs to walk westward to an unknown destination. Our Dutch commander refused: it was much safer to be in a POW camp than in a column of men in green uniforms (similar to the German uniform) on the road. Our commander had to sign a document stating that we were staying at our own risk. [The German camp officials left, so at this point the prisoners were, in fact, free.] We got shovels and dug trenches, and we painted "POW" in large letters on the roofs of the army huts. At our gate, several of our officers who were fluent in Russian stood ready to explain to the Russian troops that we were POWs.

In the night, the first Russian tanks arrived. All went well. These were "crack" troops, very disciplined. They took axes and chopped the gate posts down as a sign of liberation. Then they went on. Next day, disorganized Russian soldiers and their women came walking along the road, with little wagons with poor horses, and with some supplies. A Russian officer stayed as their commander for our camp. Our Dutch commander asked about food supplies. The Russian commander said that they did not have any but told us to go into the countryside and get it.

In April, in starved Germany, there was nothing except cows to slaughter, so we had meat. Cows were butchered; the meat was inspected by veterinarians among the POWs—as in an abattoir—before being eaten. No bread, potatoes, or anything else. The Germans had partly demolished the power plant in the small city, so we had no water, no light. We had to use water from a shallow pool where the Russian horses waded to drink and the women did the washing. We boiled the brown water, of course. Then our Dutch army engineers repaired the power plant; there was only a little fuel, but we did get water for very short moments.

There were a lot of people with stomach ulcers among us who needed milk, so a "milking crew" was organized. I was one of them, and we went with a little cart and a poor horse to a nearby valley where the cows had not been milked for days.

All the Germans were hiding in the woods, and some of my friends found a barn where a great many of the local population had hanged themselves from the joists. The Russians treated the local people terribly, but so had the Germans done in Russia.

I roamed around and came upon a shoe-cobbler shop, where Russian POWs had repaired German army boots and were now fixing their own. They taught me how to re-sole shoes, and I took some leather to do the shoes of Madzy and the children. I also took a small hammer (which I still regularly use), a knife, and an awl.

Our Dutch kitchen staff had cooked all our food during those three years so all supplies were properly stored and cooked, and not stolen. So now they [the kitchen staff] needed transportation to get whatever food they could find in the countryside, and firewood. For this they needed horses. The only ones available were the ones which the Russian army had abandoned because of poor hooves. In our camp were two sergeant farriers from my original pre-war regiment, so I knew them well. Our camp was on a huge farm, or rather an estate, with large stables and its own blacksmith shop. So our two farriers went to work [attending to the horses' hooves], and I went there to learn blacksmithing from them—having emigration very much on my mind.[61]

---

61 This does not mean that Wim was planning to be a blacksmith. Here, as in the earlier passage about learning how to repair shoes, he was simply, in his magpie way, picking up any skills and information that related to a

So the weeks of waiting passed.

I forgot to tell that about six weeks before liberation an order from the Allied Commander, General Eisenhower, had been delivered by the underground to our Dutch camp commander. It said that no POW was allowed to go home on his own (on foot or a stolen bike or by whatever other means). Hence we waited for orderly transport.

During those years we had all lived in small groups which we called "kongsies," probably an Indonesian word.[62] They were almost like families. Our group had decided that we would stay together till our arrival back in Holland.

One afternoon there was great excitement as some fifty Russian trucks drove into the camp (all American-made). Immediately orders were issued about which army hut's occupants would go in which trucks, all numbered. We gathered up our belongings, whatever we wanted to take. I had made, long before, a knapsack from my [leather] suitcase, with straps.

Our group was slow and when we came to our assigned truck it was full, taken by others who officially should have had to wait for the next transport. They said it would be coming the next day. There were not enough trucks for all of us, probably only for a little more than half the total POWs in the camp. They drove off and we stayed behind.[63]

Next day the Russians said "no trucks," as later the railroad would be repaired. So we walked to the station in the little city. No train. We slept and waited all night on the platform. Then a

---

simple rural life. Much of this miscellaneous knowledge was to be useful on our pioneer farm in Terrace.

62 The Dutch had adopted words and other aspects of culture from the Dutch East Indies, now Indonesia.

63 Bill told me when we were sorting out the chronology (see below) that he was in fact on time to take the space assigned to the members of his group, and one of his friends said, "Come on, Wim, we'll make room," and shoved over. But because Wim's "kongsie" had resolved to stay together to the end and the rest of the group had not yet reached the trucks, he said no.

freight train with empty open coal cars came and we stood up during [this part of] the trip, which was really not very long.[64] The bombed railroad yards were unbelievable. So we were stranded again until finally some trucks came which brought us to the Elbe River demarcation line. After a short wait, a convoy of British trucks came which brought us to a huge army complex in Lüneburg, just south of Hamburg. We each got a puff of DDT blown under our clothing against lice and fleas, which we did not have. Then we had a shower, a good meal, a night's sleep in good cots, and English breakfast—all looked after by many German women.[65]

Then we were off in trucks again, to a very small dirty army barracks close to the Dutch border. There was no furniture at all; we slept like sardines on the floor. There was no food at all either, as the Belgian cook had run off with all supplies. Next day we were off in trucks again to Holland—but only as far as the border, where we were supposed to be cleared. But the Dutch authorities, though knowing that we were expected, had got tired of waiting and had gone home because it was a Sunday. (A nice day.) We sat on the grass, and somebody from the Dutch border office gave each of us a cigar.

After all the delays we had become very impatient. But later that day we were brought to Oldenzaal [in the Netherlands], a medium-size industrial textile city, and billeted—with the announcement that next day we would have to stay and wait a day. I was at the house of the owner or editor of the local newspaper, where I was very nicely treated. I gave them a cake of soap I had saved for home. (I had saved also, from American food parcels, Nescafé, Prem, chocolate, and other things—all

---

64 "Not more than an hour," Bill told me when we were preparing the chronology.

65 All of this sounds fragmented and haphazard - and was - but it's a wonder that it happened at all. There clearly was someone, somewhere in that chaotic and devastated country, who organized this food and found the train and the trucks to take the POWs back to the Netherlands.

packed in the homemade knapsack, which served the purpose very well.[66])

We walked around in the city, but it was again a day lost. We were fed up with the endless delays and waiting. We were told that next day we were not going to southeast Brabant[67]—where the first convoy had gone, and from where it would be hard to get home as all the bridges over the large rivers (the Meuse, Rhine, and Waal) had been demolished—but to a conference centre called Woudschoten near Austerlitz, very close to Maarn. Of course I knew the location well, having passed by there many times. So I asked my host for a large yellow envelope or something like that, and he gave me one. I wrote a message to Madzy, and on the outside of the envelope I wrote that it was a message from a POW to his wife, with address and directions and a request to deliver it. In the envelope I put some pebbles for weight.[68]

Next day was a triumphant trip through Holland. We cheered at every living soul on the road. Taking the route from Amersfoort over the Leusderheide, we would come to the junction with the road from Woudenberg to Zeist, where we would turn right (a sharp corner) to Austerlitz. When the trucks were making the turn, a man jumped off his bike because of our cheering. I flung the envelope (between some trees) towards him where he was standing on the bicycle path. The envelope dropped literally at his feet. I saw him pick it up and read the address (with my

---

66 Interestingly, I have no memory of seeing this knapsack. Perhaps it was cut up and the leather put to other uses.

67 The southern part of the Netherlands.

68 As we know from Madzy's diary, she received two messages from Wim, of which this was the second. Bill, writing this memoir in his old age, had evidently forgotten that he had written another one a day earlier (see entry for 2 July 1945). There is no indication how that earlier message reached Dick Kolff, who arranged for his gamekeeper to deliver it; possibly one of the other officers in Wim's group found a way to get a message to Amersfoort and Wim asked the messenger to take his along as well and deliver it to Dick.

request to deliver it) and get on his bike. We know from Madzy's story that he indeed delivered it.

We were soon at the conference centre and jostled in line to get registered as quickly as possible. Then, while I was still waiting, a cavalry friend, Chris Henny, came and said, "Your wife is at the gate." So I went and met Madzy, and was surprised that Father and Jet with the mini-truck were there also; they would take Chris Henny back to Wassenaar, near their house.

It was of course a delightful moment for which we all had waited all those years. I was so overcome that later I realized that my first embrace was not as passionate as it should have been. I said good-bye to Father and Jet, who went home, and I took Madzy inside with the two bikes. (Willem de Bruin, Madzy's faithful helper, had brought my bike. In Holland every man can wheel an empty bike with one hand while riding his own.) I pushed my way to the desk and asked if I could come back next day for the formalities, which was OK.

So Madzy and I bicycled home through the beautiful woods on the little picturesque bicycle path I had ridden so often. When we neared home, we saw Juus, Marianne, and Gerard standing in front of the house, looking out for us. It was a wonderful homecoming, but Gerard was afraid of me as I was in uniform and looked very much like a German.

I think that I arrived home 5 or 6 days after Piet van Notten had come home. Madzy had waited all those days in frantic uncertainty, and I in endless frustrations because of all those delays. Anyhow we were both so thankful that I was home and that Madzy and the children (and other relatives) had survived the dangers and hardships of the war. Strangely I don't remember at all what I did in the following days, while remembering this story in the smallest details.

*****

When I was working on *Frontiers and Sanctuaries*, I asked Bill if we could precisely reconstruct the time line of his liberation and the journey home from the camp. We worked out the following:

The night of 27–28 April 1945 (Friday-Saturday): The Russians liberated the camp. The POWs spent the next 4½ weeks fending for themselves and waiting for transport.

Wednesday, 30 May: The first convoy of Russian trucks arrived, but Wim's group was left behind.

Thursday, 31 May: Wim's group, and the others who had not been taken the previous day, walked to the railway station and slept on the platform.

Friday, 1 June: A train of coal cars came for them and they travelled to the location at the Elbe River. There they transferred to British trucks and were taken to Lüneburg.

Saturday, 2 June: They travelled to the small camp where the Belgian cook had run off with the supplies.

Sunday, 3 June: They crossed the Dutch border and went to Oldenzaal, where they spent the night.

Monday, 4 June: They waited all day and spent a second night there.

Tuesday, 5 June: They were taken to the camp at Austerlitz, where Madzy met Wim with the bicycles.

Appendix B

<u>A passage from Madzy's wedding-honeymoon narrative:</u>

As mentioned in the Introduction and the Chapter Five headnote, Madzy and Wim married in the United States. Because no relative from either side was present, Madzy wrote a detailed account and sent copies to friends and family.[1]

It is a mostly lighthearted and amusing narrative, and it is full of observations about what was to Madzy a world and a life very different from what she was used to. As is also evident from the columns titled *Impressions of a Dutch Housewife in America*, these differences between the Netherlands and the United States were substantial, and American ways would be of interest to her readers.

In the months leading up to the wedding, Wim was living in a boarding house in Montclair, NJ, and commuting to his office in Manhattan. Madzy, when she arrived, would need appropriate accommodation, so he arranged for her to stay with Cornelius and Mimi Kolff (see Chapter Five headnote) on Staten Island, while he stayed with friends of theirs nearby. The wedding took place in Montclair, and after the honeymoon they returned there to live in a small flat that he had rented.

On the morning of the wedding, therefore, they set off from the Kolffs' house, in the car they had borrowed from Mimi Kolff, to go to Montclair. Madzy wrote:

It was about 2 hours of driving before we were in Montclair. There we first went to the Gas and Electric Company to request

---

1   The translation is mine.

that the gas and electricity be hooked up in our little flat when we came back. Then we went to the Board of Health to pick up our [marriage] licence, and then Wim brought me to the minister, because I was allowed to change my clothes in his house. To prevent wrinkling, my gown lay at full length over the tops of the luggage in the back of the car. I changed in the bedroom of the minister and his wife, while the minister's wife lay in bed with sciatica, but she said that she did want to get up because she wouldn't miss the wedding for all the gold in the world. She did up my gown at the back while I sat on the edge of her bed, and she called me "Dearie." I was allowed to look in all the mirrors in the house to see if everything hung right on me. And then the minister came upstairs proudly with the wedding bouquet, which Wim had in the meantime fetched and which he had just dropped off, because he just had to drop in to see his former landlady, Mrs. Smith, who lived across the street, a very nice lady, and make an arrangement about his dirty laundry![2]—and came running in at the last moment for his own wedding!

Meanwhile all kinds of wedding guests had come to the rectory and greeted me,[3] first the Bakkers with Mevr. van Staveren. Miss Kolff and Mrs. Verbeet came in Mrs. Verbeet's car.[4] And while the others went to the church, we (that is, Mr.

---

2   According to a note in Bill's memoirs, he dropped off his dirty washing at the Chinese laundry; in the confusion and excitement of that morning, it's not surprising Madzy didn't get the details quite right.

3   The wedding guests, as I mentioned in the headnote to Chapter Five, included several of the acquaintances Madzy had made on the crossing in the *Statendam* and also two elderly friends of Iete's who happened to be on the ship. Wim had invited some people from a folk-dancing group he had joined in Montclair. I don't know which names refer to which people, except in the case of Mimi Kolff and Mr. Bakker (the latter had been on the *Statendam* and would be the best man).

4   For some reason, Madzy used "Mevr." van Staveren but "Miss" Kolff and "Mrs." Verbeet. Perhaps Mrs. Verbeet was, like Mimi Kolff, American (though the name is Dutch). Mevr. van Staveren may have been one of the Dutch ladies from the ship.

Bakker, the minister, Wim and I) still had a small rehearsal so that everything wouldn't be a mess. Then Mr. Bakker and I walked to the back of the church, while the minister took Wim along to the other entrance. Mr. Bakker and I had to wait until Wim and the minister stood by the altar. The verger would give a sign when we had to enter. I was surprised to see that the verger was black, but that is very common here with the large number of coloured people that you see here.

At the right moment, to the tones of the wedding march, I walked in on the arm of Mr. Bakker. The light in the church was dim, but at the altar there were candles and an abundance of flowers. It was beautiful. And then followed the service, which went perfectly; when Wim and I knelt in front of the minister to receive the last blessing I thought of you all ....

Congratulations and jubilation. The marriage certificate, which had to be signed by two witnesses: Mr. Bakker and Miss Kolff. And then in the garden of the church the film, which you will see.[5] It was all so strange and overwhelming; I didn't take it all in but let myself just 'live it.'

[They had the wedding breakfast at a restaurant and then Madzy changed her clothes at the rectory.]

And after drawing a long, deep breath we started the Ford and, waved off by the minister and his wife, we cheerfully drove away.

That night we slept in Greenwood Lake, somewhat to the north. But it was very lugubrious, cold, and wet, and the next day we quickly headed south.

*

Bill, in his note on the wedding-anniversary passage in the diary, wrote:

The next day we went south because of the cold weather, not really knowing where we were going except on the map. We came

---

5   I have so far been unable to find this film.

to the Shenandoah Valley in the mountains of Virginia [a national park] and rented a small log-cabin guest house belonging to a lodge with dining room. There was [in the cabin] an open fireplace attended by a black servant; this fireplace also supplied hot water. The black man came into the living room before we got up [in the morning] to start the fire. [These were] all new experiences to us. The cottage had a porch with a beautiful view over the valley. It was very cozy and secluded and just right for a honeymoon. We went shopping in a little village miles away [for groceries] to make our own breakfasts and lunches.

For both of them, those days were a never-forgotten experience of rest and tranquility. In the remainder of their lives, there were very few holidays and never anything to compare with this.

*****

The poem written for Sinterklaas 1944

Madzy wrote this poem for the Sinterklaas party held at Huis te Maarn in December 1944 (see Chapter Ten). As indicated there, I found it in the typescript of Dientje Blijdenstein's war diary. The typescript of the diary was apparently not prepared by Dientje herself, so the text of this poem has gone through several copyings. I've made no attempt to translate it in verse form; I concentrated on the content and tried to capture something of Madzy's tone of voice. The poem was meant to be read aloud and was punctuated accordingly. It is a picture of the lives we were living, and it was no doubt greeted with laughter—half grim and half delighted—as people saw their lives reflected in the verse.

Following the prose translation of the poem I give one verse in Dutch to show the verse form and because it might be interesting for Dutch-speaking readers. The poem is untitled.

The days they run past us one after another; they crawl or they fly. And still there's irritation from the Huns,[6] who only lie. The Hun who steals, the Hun who grabs. That shoe's wearing out, that bicycle tire bursts, and yet, really, yes, how is it possible: We're still alive!

By day everyone runs full speed to use the daylight. We slog around with the milk-can and then … we even have to pay! Here still one loaf of bread, there's still one coupon, [unintelligible phrase]. We're out of breath … and yet … we're still alive!

We look anxiously at the sky while furiously pedaling on bicycles without tires or brakes (so that they don't get grabbed). A plane?!?! I'm not happy about that! Over there … from that nest of Huns … shooting! bombing! Boom! Boom! Och, och, we're still alive!

When day is gone and darkness comes we muddle around in the dusk to make the most of it. Here's a chair! Watch out! What's that? Oh, the cat's tail! Ouch, ouch, my head! What's that you say? We're still alive!

We get tired, we get dirty, and all our clothes wear out. We're packed with refugees and … with lice, that don't bite.[7] We eat but … we remain hollow. We sleep a lot; our heads are frantic. We don't think, our brains are muddled anyway. We're still alive!

Bos nearly sets fire to our houses because we don't go and dig. We no longer get a scare when we see him galloping up our

---

6   I use this now-unacceptable term to translate the Dutch word "moffen," the then-colloquial term for Germans. Translating it as "Germans" would not capture the colloquial tone.
7   The lice that don't bite may be the Germans again.

driveway. With bag and baggage and kitbag we look for another roof. Well, there are still the chicken houses. We're still alive![8]

At least thirty Huns come and bivouac for a night. Their meat[-eating?] and their yammering are really more than Chris can bear. It's not actually billeting, but still, they leave behind a heap of horse-manure. But they'll be leaving at six a.m., after all.[9] We're still alive!

Electricity! It's also taken away, and we have to sweat a lot before we can take a bath and be considered clean again. No news! ... that's a big loss, because news, that's what we live on. What now? Paper?[10] There's still that. We're still alive.

All the same, there'll be a better time and a more cheerful future coming. Sometime our men will be here again to ask us about our sorrows and burdens. When? Yes, really, just be patient. The time isn't ripe yet. Be grateful for this one thing: We're still alive.

---

8   This refers to the incident Madzy dealt with in the diary on 31 October 1944.
9   This refers to an incident Madzy recorded on 27 November 1944.
10 This probably refers to the underground newspapers.

Here is the eighth verse in the original:

Electra! ...
    't word ons ook ontzegd,
En men moet eerst gaan zweeten,
Alvorens in het bad te gaan
En men weer schoon mag heeten.
Geen nieuws!! ...
    dat is een heele strop!
Want 't nieuws ...
    daar leefden wij nog op!
Wat nu?
    Papier!
        Dat is er toch!
    WE LEVEN NOG!

Bibliography

Primary Sources

This book is based largely on our family archives. For anyone interested in more information, *Frontiers and Sanctuaries: A Woman's Life in Holland and Canada*, gives details. At this time (2019) it is still in print, and there is an e-book edition. The family archives are now in my possession and will eventually go to the archives at McMaster University in Hamilton, Ontario. Inquiries may be addressed to me at mariannebrandis@cyg.net

These are the family archives and related resources on which I have drawn:

Madzy's writings:

- The war diary
- The note Madzy put with the Christmas decorations
- The report giving information that Mrs. LeHeux passed on from the army doctor
- The report from the unnamed doctor who visited Madzy
- The baby book Madzy wrote for/about me
- The 1976 taped narrative based on the war diary, which I transcribed
- Two narrative tapes that Madzy made for me in her old age: "Memories for you and me" and "Marianne's health history"

- The account that Madzy wrote of her and Wim's wedding
- Short stories and memoirs that are relevant to the war years:
  o "Uncle Sebastien's Pet" (the story of the requisitioning of the radios)
  o "Bacon on the Moors" (the story about the Canadian soldiers' canteen in spring 1945)
  o "Our Dominee" (the story about the elderly clergyman working with the Resistance)
  o "Four Hours to Spare" and "Curfew." These are two versions of the same story; the narrator is a woman in the wartime Netherlands whose husband, a spy for the Allies, visits her secretly one night.
  o "De Levende Kerstboom" ("The Living Christmas Tree")
  o The columns for *De Nederlandse Courant in Canada* ("The Dutch Newspaper in Canada")
  o "Never Say Die" (a fragment of a novel)
  o The poem for Sinterklaas 1944 (see Appendix B)
  o The family memoirs Madzy put on tape and had transcribed

Madzy's published books relating to this period:

Land for Our Sons. Note that this was published under the name Maxine Brandis. The publisher considered that "Madzy" was too odd a name. Madzy hated "Maxine" and rarely used it again except for the Dutch translation of this work.

Land voor onze zonen: Belevenissen van een emigrante in Canada. ("Land for our sons: experiences of an emigrant in Canada.") As this was a direct translation, it was also published under the name Maxine Brandis.

<u>Bill's writings:</u>

- His very rough translation of the diary, with annotations and explanations
- Three letters written from the POW camp
- The narrative of his liberation and return home in 1945
- "Memories of Maarn" (a short memoir)
- Several memoirs dealing with his youth and early manhood up to emigration to Canada in 1947, including his experiences of the war period and the POW camp

There are also notes that I made on my discussions with him while I was working on *Frontiers and Sanctuaries.*

<u>Other primary sources:</u>

Mej. B. Th. W. Blijdenstein. *Dagboek van Dientje Blijdenstein, 17 Sept. 1944–7 May 1945* ("Diary of Dientje Blijdenstein"). This is a diary written mostly during the war; later, when it was safe to do so, Dientje added more material and prepared the whole document as a gift for her sister and brother-in-law, Christie and Piet van Notten. I used it with the generous permission of Jim van Notten.

Margaretha Laurentia Blijdenstein de Beaufort. *"Herinneringen aan het leven in Maarn en Maarsbergen"* ("Memories of Life in Maarn and Maarsbergen"). http://www.mmnatuurlijk.nl/jml/index.php/actueel/654-herinneringen. This is an interview with Greet Blijdenstein (Wim's cousin, daughter of Betsy and Ferd de Beaufort) done at about the time of her hundredth birthday in 2010.

The correspondence between Madzy and Virginia Donaldson and Rosalie Worthington.

I used some genealogical information about the Brender à Brandis family published by August de Man on his website: http://home.online.hl/audeman/BRaBR/BRaBR.htm. I also corresponded with him.

I drew on notes that I made during a trip to the Netherlands in May 2001 to do research and interviews for *Frontiers and Sanctuaries*, and on correspondence with family and Madzy's friends, both for that book and for this present one.

Secondary Sources (print)

NOTE: Information about internet sources is given in footnotes where the material is used.

Bailey, Ronald H. *The Air War in Europe.* Alexandria, VA: Time-Life Books, 1979.

Beevor, Antony. *The Second World War.* New York, NY: Little, Brown and Company, 2012.

Brandis, Marianne. *Frontiers and Sanctuaries: A Woman's Life in Holland and Canada.* Montreal, QC: McGill-Queen's University Press, 2006.

Brandis, Maxine [Madzy]. *Land for Our Sons.* London, UK: Hurst & Blackett Ltd., 1958.

Brandis, Maxine [Madzy]. *Land voor onze zonen: Belevenissen van een emigrante in Canada.* ("Land for our sons: experiences of an emigrant in Canada.") Utrecht: Het Spectrum, 1960.

Briedé, J. P. *Maarn-Maarsbergen in de loop der eeuwen* ("Maarn-Maarsbergen through the centuries"). Maarn, NL: Lions Club, 1993.

Brittain, Vera, *Testament of Experience.* USA: PEI books, Inc., 1981. Originally published by Victor Gollancz in 1957.

Caspers, Loek. *Vechten voor vrijheid: Oorlog en verzet op de Utrechtse Heuvelrug* ("Fighting for Freedom: War and

Resistance in the Utrecht area") (2nd edition). Hilversum: NL Verloren, 2008.

Cook, Tim. *The Secret History of Soldiers.* Canada: Allen Lane, 2018.

Hackett, General Sir John. *I Was a Stranger.* London, UK: The Hogarth Press, 1988.

Haley, K. H. D. *The Dutch in the Seventeenth Century.* London, UK: Thames & Hudson, 1972.

Hazelhoff, Erik. *Soldier of Orange.* London, UK: Hodder and Stoughton, 1972.

Howarth, David. *Dawn of D-Day.* New York, NY: Skyhorse Publishing, Inc., 2008.

Jacobs, Maria. *A Safe House: Holland 1940-1945.* Hamilton, ON: Seraphim Editions, 2005.

Judt, Tony. *Postwar: A History of Europe Since 1945.* London, UK: Penguin Random House, 2005.

Kaufman, David, and Michiel Horn. *De Canadezen in Nederland, 1944–1945* ("The Canadians in the Netherlands, 1944–1945"). Laren, NH: Uitgeverij Luitingh, 1980.

Keith, Janet. *A Friend among Enemies: The Incredible Story of Arie van Mansum in the Holocaust.* Richmond Hill, ON: Fitzhenry & Whiteside, 1991.

Kitchen, Martin. *Nazi Germany at War.* London and New York: Longman, 1955.

Lägers, Hans, and Karen Veenland-Heineman. *Maarn: Geschiedenis en architectuur* ("Maarn: History and Architecture"). Zeist, NL: Uitgeverij Kerckebosch BV, 2003.

Maass, Walter B. *The Netherlands at War: 1940–1945.* London, UK: Abelard-Schuman, 1970.

Mak, Geert. *De eeuw van mijn vader* ("My father's century"). Amsterdam/Antwerp,: Uitgeverij Atlas, 1999.

Nederland's Patriciaat ("Patrician families of the Netherlands"). The Hague NL: Centraal Bureau voor Genealogie, 1967.

Olson, Lynne. *Last Hope Island.* New York, NY: Random House, 2017.

Overy, Richard. *Why the Allies Won.* New York & London: W. W. Norton & Co., 1995.

Ryan, Cornelius. *A Bridge Too Far.* New York, NY: Simon and Schuster, 1974.

Seaton, Albert. *The Fall of Fortress Europe 1943–1945.* New York, NY: Holmes & Meier Publishers, 1981.

Time-Life Books. *WWII: Time-Life History of the Second World War.* New York, NY: Prentice Hall Press, 1989.

van der Donck, Paul, Walter Scholten, David Vroon, and Bertjan Sneller. *Vrijheid geef je door: oorlogsmonumenten in Maarn en Maarsbergen* ("Freedom: you pass it on: war monuments in Maarn and Maarsbergen"). Maarn, NL: Lionsclub Maarn Maarsbergen, 2018.

van der Zee, Henri A. *The Hunger Winter: Occupied Holland 1944–1945.* Lincoln, NE: University of Nebraska Press, 1982.

Warmbrunn, Werner. *The Dutch under German Occupation 1940–1945.* Stanford US: Stanford University Press, 1963.

Wilhelmina [Queen]. *Lonely but Not Alone.* London, UK: Hutchinson & Co. Ltd., 1960.

About Marianne Brandis

Marianne was a child in the wartime Netherlands and is one of the characters in the story narrated in her mother's diary; she brought her own memories to the translating and editing of this work. She also drew on the extensive research that she conducted for *Frontiers and Sanctuaries: A Woman's Life in Holland and Canada*, the biography of Madzy's whole life.

Growing up in Canada, Marianne knew she was going to be a writer. While working in radio and teaching English Literature and Creative Writing, she wrote fiction, including award-winning historical fiction for young readers. She has also written works of biography, autobiography, and creative non-fiction—a total of fourteen book-length works, in all of which there is a strong historical element. In working on her mother's diary, she drew on this extensive experience of doing historical research and bringing the past to life.

She is a full-time writer living in Stratford, Ontario.

Visit
www.mariannebrandis.ca
for more information.

Index-Glossary

Anderstein. Home of the van Beuningen family, near Maarsbergen. About 3 km [2 mi] from Maarn. 229, 248, 253

Anna Toos. See *Toos family*

Anneke de Jonghe. See *Jonghe*

Annetje Nahuys. See *Nahuys*

Antigonish. Town in eastern Nova Scotia, Canada, where the Brender à Brandis family lived from 1958-1959. 314, 316

Arnhem, battle of. See *Operation Market Garden*

Arnhem, evacuation of and refugees from. 181, 186ff

Arnhem, looting of. 235

Austerlitz. Location where returned POWs were registered, about 4 km [3 mi] from Maarn. 305, 341

Automobile, Madzy and Wim's. 71, 221

BBC. British Broadcasting Corporation. 6, 62, 81, 162, 336. Also see *Radio Oranje*

Beaufort, Ernestine de. Daughter of W. H. de Beaufort of 't Stort. 89

Beaufort, Henrica Volrada Julia Elisabeth de Beaufort (Betsy) de. Wim's aunt, sister of Gerard Brender à Brandis. Lived at de Hoogt. 13, 87, 121

Beaufort, J. F. de. Joachim Ferdinand de Beaufort, owner of de Hoogt and director of de Nederlandsche Bank. Husband of Betsy de Beaufort. 13, 303

Beaufort, W. H. de, and/or Mevrouw. Owners of 't Stort. Mr. de Beaufort was the brother of J. F. de Beaufort. 89, 332

Bem(me) van Notten. See *Notten*

Bent, Mevrouw van den. (first name never given) Acquaintance of Wim and Madzy. 93

Bentinck, Baron R. F. C. and Baroness (Mevrouw). Friends of Madzy and Wim. Owners of Landeck. 69, 167, 259-60

Berg, Sam and/or Kuuk van den. Friends of Madzy and Wim. 102-3, 333

Bernard, Prince. Consort of Princess Juliana. 62, 160, 293, 300. Also see *Royal Family*

Betsy de Beaufort. See *Beaufort, Henrica Volrada Julia Elisabeth (Betsy) de*

Betuwe. Area south of Maarn, famous for fruit production. 100, 228

Beuningen, C. S. and/or Mevrouw van. Owners of Anderstein, near Maarsbergen. Lot Hudig was their daughter. 229, 252

Bill Brender à Brandis. The name by which Wim was known after immigration to Canada.

Black market. 61, 186, 214, 215, 252

Blijdenstein family. 15, 35

Blijdenstein, Mejuffrouw B. Th. W. Blijdenstein (Dientje). Friend and neighbour of Madzy and Wim, sister of Christie van Notten. 35, 348

Bob and Jet Hudig. See *Hudig* and *Beuningen*

Boer, Suus de. Friend of Madzy. 68, 104-5, 184, 195

Boerderij, de. Home of VaVa and Edward Hoogeweegen. 49

Bomb shelters. 173, 190

Bos, G. 207

Boy Ruys de Perez. See *Ruys de Perez, Pierre Jean Baptiste*

Brandstead. Home of the Brender à Brandis family in Carlisle, Ontario, Canada. 315

Bread containing sawdust. 195-6

Brender à Brandis, Augusta (Gusta). Wim's aunt. 48

Brender à Brandis, Elize (Lies). Wim's sister. Monica was her daughter. 39, 106, 147, 222

Brender à Brandis, Gerard and/or Jet. Gerard was Wim's father, and Jet was his second wife, Wim's stepmother. 13, 31, 43, 70, 193, 305

Brender à Brandis, Gerard Willem. Madzy and Wim's son, born two days before Wim's imprisonment.

Briedé, J. P. Secretary in the municipal office of Maarn. 202

Broekhuisen. Estate about 7 km [4½ mi] east of Maarn, where Wim worked before being imprisoned. Owned by Jkh. and Mevrouw Stratenus. 16. Also see *Stratenus*

Bruin, de, family. 94, 125

Bruin, Marietje de. Madzy's neighbour and part-time household helper. 24. Also see *Bruin, de, family*

Bruin, Willem de. Madzy's helper. 163, 198, 202, 244, 263, 306, 342. Also see *Bruin, de, family*

Driebergen. Town about 6 km [4 mi] west of Maarn

Ds. (Dominus). Title used for the clergy. 75

Dus Fabius. See *Fabius*

Dutch SS. A Dutch police force under German control. 285, 289, 292

Eddy and Annemarie van Vollenhoven. See *Vollenhoven, Eddy and Annemarie van*

Ede. Town about 20 km [15 mi] east of Maarn

Edward Hoogeweegen. See *Hoogeweegen*

Egner, Juus. Nanny in the van Vollenhoven family. 11, 32, 46, 129, 212, 222, 245, 261-2

Electricity discontinued. 173, 188, 201, 202, 204

Els van Ketwich Verschuur. See *Ketwich Verschuur, van*

Emiel de Jonghe. See *Jonghe, de*

Emigration, thoughts, plans, decisions. 234, 244-5, 312

Erna van Heuven Goedhart. See *Heuven Goedhart, van*

Ernestine de Beaufort. See *Beaufort, Ernestine de*

Everwijn Lange, F. E. and/or Mevrouw. Mr. Everwijn Lange was mayor of Maarn from 1924 to 1951, replaced during the war by J.P.A. de Monyé. 44, 136, 232, 291

Fabius, Dus. Friend of Wim. 137-9

Fabricius, Johan. 182

Ferd de Beaufort. See *Beaufort, J. F. de*

Floris Kool. See *Kool*

Food drop. See *Relief flights*

Food requisitioned for Germany. 74

Food, embargo on shipments of. 200

Geneva Convention. 33, 336

Gerard Brender à Brandis. Wim's father. See *Brender à Brandis, Gerard and/or Jet*

Gerard Willem Brender à Brandis. Madzy and Wim's son. See *Brender à Brandis, Gerard Willem*

Gerbrandy, P. S. Prime Minister in the Dutch government-in-exile. 160, 256-7, 269

Gerrit Heerikhuizen. See *Heerikhuizen, Gerrit*

Gijselaar, Jkvr. Cornelia Sophia de. Madzy's aunt. 37

Gleichman, Juffrouw. (first name never given) Madzy's former music
  teacher. 231

Grebbe Line. A line of defence installations just east of Maarn. 169, 195,
  199, 202, 270

Green Police. Executive branch of the German SD. 34. Also see *SD*

Greeve, Zuster. (first name never given) 277

Gusta Brender à Brandis. See *Brender à Brandis, Augusta*

Hackett, General Sir John. 243

Halm, de. Neighbouring farm.

Hans Hoogewerff. Wim's mother. See *Hoogewerff, Anna Nancy*

Hans van Ketwich Verschuur. See *Ketwich Verschuur, van*

Hansje van Vollenhoven. Madzy's sister. See *Vollenhoven, Johanna van*

Heerikhuizen, Gerrit. Postman. 126, 178, 179, 180

Heuven Goedhart, Gerrit Jan and/or Erna van. Erna was a friend of
  Madzy. 64, 68

Heydrich, R.T.E. 57

Highway (east-west) through Maarn. 22, 191

Hilversum. City about 21 km [16 mi] northwest of Maarn

Hitler, Adolf. 156, 288

Hoogeweegen, Edward. 30, 42, 295

Hoogeweegen, VaVa and Edward. Friends and neighbours of Madzy and
  Wim. Both mentioned on 18, 30. Also see *Hoogeweegen, Edward* and
  Hoogeweegen, VaVa

Hoogeweegen, VaVa. 18, 30, 241-2, 245, 271, 289, 292, 300, 303

Hoogewerff, Hans ("Moeder"). Wim's mother. 13, 28, 77, 122, 147

Hoogt, de. Home of Ferd and Betsy de Beaufort, about 4 km [3 mi] from
  Madzy's house. 13, 74, 177, 187

Hostages. 23, 110, 157. Also see *Reprisal killings*

Hudig, Bob and/or Jet. Friends of Madzy and Wim. 248, 253. Also see
  Beuningen, van

Huis te Maarn. The principal house on the Blijdenstein estate. 18, 226, 280

Hunger Winter. The winter of 1944-1945. 154, 200, 220

Ida Roest van Limburg. See *Roest van Limburg, Ida*

Idenburg family. Caretakers at Huis te Maarn, active in the Resistance. 208, 242

Iete ("Moeder"). Madzy's mother. See *Vollenhoven, Marie Louise van*

Irma Pahud. See *Pahud, Irma*

Jet Brender à Brandis. See *Brender à Brandis, Gerard and/or Jet*

Jim van Notten. See *Notten, van, family*

Jonghe, Emiel and/or Anneke de. Emiel de Jonghe was an estate manager working in the Maarn area. Anneke was his wife. 34, 54, 82

Joost van Vollenhoven. Madzy's brother. See *Vollenhoven, Joost van (junior)*

Josselin de Jong, J. P. and/or Mevrouw de. Friends of Madzy and Wim. 197, 250

Julia ter Kuilen. See *Kamp, Nico, and Julia ter Kuilen*

Juliana. Crown princess of the Netherlands. 62, 165, 290. Also see *Royal Family*

Juus(je) Egner. See *Egner, Juus*

Kamp, Nico, and Julia ter Kuilen. Friends of Madzy and Wim. 233, 247

Kekem, Ad and/or his wife Dick van. Ad was the family doctor; they were friends of Madzy and Wim. 18, 28,35, 123

Ketwich Verschuur, Els and/or Hans van. Els was Wim's cousin, daughter of Ferd and Betsy de Beaufort. 44, 74, 124, 177, 296

Kidnapping of children. 59

Kleffens, Eelco van. 191

Kloppenburg, Wia and/or Wim. Friends of Madzy and Wim. 73, 141

Kolff, Cornelius and/or Mimi. Friends of Wim and Madzy in the United States. 115, 345ff

Kolff, Dick and/or Charlotte. Friends of Madzy and Wim. 16, 27, 32, 145, 221-2, 272, 295, 304

Kool, Floris. Friend of Annetje Nahuys. 172, 202, 280

Koolemans Beijnen, de heer and/or Mevrouw. Friends of Madzy's parents and of Wim and Madzy. 66, 100, 167, 221

Koolhaas, Ds. Assistant "predikant" at the Hervormde church in Maarn which Madzy attended. 124, 135, 293

Kuch. Bread baked specially for the military. 266

Kuilen, Julia ter. See *Kamp, Nico, and/or Julia ter Kuilen*

Kuuk van den Berg. See *Berg, Sam and/or Kuuk van den*

Labour draft and labour camps. 43, 82, 125, 126, 169, 180, 195, 198, 206, 246, 329, 334

Lambalgen. A house/estate about 9 km [6 mi] from Maarn.

Landeck. Home of Baron and Baroness Bentinck.

Landwacht. A military police force set up by the Germans in the Netherlands. 185, 194, 207

Lanoy, Miss de. (first name never given) Owner of the finishing school in London which Madzy had attended. 72

Leeuwarden. City in north-eastern Netherlands. 15, 233

LeHeux, Mevrouw. (first name never given) Acquaintance of Madzy. 58, 86

Leusden camp. See *Amersfoort transit camp*

Leusden. Town where Dick and Charlotte Kolff lived, southeast of Amersfoort, about 9 km [6 mi] from Maarn

Lies Brender à Brandis. See *Brender à Brandis, Elize*

Lighting (substitutes for electric light). 204, 222, 231, 238

Looting and destruction. 154, 166, 234, 235, 284. Also see *Dikes, destruction of*

Lot Roest van Limburg. See *Roest van Limburg, Lot*

Lotje Suermont. See *Suermont, Charlotte Elize*

Luchtbeschermingsdienst. 260

Maarsbergen. Town 3 km [2 mi] east of Maarn

Madzy Adama van Scheltema. See *Adama van Scheltema, Madzy*

Man, August de. Creator of extensive genealogy of the Brender à Brandis family

Marietje de Bruin. See *Bruin, Marietje de*

Molhuizen family. Refugees from Arnhem. 189, 199, 213, 217

Monica. See *Brender à Brandis, Elize*

Monyé, J. P. A. de. Nazi-appointed mayor of Maarn during the years of German occupation. 198

Nahuys, Annetje. Friend of Madzy. 34, 172, 280

Nel Slag. See *Slag, Nel*

Netherlands, liberation of. 285 ff

Neubrandenburg. Third camp where POWs were imprisoned (January–June 1945). 152, 336, 337

Nico Kamp and Julia ter Kuilen. See *Kamp, Nico, and Julia ter Kuilen*

Nieuwenhuizen. (first name never given) Maarn postmaster. 48, 179, 180

Noordam, Dr. (first name never given). 162

Noordhout. Wooded area near de Hoogt, site of German anti-aircraft installation. 22, 66

Notten, van, family. Piet and Christie van Notten were friends of Wim and Madzy; their sons were Jim and Bem(me). 15, 35, 145, 300, 301, 304. Also see *Blijdenstein family*

NSB. Nationaal-Socialistische Beweging, Dutch political party that supported the German Nazis. 39, 157, 158, 160, 185, 326

Nuremberg. First camp where POWs were imprisoned (May–August 1942). 77, 324

Operation Market Garden. The Allied offensive intended to capture bridges across the Rhine in and near Arnhem. 153, 155, 168-182

Organization Todt. A German military engineering organization working on defence installations. 195

Pahud. (first name never given) Husband of Irma Pahud. 63, 128

Pankie. Nickname for Marianne

Pater, de, correspondence. 63, 88, 321

Paul Adama van Scheltema. See *Adama van Scheltema, Paul*

Pauw van Wieldrecht, Jeanne. Acquaintance of Madzy and Wim. 184-5

Piet van Notten. See *Notten, van, family*

Pillarization of Dutch society. 219

POW camp, liberation of. 284, 299, 303, 336ff

Press, underground. 61, 153. Also see *Idenburg family*

Primitive conditions, 1944-1945. 233, 256. Also see *Hunger Winter*

Prisoner of war camp, conditions in. 321ff

Radio Oranje ("Radio Orange"). BBC Dutch-language program. 61-2, 152

Radios, confiscation of. 134

Rauter, Hanns Albin. 264

Razzias (raids). 2, 23, 31, 145, 259, 261

Relief flights. 269, 287, 288-9

Renswoude. Town about 12 km [7 mi] east of Maarn

Reprisal killings. 163, 201, 264. Also see *Hostages*

Resistance. 2-3, 133, 158-9, 241-3, 333-4

Rheumatoid arthritis. 314ff

Rhine-Maas-Scheldt estuary. 153

Rietie van Vollenhoven. See *Vollenhoven, Maria Catharina van*

Rika. (surname never given) Madzy's former household helper. She lived in or near Renswoude. 147, 229-30

Rinkes, Dr. (first name never given) Maarn doctor

Roest van Limburg, Ida. Aunt of Wim. 48

Roest van Limburg, Lot. Aunt of Wim. 230

Roest van Limburg, Wim and Caro. Friends of Madzy and Wim. 48

Royal family. 61

Rumelaar, de. Farm where Madzy went to try to obtain food. 249

Ruys de Perez, Pierre Jean Baptiste ("Boy"). Friend of Wim and Madzy. 95, 110

Rye bread, making of. 204-5

SA [Sturmabteilung]. The original paramilitary organization of the German Nazi party.

Salary, Wim's military. 40, 76, 95

Sam van den Berg. See *Berg, van den*

Sandberg, Tini. Friend of Madzy. 53

Schools and schooling. 161, 185-6, 197, 237, 250, 265, 309

Toos family. Juffrouw Toos was the caregiver, for most of the war, of Madzy's brother Joost, assisted by her sisters Anna and Dina. 94, 247, 249, 257

't Stort. Home of W. H. de Beaufort and family. 89, 178, 180

Tuinmanshuisje ("the gardener's cottage"). Name of the house in Maarn in which Wim and Madzy lived. 16-17

Tuyll van Serooskerken, Wendela van. Private nurse attending Madzy for the birth of the baby. 24

Tuyll, Cornelie van. See *Tuyll, Willem van, and/or Cornelie*

Tuyll, Willem van, and/or Cornelie. Cornelie was the daughter of W. H. de Beaufort of 't Stort, and Willem (Wim) was her husband. 89, 305, 322, 333

TWED ("tegen wil en dank"). Home of Mr. and Mrs. Koolemans Beijnen. 167

UBC. The University of British Columbia, in Vancouver, Canada, where Madzy and Bill studied. 314

Underground. See *Divers*

Utrecht. City about 18 km [12 mi] west of Maarn

V weapons (V-1 and V-2). The V-1 was a pilotless bomb, the V-2 was a rocket

Valkenheide. 162

VaVa Hoogeweegen. See *Hoogeweegen VaVa*

Vlastuin. (first name never given) Farmer in Maarn. 29, 31, 54, 56, 74, 228, 273, 281

Vollenhoven, Catharina Maria ("To") van. Aunt of Madzy. 37, 139

Vollenhoven, Eddy and Annemarie van. Friends of Madzy and Wim. 53

Vollenhoven, Johanna ("Hansje") van. Madzy's sister. 12, 18, 37, 219-221, 223-4, 237-8

Vollenhoven, Johanna Cecilia ("Zus") van. Aunt of Madzy's, who lived in St. Tropez, France. 156

Vollenhoven, Joost van (junior). Madzy's brother, who lived in Driebergen. 12, 18, 94, 167, 181

Vollenhoven, Joost van. Madzy's father. 11-12

Vollenhoven, Maria Catharina ("Rietie") van. Aunt of Madzy. 159

Vollenhoven, Marie Louise ("Iete") van. ("Moeder") Madzy's mother. 11, 37, 81, 82, 145, 155, 171, 225, 235, 240, 249, 252-3, 259, 294

Vucht concentration camp. 157-8

Wendela van Tuyll van Serooskerken. See *Tuyll van Serooskerken, van*

West family. Refugees from Arnhem. 189, 202, 203, 217, 220-1, 235, 258-9, 297-8

Wia Kloppenburg. See *Kloppenburg*

Wilhelmina, Queen. 48, 61, 160, 193, 269, 290, 311. Also see *Royal Family*

"Wilhelmus." The Dutch national anthem

Willem ("Wim") van Tuyll. See *Tuyll, Willem van, and/or Cornelie*

Willem de Bruin. See *Bruin, Willem de*

Willy (Wilhelm) Schüffner. See *Schüffner*

Wim and Caro Roest van Limburg. See *Roest van Limburg, Wim and Caro*

Wolfswinkel, Kees. Farmer to whom Madzy went in search of food. 250

Worthington. See *Donaldson-Worthington correspondence*

Zeist. Town about 8 km [5 km] west of Maarn

Zus van Vollenhoven. See *Vollenhoven, Johanna Cecilia van*